The Art Direction Handbook for Film

The Art Direction
Handbook for Film

Michael Rizzo

Amsterdam Boston Heidelberg London New York Oxford
Paris San Diego San Francisco Singapore Sydney Tokyo

Acquisitions Editor: Elinor Actipis
Project Manager: Jeff Freeland
Assistant Editor: Cara Anderson
Marketing Manager: Christine Degon
Cover Design: Susan Shapiro

Focal Press is an imprint of Elsevier
30 Corporate Drive, Suite 400, Burlington, MA 01803, USA
Linacre House, Jordan Hill, Oxford OX2 8DP, UK

Library of Congress Cataloging-in-Publication Data
Rizzo, Michael.
    The art direction handbook for film / Michael Rizzo.
        p.   cm.
    Includes bibliographical references and index.
    ISBN-13: 978-0-240-80680-8   ISBN-10: 0-240-80680-8 (alk. paper)

  1. Motion pictures—Art direction—Handbooks, manuals, etc.   I. Title.
    PN1995.9.A74R58 2005
    791.4302'5—dc22

                                                                    2005040563

British Library Cataloguing-in-Publication Data
A catalogue record for this book is available from the British Library.

ISBN-13: 978-0-240-80680-8
ISBN-10: 0-240-80680-8

For information on all Focal Press publications
visit our Web site at www.books.elsevier.com

10   10 9 8 7 6

Printed in the United States of America

For Allan White, a partner for all ages

Contents

COLOR PLATE SECTION: Between Pages 142 and 143

Preface

An updated version of an art direction handbook for film is long overdue. In the past, an aspiring art director could study architecture or theater, learn construction theory or stagecraft, discuss a bit of design theory in film class, and emerge from a four-year program feeling fairly confident with a modicum of hands-on experience. The advent of 3D animation for video games and a related explosion of visual effects for digital filmmaking—in short, a new demand for computer assisted movie making and its inherent speed—has redefined how we do our jobs, given the demands of that technology. Otherwise, nothing has fundamentally changed. The historical, filmmaking techniques with which some readers are already familiar have been updated and recycled into a more exciting, more believable cinematic product. Not only will this handbook demonstrate that evolution in terms of how an art director's job has been impacted, but it will also establish a comfort level with state-of-the-art technologies now used in cinema.

As a straightforward manual of how to become or perform the job functions of an art director, this book is perfect for the newcomer. In addition to the fundamental information it provides, the first edition of *The Art Direction Handbook for Film* has been written to meet the needs of newly graduated students and other aspiring filmmakers eager for some first job experience. Networking within the low budget and Indie filmmaking realm is presented from firsthand experience of art directors established in successful careers by providing various, entry level viewpoints and how-to scenarios. This information derived from direct experience is delivered regularly throughout the book and is invaluable. Sometimes offered as a helpful anecdote or directly as advice, the newcomer can easily put the pieces together and navigate the beginning of a new career.

This handbook also exposes the primary function of the art director as design manager. It begins by clearly and finally drawing the distinction between the terms "production designer" and "art director" and then explains how the innate creative and aesthetic qualities of who an art director is must be combined with the practical and business aspects of what an art director is expected to do. Four levels of responsibility to the production designer, the art department, the director, and the studio are detailed in terms of relationships and political expectations. Hands-on aspects of how an art director functions during the three phases of film production—pre-production, production, and post-production—serve as technical, straight-ahead extensions of day-to-day scenarios on any film project experience that might be encountered. This guide concludes with a comprehensive appendix of reference and source lists, contracts and forms, production lists, list of figures supporting text, expanded glossary, and index.

My intention, by writing this guide, is not to make the job of art direction any more complicated or important than it really is. As a matter of fact, the job of an art director is as straightforward as any creative manager. The workday is long, and the work intensity reflects the rigors of this demanding position. And now, the quickly evolving layers of technology offer additional challenges. But what differentiates this creative/managerial job from those in the civilian population is its caché of privilege and entitlement. Moreover, the thrust of this handbook strives to contemporize what the art director does within the context of the 21st century.

The question of where to begin took the form of a detailed outline in the initial stages. From there, the process was not as direct as one would imagine. Basic information quickly filled the growing chapters, and then my journey became a surprisingly organic one, as the book literally took on a life of its own. Within the parameters of the basic structure, the need for other voices to play in counterpoint to mine inspired interviews and supportive imagery. I worked along, amused by all of this, and clearly imagined this book as a large, carnivorous plant. As the reader will soon realize, the creative activity of designing a film is to extract imagery from the text of the screenplay. In this case, I was compelled to create text from the imagery demanding further recognition. Creativity-in-reverse was a worthwhile skill to master. Relearning the steadfastness to an idea, the delight of happy accidents, and surpassing a goal were the landmarks of this unique and sobering experience. I can only hope that this handbook might inspire other people to do other unexpected or extraordinary things.

Acknowledgements

The task of writing a definitive guide on a subject as specialized as art direction is daunting. In order to include as much information as necessary to complete such a comprehensive undertaking, I relied on personal wisdom gleaned from working in the collaborative art of filmmaking, which has taught me to trust the collective experience and knowledge of my peers. Other art directors whom I admire and have helped fill in the gaps are Linda Berger, Gae Buckley, Phil Dagort, Christa Munro, and Steve Saklad. Big thanks to all of you for your personal insights, recollections, information, and unique personalities, making this book a reliable guide for future generations of eager filmmakers.

Special thanks to Linda Berger for her preternatural love for the moving image. Within the short span of two years as chairman of the Film Society, she has presented tribute programs focusing on accomplished art directors as a way to educate the art direction guild membership and the public at large. The introductory presentations, interviews with honored guests, and screening of their works have been nothing less than inspiring. Her gift to me, aside from some of the imagery for this book, is her drive to honor visual excellence. It is contagious. I thank her for her zeal and steadfastness.

Allan White is another key player who requires special thanks. He is not a filmmaker, but an extraordinary partner willing to go the distance at all costs. He is a spiritual guardian allowing little negativity, a resilient sounding board, an unconditional financial supporter, and someone who believes in me when I do not. Without his towering presence, this book would not exist.

Christine Tridente is my editor at Focal Press, who spearheaded this book and went to battle for me when changes were inevitable. She is professional, steadfast, unwavering, and everything an editor should be. Her effort and dedication have shaped this book.

Certain factual and spiritual support from production designers, directors, cinematographers, and producers encountered along the way has encouraged my own excellence and function as a film professional. They are the following: Charles Bennett, Lark Bernini, Jim Bissell, Richard Crudo, John Gray, John Graysmark, Catherine Hardwicke, Gemma Jackson, Victor Kempster, Debra Lee, Alex McDowell, Harold Michelson, Ron Nash, Victoria Paul, Kirk Petrucelli, Richard Prince, Ida Random, Tommy Schlamme, Dean Semler, Roy Forge Smith, Craig Stearns, Oliver Stone,

Veronique Vowell, Bernie Williams, and Stuart Wurtzel. In one way or another, you have all had a hand at the forge.

Very special thanks to Henry Bumstead, John Gray, and Frank Stiefel. They didn't have to provide book cover quotes; they wanted to. I thank them for their generosity.

Although challenging, writing the text between the covers of this book was not my most difficult task. Nor was gathering the extraordinary images that support the text. Every art department artist I spoke with and interviewed for quotes was forthcoming and generous with any of the imagery created for a specific film project I was referencing. In effect, everyone was willing to share the contents of his or her portfolio with me. The essence of that collaborative spirit permeating the movie industry from where all creative participants stand and work is what kept me going through the rough spots. I began to stumble when I was requesting studio permissions to use their "intellectual property" illustrating the pages of this book. Studio guidelines are strict and rarely flexible; for the most part, I was met with cooperation and willingness toward a mutually satisfying outcome of reasonableness and fairness. In one arduous moment when I was flatly refused permissions, I had a hero. Alex McDowell, production designer, interceded by calling a former boss—together, Steven Spielberg and he became single-minded champions who helped secure permissions for some of the book's more important digital images. I am indebted to them. I am also deeply moved by the palpable effect of that same collaborative love and tremendous effort that imbues the making of the films we watch.

While thanking champions, I must also acknowledge the tireless effort of Patty Mack, owner of The Mack Agency, Los Angeles, in helping to secure the final permission for these same difficult images. She is an ardent and resilient supporter of all creative folks in Hollywood.

Art department crewmembers I have worked with or met in passing whose effort, conversation, or willingness to contribute images and interview text must be acknowledged: Beany Barnes, Jim Bissell, J. Andre Chaintreuil, Laureen Clarke, Beat Frutiger, Stephanie Girard, Colin Green, Luke Freeborn, Jeff Jarvis, Victor Martinez, Harold Michelson, Harry Otto, Maya Shimoguchi, Dan Sweetman, and Dennis Welch. These individuals and others like them can always be counted on to run interference and support me as an art director. Along with the satisfaction of another film in the can comes the knowledge of what creative interchange and true collaboration can produce. It is the most precious gift to take away from a project, not a baseball cap or jacket.

Individuals at institutions providing access to images include Amy Jelenko at the Art Directors Guild—Local 800 in Studio City; Lillian Michelson of the Lillian Michelson Research Library at DreamWorks SKG; Barbara Hall at Dorothy Herricks Research Library at the Motion Picture Academy of Arts and Sciences in Los Angeles; Helen Cohen and Ms. Presley at the Cecil B. DeMille Foundation; Ricky and Jamie at The Kobal Collection in New York City; and Donovan Brandt at Eddie Brandt's Saturday Matinee in North Hollywood.

Lillian and Harold Michelson were particularly supportive in my image search. As newly made friends, the Michelsons are welcoming and willing to share their individual and collective experience, friends, stories, wisdom, and time. Harold's extraordinary storyboards and sketches will continue to provide inspiration for generations of creative filmmakers.

The bulk of the visual material within these covers was cleared for use through the efforts of Andy Bandit for 20th Century for Films, Margarita Harter of Columbia Pictures, Margaret Adamic at Disney Studios, Melissa Hendricks of DreamWorks SKG, Albert J. Parks of MGM/United Artists, Larry McCallister of Paramount Studios, Roni Lubliner of Universal Pictures, and Marlene Eastman at Warner Bros. Clip & Still Licensing.

Additional help of reviewers includes Jill Bream, Balint Birkas, Tobias Frank, Giovanni Guarino, and Tim Keates, and it is much appreciated.

Finally, there are the civvies who have had a profoundly quiet impact on this yearlong project—they are Brian Ashby, Joan Greco, Fran Jacobson, Troy Kivel, Camille Mottet, Mark Penfield, Mark Quinlan, Jane Rizzo, Len Talan, Elizabeth Tullis, Evelyn Uhlig, Nancy Weems, Allan White, and Oscar, the Boston terrier.

SECTION I

Pre-Production Process

CHAPTER 1

Introduction

Art directing is somewhat like snowboarding or skydiving—the essence of the activity is in the doing. In that way, an art director is by nature an action figure. The definitive art director is also a unique amalgam of contradictions. On one hand, creativity reigns with few boundaries; on the other hand, practicality takes primary focus. Balancing pairs of opposites, like art and commerce, make the job of art directing unique and challenging. Getting right down to it, an art director is best described as a design manager.

How can this be? Doesn't the job description of art direction include phrases like "seminal creative force" or "visionary?" It certainly does, but indirectly so. As a design manager, the art director on a film project operates as a department manager in form but as an artist in substance. In other words, business decisions for the art department are made on a daily basis, enabling the physical side of creative film production to happen according to schedule, while creativity provides the foundation for those decisions. Before we venture too far, perhaps it's best to establish a fundamental difference between the "production designer" and the "art director."

CLARIFICATION

Talent and title are important aspects of filmmaking, generally referred to as *billing*. When we examine the art department hierarchy, the production designer is found at the top with the art director close at hand (see Fig. 1-1). As a side-by-side relationship, the production designer and art director complement one another. Although the terms "production designer" and "art director" are constantly used in substitution for one another, they are not interchangeable or synonymous. Why? Sharing the same hierarchy level of the film pyramid with the director and cinematographer, the production designer delivers the visual concept of a film through the design and construction of physical scenery. In this sense, the designer *is* the seminal, creative force of the art department. Referring back to the image of the action figure, the art director *drives* the process of design from sketch to actual physical scenery. The art director, or design manager, heads and runs the art department, interfaces with all other departments, supports the art department arm of the shooting crew, oversees scenery fabrication, and controls

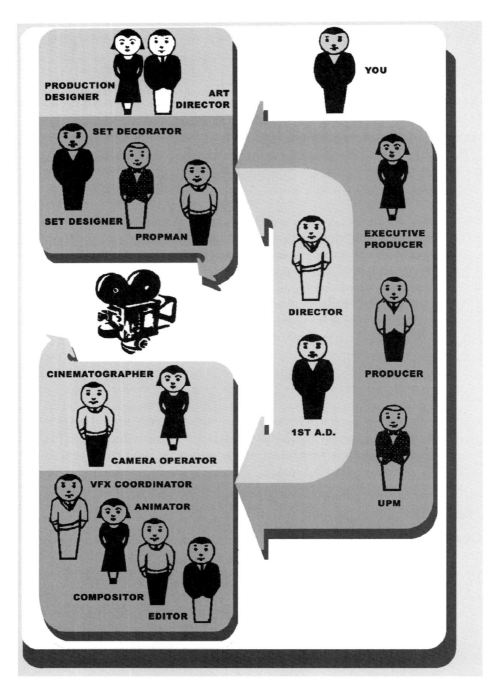

Figure 1-1 Film hierarchy (simplified).

all aspects of the department expense and scenery budgets. Although an art director's creative input is essential to support the initial creative ideas of the designer, the totality of the design in terms of conception and responsibility belongs solely to the designer. This idea of symbiotic, creative support is echoed in a recent interview with art director **Linda Berger** (*Angelmaker, Forrest Gump, Death Becomes Her*):

☐ *Why are you an art director?*

I have been thinking about the silent film designers most of my adult life. In the last ten years, especially through my work with the Art Directors' Film Society, I have begun to look at them within the whole context of art direction. As a professional in the field of movie making who started out in the theater, my earliest adventure in the networking process was to go to New York City right out of design school at The Goodman and The Art Institute of Chicago—with no connections, no anything—except my education, a handful of very close friends, and two seasons of professional summer stock in Pennsylvania and upstate New York. When I arrived in New York City, I did everything I could to find my way and continue to learn. I was an Off-Broadway lighting electrician, a lighting designer's assistant at the Brooklyn Academy of Music for the ballet and modern dance, and worked in costume shops at Lincoln Center and in the individual shops of costume designers. I worked props and painted scenery. I also worked in television as an animation assistant and did lots of commercials. Eventually, I became an Off-Broadway theatrical designer. The first time I saw my name on the marquee from across the street, I almost fainted. Regardless, I challenged myself to meet people and explore the possibilities. It thrilled me to walk around the city and actually stand in the places where great designers stood. Now many years later, I continue to do exactly that when I work with a production designer. And, to have eventually met some of them, I allow myself to climb within their skins so I can see from their angle of vision in order to fully understand how to contribute to their vision. That's how I view art direction.

I can't speak for everyone, but I think most people look at art direction from the outside in. There's nothing wrong with that. I tend to do it from the inside out; it's my instinct to do it that way. Expressing myself as an art director in this way allows me to leapfrog through time and enter the mind and spirit of any great artist or designer. Oftentimes, certain art directors have such a difficult time doing their jobs because they are in competition with the designer. Most importantly, they're missing a great opportunity. In its own way, projecting myself into the designer's mind that way is very gratifying because I learn so much about myself in the process. It's thrilling to make another person's vision a reality.

☐ *Art directors share a great creative component with the designer, but do you also see yourself as a creative manager, for the most part?*

I'm not fully doing my job if I'm just nuts-and-bolts managing the art department. The daily process is a creative process in how I deal with people, how I process instructions from above, how I convey ideas to those who need answers from me, and how I think on my feet when I'm on set. Any film I work on is not just my film, but the designer's film first. Again, I can only be creative in my position if I'm seeing the project through the designer's eyes, as a proxy. Understanding my designer's tastes and aesthetic responses supports how I supply what is needed at any given moment—how I contribute ideas and follow through to completion all those details that we all collaborate on. So, if I am a creative manager, then it happens on a continuing, organic basis. How I fulfill my job changes slightly as I work with different designers, given the differences in perspective. In the same way, the designer has to think the way the director thinks in order to do his or her job properly. There's a line of thought and function that connects everything in a collaborative environment like a movie.

Storytelling drives what we do. Two questions are always asked. What is the story we want to tell, and how are we going to tell it? The biggest part of my job, then, is storytelling through the interpretation of the production designer and director's vision.[1]

Together, both the designer and the creative manager strategize about the functioning of the art department and scenery output, but the art director alone spearheads design management on a tactical level by delegating responsibility and guiding each task to completion. With the creative integrity of the art director kept in strictest respect, this book will deconstruct the art director more as a marketing and operations manager rather than a seminal creative force. In the end, the reader will view the art director not only as a peerless, organizing force for the art department but also as a powerful shaper of policy and systems management for the larger film project.

SOME HISTORY: WILFRED BUCKLAND

All production designers are art directors, and formerly, there were no production designers at all—there were *only* art directors. In earliest film memory, the first creative moviemaker to be given the title of "art director" was Wilfred Buckland (see Fig. 1-2). "By 1916 when *Photoplay* (magazine) commented on the rise of the 'artistic executive or art director,' Wilfred Buckland had already been working for Cecile B. de Mille and Paramount since 1914 and would continue to 1927."[2]

Previously, he had designed Broadway theatrical productions, and later for the fledgling movie business developed a form of minimalist, a Carravaggio-like lighting that engulfed the characters in darkness except for a single source of side illumination. This dramatic theatrical effect quickly became a silent film trademark known as "Lasky lighting," after the **production** company that made *The Cheat* (1915), his most successful film (see Figs. 1-3A and B). It was also one of Cecil B. DeMille's masterpieces, shot in Standard 35 mm spherical 1.37 : 1 format, combining all the ingredients typical of the infamous DeMille style "a mixture of sex, sadism, and sacrifice, washed down with lurid melodrama."[3] Buckland's lighting contribu-

Figure 1-2   Wilfred Buckland, the first Hollywood art director.

tions were groundbreaking. Two signature scenes in the film—the branding of the heroine by her wealthy Japanese paramour and the subsequent shooting scene—are lit with such theatrical richness and integrity that our attention is just as adroitly manipulated today as it was during its initial release.

This early maverick's scenic designs created an equally powerful *tour-de-force* for film-going audiences in the early twenties. Towering 40 feet above Santa Monica Boulevard and La Brea Avenue, King Richard's castle, the centerpiece for Douglas Fairbank's *Robin Hood* (1922), is arguably the largest set ever constructed in Hollywood history. It took 500 workmen three solid months to build. Considering Los Angeles was more of a wide spot in the road then, the silhouette of the completed castle set could be seen for miles. It exemplified W. Buckland's penchant for creating extravagant, naturalistic sets, and it attests to his flair and flexibility as an early art director. Allan Dwan, director and trained engineer, recalled, "We worked

A

B

Figure 1-3A Production still from *The Cheat*, designed by Wilfred Buckland.
Figure 1-3B An example of a "Lasky Lighting" effect for the same scene, designed by Wilfred Buckland.

out a couple of interesting engineering stunts for the big sets. On the interiors, the walls meshed together with a matrix, which we designed and built, so they could be put together rapidly in sections. The interior of the castle was very vast—too big to light with ordinary arcs. We didn't have enough. It was an open set, and certain sections were blacked out to give the right atmosphere. So to light them we constructed huge tin reflectors, about twenty feet across, which picked up the sun and shot the light back onto the arches inside. Then we could make effects."[4] This set was larger than life in all ways—from the completion of the steel-frame, reinforced, working drawbridge, signifying the end of set construction, to the fact that the shooting of the film on its massive sets was a big tourist attraction—the magic of the Dream Factory continues to stir our imaginations (see Figs. 1-4A–F).

Under the steady but tumultuous employ of Cecil B. De Mille, Buckland was a prolific film designer—79 films listed on www.imdb.com—spanning 1914–1927 (see Appendix A, Buckland Filmography), rivaling the overlapping accomplishments of a younger upstart, William Cameron Menzies. Incidentally, as supervising art director Buckland ran the art department for *Robin Hood* overseeing Anton Grot and William Cameron Menzies, not credited as assistant art directors. The practical vision of Buckland, the little-known Hollywood art director and initiator of the use of controlled lighting within studio environments, set a standard in the first decades of the twentieth century that has become as commonplace as shooting film sequences in Hollywood sound stages today. He stands as an art-directing giant; his creative ingenuity ennobles the craft of film design even now.

The stills shown here illustrate the enormous sense of theatricality belying his earlier, formative years in New York City. His exuberance for designing these impressive, interior castle shots matches that of the swashbuckling star and sole producer of the film, Douglas Fairbanks.

PAST CHANGES

The function and title of art direction continued into the next decades before the landscape of the art department was changed forever. Since Buckland's inauguration, Hollywood's creative visual managers were simply called *art directors*. Each of the existing studios including 20th Century Fox, Columbia Pictures, Paramount Pictures, Metro-Goldwyn Mayer, and Warner Brothers contained stables of art directors overseen by a supervising art department head. The paradigm shift began in 1939 during the Golden Age of the American Studio System. William Cameron Menzies, having grown up under Buckland's tutelage, set a new standard for visual excellence by mapping the film epic, *Gone With the Wind*, with detailed concept sketches and storyboards, and adamantly insisting on using them as guides for shooting the film. David O. Selznick, the film's producer, rewarded Menzies' efforts of managing every detailed aspect of *GWTW* from a visual standpoint by crediting him with the title of "production designer." By the way, *GWTW* was art directed by Lyle R. Wheeler and set decorated by Edward G. Boyle.

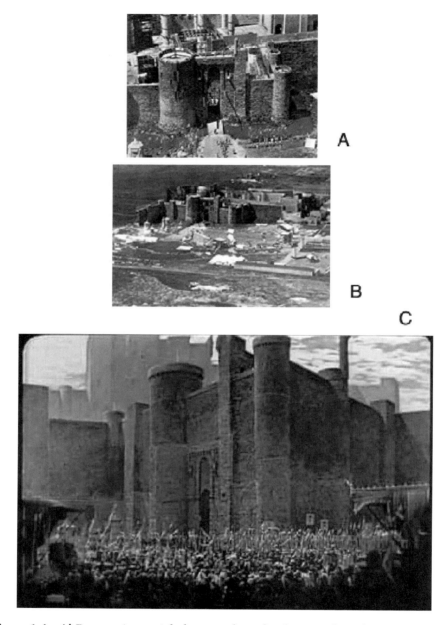

Figure 1-4 **A)** Perspective aerial close-up shot of Robin Hood castle. **B)** High aerial shot of Robin Hood castle. **C)** Production shot of the Robin Hood castle: The glass painted matte above the existing set suggests additional architecture within or beyond.

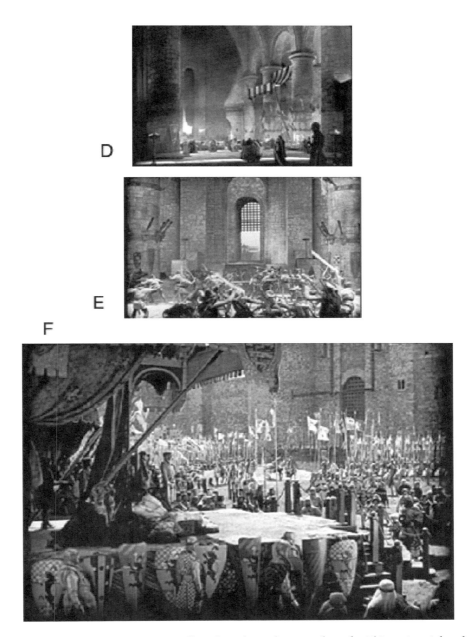

D

E

F

Figure 1-4   D) Interior: Great Hall within the Robin Hood castle. **E)** Interior: A battle scene is fought just inside the main courtyard entrance of the castle set. **F)** Holding court just outside the Robin Hood castle walls.

This distinction continues to the present. Regardless, the titles continue to be blurred. Why is that? One logical reason is that the Academy of Motion Picture Arts and Sciences annually presents an Oscar for "Best Art Direction for a Film," never having taken the leap to make the correction. Another explanation reminds us that the television industry has consistently maintained the original label for the designer as "art director." Despite the confusion of terms between industries, one fact remains: two different titles refer to two separate job descriptions—plain and simple. When in Hollywood, speak specifically.

PRESENT CHANGES

Several years ago, the Art Directors' Guild in Los Angeles was in a minor uproar when the title of our union, Local 876, had come up for review and subsequent vote by the membership. As we have just seen, the battle of who's who had gone on intermittently in an informal way during the many years since Hollywood's Golden Age. A handful of committed members called for a formal discussion and vote to resolve the squabbling for a truly descriptive title for the Guild, once and for all. After a lengthy debate, the name of the art directors' union was changed from Society of Motion Picture and Television Art Directors to LOCAL 800 ART DIRECTORS GUILD & SCENIC, TITLE AND GRAPHIC ARTISTS or, The Art Directors' Guild, informally.[5] Holding title in a designing capacity or not, art directors continue to occupy a vital place within the context of cinema's creative operatives. Formally being called an "art director" now more than ever personally connects us to our glorious past and reminds us of our historic roots without pretension.

One would think that after all this, the issue would be resolved. Friend and fellow art director **Phil Dagort** (*Six Feet Under, X-Files, The Stupids, Hard Target*) reminded me of this small piece of information:

☐   *In your understanding of it, Phil, is there a distinct difference between PD and AD?*
   That's an interesting point. A producer is not required to hire both a designer and an art director in terms of fulfilling the needs of a typical project. Officially, the studio considers the designer as the art direction lead on a film project and "designer" is the given title. For your book, you might want to consider this in defining the terms.[6]

For the purpose of this book, I will continue to refer to the production designer as the titular visionary guiding the course of the entire physical, visual look of a film. Art directors make the vision real. We are the art cops, the watchdogs who preserve the vision and ensure its delivery.

DIGITAL COMPETITION

It is also important to address the most recent challenge to film designers and art directors by and large, and that is, the evolution of the visual effects coordinator, supervising 3D animation and **CGI** prevalent in Hollywood's crossover comic book and videogame-inspired films. These digital magicians wielding technology's newest tools have the director's ear and fascination. Suddenly, the designer and art director are faced with the supervision of the limits of physical background, instead of creating ancient Rome with glass paintings and foreground miniatures, the historical secrets of celluloid alchemy. As this current benchmark in film creation initially horrified designers, it has also emboldened them, inspiring a sober rethinking of their contribution and a healthy competitive attitude toward their visual effects counterparts. Digital filmmaking has inadvertently done a good thing. By default, it has created a new playing field where designers are embracing the new technology and reclaiming visual control of the moviemaking process. **Victor Martinez**, conceptual modeler, added his response to the question about the merging of traditional and digital techniques at an Art Directors Guild lecture and workshop held in the spring of 2003:

> That is how an efficient art department should be organized—it should take the best of what is already there and use digital tools to expand upon that foundation, and vice versa, allowing the art department to broaden its capabilities. Here, there is no longer the notion of "mixed media," but rather, "cross-media." This implies that there is an active exchange of ideas through the use of different techniques (i.e., hand/analog vs. computer/digital) and that this exchange produces work that transcends any original gesture by either hand or computer. It becomes about the design. More importantly, under such a process, the art department can engage more complicated design projects, whether technical, physical, or artistic, and bring more control back into the art department in terms of development of work most often reserved for post-production—and do so more efficiently and critically.[7]

Currently, there are a handful of designers who have done just that. **Alex McDowell** (*The Terminal, The Cat in the Hat, Minority Report, Fight Club, The Lawnmower Man*) has forged a solid career as a visual effects production designer. Mavericks like McDowell have begun to cut serious inroads into the reorganization and redefinition of what the art department is and how it must operate at the center of the new paradigm. His successful hybrid status offers authority when addressing questions at the same workshop on his experience as a digital designer:

> To date the perception, language, and understanding of digital technology for film production comes largely from post-production and visual effects. That usage applies only remotely to the new applications of these tools in pre-production. Although we are using many of the same tools, our use of digital technology in the art department has very specific applications and to a large extent a different organizational language.[8]

TYPECASTING: A FULLER PICTURE

Basic personality traits define the working style of every art director. Despite the marker traits that make an art director unique, there are other indications that are universal to all. As described briefly in the introduction, the basic personality of an art director is creatively practical; without it, this person is most likely a production designer. I'm not inferring here that production designers are impractical, but without a highly developed sense of practicality, an art director is ineffective. This hybrid marker trait also compels some art directors to question just how creative they should be. When in doubt, leave the realm of full creativity to the **PD** and concentrate on the practical aspects of film design work: the flawless designing, drafting and building of scenery, its placement onstage, or retrofitting it into a location.

If you are a list maker, you undoubtedly have an art director gene lurking somewhere in your chromosomal patterns. Not organized? No inclination for insisting on detail and controlling every aspect of a project with anal-retentive fervor? Then keep your day job and stop the daydreaming. My point is that you cannot do this job correctly without a sharp sense of priority when strategizing a process. Unless that sensibility is firmly in place, there is no way you will be able to shoot from the hip in your daily participation in the game, The Quick and the Dead. A strong ability to make an effective priority list enables improvisation and the exercising of sharp reflexes. Consider this scenario: the PD and shooting crew have flown off to the next location on the schedule leaving you and the **second unit** behind to get some pick-up shots of a new Lexus crashing into a plate glass window in a downtown Baltimore storefront. Two hours before **call time** you learn from the assistant **transpo** captain that the car was not delivered the night before as everyone expected. Most importantly, it has to be a Lexus because of what has been established in previous **dailies**. The camera crew is beginning to set up the three-camera shot. What do you do? You meet with the **2ⁿᵈ unit director** and based on your knowledge of the **shooting schedule**, determine if you can wait an extra day to shoot with the proper car in Baltimore, or **wrap** it and figure out if you can replicate the scene in one of the other subsequent cities on the shooting schedule. A quick call is made to the UPM for decision approval and an announcement is made to the attending crew. This decision could not have happened without the ability to be flexible and inflexible simultaneously. Like it or not, you're also a tightrope walker.

The film business attracts extroverts, and this includes art directors, being part and parcel of such a collaborative medium. What's more, the willingness to be a solid team player, possessing a high level of energy, is another prerequisite. The charming caricature in Fig. 1-5 of the AD is a relic of the Hollywood studio system. Some qualities omitted from this chart are currently found in the digital art department. **Phil Dagort** provides additional commentary:

> The art department is still built on job descriptions and breakdowns created in the studio system of the 1930's. In terms of the digital art department now, it's still surprisingly antiquated. What's significant about the digital art department is that job descriptions are beginning to run together, creating a more flexible and maybe even more creative overall experience. The old

The MOTION PICTURE ART DIRECTOR
• HIS RESPONSIBILITIES, FUNCTIONS, AND ACCOMPLISHMENTS •
The Society of Motion Picture Art Directors, Local 876 - IATSE

7715 Sunset Boulevard   Hollywood, California 90046

ART DIRECTOR IS ASSIGNED TO STORY BY THE PRODUCER.

SET CONFERENCE WITH THE PRODUCER AND THE DIRECTOR.

THOROUGH STUDY & RESEARCH FOR PURPOSE OF AUTHENTICITY.

ART DIRECTOR GIVES GRAPHIC FORM TO HIS CONCEPT OF SETTINGS.

COMPLETE ARCHITECTURAL DRAWINGS MADE BY SET DESIGNERS.

SKETCH ARTISTS SHOW, IN SKETCHES, HOW SETS WILL LOOK ON SCREEN

SCALE MODELS OF ALL SETS ARE BUILT BY MODEL ARTISTS.

PROPOSED SCHEMES FOR SETS APPROVED BY PRODUCER & DIRECTOR.

ESTIMATED SET COSTS ARE BUDGETED BY THE ART DIRECTOR.

ART DIRECTOR'S PLANS ARE APPROVED BY PRODUCTION MANAGER.

ART DIRECTOR AIDS IN "LOCATION" SELECTION OUTSIDE OF STUDIO.

PROGRESS OF SETTING CONSTRUCTION CHECKED IN WOODWORKING MILL.

SET CONSTRUCTION SUPERVISED BY ART DIRECTOR ON STAGES

MECHANICAL UNITS DEVELOPED FROM WORKING DRAWINGS.

ART DIRECTOR SELECTS PAINTS, WALL PAPERS, & SURFACE TEXTURES.

DIRECTION OF STYLE AND PLACEMENT OF SIGNS & LETTERING.

SCENIC ARTISTS PAINT BACK DROPS FROM DETAILED DRAWINGS.

PLASTIC ORNAMENT AND SCULPTURED UNITS REQUIRE DIRECTION.

SELECTION OF TREES AND SHRUBBERY FOR LANDSCAPING.

ART DIRECTOR SELECTS PLUMBING FIXTURES & DIRECTS INSTALLATION.

CARRIAGES, BOATS AND "PROPS" BUILT FROM DETAILED DRAWINGS.

ART DIRECTOR SELECTS FABRICS AND SPECIAL DRAPERY MATERIALS.

LIGHTING FIXTURES OF PROPER PERIOD DESIGNED & SELECTED.

INTERIOR DECORATIVE FURNISHINGS SELECTED AND APPROVED.

ART DIRECTOR DETERMINES PROPER PLACEMENT OF BACK DROPS.

CONFERENCE WITH DIRECTOR REGARDING MONTAGE SEQUENCES

PROCESS AND "TRICK" SHOTS REFLECT TECHNICAL TRAINING & EXPERIENCE

CAMERAMAN AND ART DIRECTOR CO-OPERATE IN ILLUMINATION.

THE SET IS READY, AND PHOTOGRAPHY OF THE PLAY BEGINS.

PICTORIAL PERFECTION OF THE SETTING AIDS IN TELLING EVERY STORY.

R. D. WILKINS

Figure 1-5 The Motion Picture Art Director: Responsibilities, functions, and accomplishments. Courtesy of ADG—Local 800 IATSE.

breakdown won't withstand the pressures of the visual effects department as an integral part of the current art department in terms of previsualization. The old system can't last—it has to give way to the new.

☐ *Given how you choose to structure your art department, do you prefer it if people think creatively and manage themselves, or do you provide an outline for people as a supervisor?*
Someone has to manage the department. How it's managed is the choice of any AD by overmanaging or undermanaging—I've made mistakes both ways. Achieving a balance and gauging your response is the challenge. The beauty of our job is the fact that on every project we get to choose who we work with by preference. Being hired and in a position to hire comes down to the fact that this business is very personality oriented. It makes our jobs very political but also very pleasant as well. I understand that my hiring an art department crew is driven by the personality of the project. I do a lot of homework before I make calls to set up interviews because we all operate on references. Some people who might be on one person's No-No list will work surprisingly well with a different person. So, that's an important thing to remember.

☐ *Phil, what is your basic approach to art directing?*
My approach to art directing is in the question, "What are we forgetting now?" or "Why am I sitting still; what should I be doing?" I have to be constantly in motion. I admire people who can be smooth and a lot more laid-back about it. I really envy them. Not worrying is a skill to be developed. In our end of the business it's 20 percent art and the rest is organizing how it happens, although on some projects I could never get it to add up to 100 percent and on other projects it was a clear 50–50 spread. I've been fortunate in having worked with people who have allowed me to do my job by delegating responsibility and the work at hand. Having developed that experience and those people skills necessary to do my job has been really important in order to answer my question, "What am I forgetting?"

The scope of the activities of an art director is dependent on the designer's comfort level. To be effective, the designer/art director relationship has to be close and really tight—a best brothers (or sisters) kind of thing. I ask each production designer I work with to tell me everything: what has been communicated to the set decorator and construction coordinator, what has been discussed with the director, and what the up-to-the-minute details are. We have to be in sync because when I'm out there on the floor, the crew is going to ask me the same questions they've asked the designer to see if they get the same answers. They only do that to know that they are on track. There has to be a basic trust or there could be terrible problems if the designer is not constantly downloading that information. Again, it's not really about an AD setting the ground rules for the relationship, but more about how the PD is calling the shots. Insisting on open communication is what the AD can contribute.[9]

An art director also has to be a know-it-all: well versed in architecture, art history, interior design, photography, psychology, and technology, for example, and then be willing to add other categories to her/his repertoire as each project introduces itself. In short, art directing grants one the license to be an eternal student.

TWO PATHS

There is no better way to learn how the art department operates than by working for a time as an art director. For some, a solid supporting role as design manager is exciting and appeals to a more detail-oriented, hands-on personality. For others, the seductiveness of a more visible and politically dynamic role in the spotlight as a production designer offers a more feasible career direction. Both positions are equally prestigious, containing respective pros and cons, and both will be discussed briefly here.

Design Manager: The Lifers

Some art directors are career professionals—they choose not to production design or necessarily aspire to it. Instead, they are delegators of responsibility both within the art department and other departments of a film. They are judges of quality of work, arbiters of visual sensibility, and transmitters of information. As communicators and efficiency experts, they insure that whatever needs to be in front of the camera gets there through relentless attention to detail and data cross-checking. In addition to their managerial responsibilities, the Lifers also assume the role of co-creator. It is very gratifying to experience this level of art directing. It evolves as a result of a long-term and mutually satisfying relationship with a production designer. Having worked with several designers, the most notable relationship that effortlessly comes to mind was with Roy Forge Smith (*Monty Python and the Holy Grail, Mrs. Soffel, Robin Hood—Men in Tights, Bill and Ted's Excellent Adventure*). From Roy's perspective, his designer/art director relationship is ultimately founded on trust, not micromanagement. A contemporary of both Henry Bumstead and Robert Boyle, Roy is a secure designer, accepting of his art director's visual intelligence and unique creative process. In addition to his quiet generosity, he is patient and very creative. Embracing that kind of camaraderie in this business is rare. Other designers who do not possess the poise of Roy's experience and professionalism tend to be histrionic; these designers only add to the length of an already challenging day. Engaging in a relationship with a designer like Roy Smith and nurturing it signifies the hallmark of a well-rounded film career.

Production Designer-in-Embryo

The chasm separating art direction from production design is deceptive. It seems easy to be a production designer, but that assumption can be an illusion. For some aspiring production designers, it is a matter of finding the narrowest section of the stream and simply stepping over the singing water; for others, there is no boat in sight to help cross the vast expanse of the raging currents. Why? Time and place have a lot to do with it. And so does perseverance. Those art directors who successfully use their current position as a catapult from the art department guild system find that it is only a matter of time before they are hired by a director to design a first film. Again, there is no easy journey, regardless of how effortless some people make it look. The resolve to do whatever it takes is often met with other conditions that must be relinquished in order to achieve the goal. For instance, it may be necessary to make the difficult choice between having a personal life, a relationship, and a family in lieu of developing a solid career as a designer. There are many trade-offs to make along the way, and it is ultimately a highly personal affair. In any case, it is this initial, compelling dream that lures so many hopefuls into the art department in the first place. When **Steve Saklad** (*Spiderman 2, Red Dragon, The Mambo Kings*) was asked why he was an art director, he responded:

☐ *What do you or don't you enjoy about art directing?*
Like most art directors out there, I'm also inclined to want to production design. The larger projects like *Spiderman 2* are projects that I can also contribute a lot of design ideas to, even as art director. Designers like Neil Spisak, Kristi Zea, and Stuart Wurtzel want their art directors to bring a lot to the party in terms of architectural expertise, a sense of theatricality and detailing, and inspired solutions to design problems. I enjoy the application of choosing molding details for interiors, and similarly these designers appreciate my participation down to that level. Each of those people doesn't usually sketch like professional illustrators can. My ability to rough sketch or doodle quickly what I interpret as their idea is not only invaluable to them but a pleasure for me.

☐ *Did you stand out as a young art director because of those abilities or was it because of your organizational and management skills?*
The easy answer is that it is always about the creative. There have been times that I've had to apologize for having to catch up on the management aspects, although each of those designers has been happy with my organizational skills. I hate to say it in this day and age, but the computer is not my friend; I use it only when absolutely necessary.

☐ *Would you talk a little about the challenges you faced on Spiderman 2?*
On *Spiderman 2* there were five art directors: Scott Murphy, who dealt with all the New York locations; Jeff Knipp, who dealt exclusively with Doc Ock, his tentacles, and related equipment; Tom Wilkins and myself primarily split the Sony stage sets in L.A. as well as the L.A. locations; and Tom Valentine, who had previous experience with Sony Imageworks, and dealt with everything that overlapped between the CG world and physical scenery.

In effect, three of us were creative, but in totally different ways. Tom Wilkins supervised four of the biggest sets in the movie, including Otto's Lab, the Planetarium, the Bugle office, and the massive Pier set, plus a handful of smaller sets, and he managed the budget and memo paperwork as well. Tom Valentine had his hands full with all the photo-driven backings, all blue screen work, the Clock Tower set, the two built miniatures: one $\frac{1}{6}$th scale model of the interior Pier set, and another miniature of the entire exterior Pier and dock. Some of these sets at Sony, for example, held an array of blue screens angled above and around, engulfing the sets. In addition, large mirrors were butted against the edges of the set walls, reflecting blue screens below for digitizing. Yet, he still found time to create timeline flowcharts indicating due dates for designing, building, dressing, shooting, and striking each set.

I was responsible for a long list of mid-scale sets that were meant to show a real sense of New York City: Peter's apartment, an East Village deli, a burning tenement building, the Off-Broadway theater world, a mid-town hospital operating room, Harry's East side mansion, as well as action-filled street scenes not shot in Manhattan but on the Universal back lot or in downtown L.A. I was also the only one of the three art directors to get a chance to sketch some of the set ideas the old-fashioned way, in the form of ink-and-marker drawings on large sheets of **onionskin**.

We all played well together but would all agree that there existed a friendly sibling rivalry in terms of currying favor to get good sets. I was on the movie for 15 months, Wilkins for 18, and Valentine for 21. When we all started, there wasn't a finished script and consequently no known set list to divvy up beforehand. Neil Spisak, the designer, and I had a special relationship we garnered from our mutual work in the theater, decades before. But everyone was playing on a much more expensive field here. Things ultimately seemed to work to each person's strong suit. And the final product each of the three art directors helped to create was, I think, pretty extraordinary.[10]

Throughout this book, many points of view are presented to enrich the experience of the reader. It is deliberately done because the activity of art directing is, in the final analysis, more subjective than following a list of procedures or clutching to a fistful of rules. Via the process of interviewing several art directors and art department creatives, our combined perceptions have drawn a more dynamic picture of our filmmaking process.

ENDNOTES

1. Linda Berger interview with the author, 8/16/04, N. Hollywood, CA.
2. Mann, William J, 2002. *Behind the Screen: How Gays and Lesbians Shaped Hollywood, 1910–1969*. New York: Viking Press, page 32. (ISBN: 0142001147).
3. Brownlouw, Kevin, 1968. *The Parade's Gone By*. Berkeley, Los Angeles: University of California Press, page 180. (ISBN: 0520030680).
4. Op. cit, page 250.
5. Since the Art Directors Guild adopted its new name, it has merged since 2003 with two other IATSE guilds: Scenic Artists, and Title and Graphic Artists, all collectively known as IA Local 800.
6. Phil Dagort interview with the author, 6/06/04, Toluca Lake, CA.

7. Art Directors Guild Workshop. *Post Digital: The Redesign of Pre-production through the Digital Art Department*, Victor Martinez interview, April 5, 2003, Panavision Screening Room, Woodland Hills, CA.

8. (Ibid.): Alex McDowell interview.

9. (Op. cit.): Phil Dagort interview, 6/06/04, Toluca Lake, CA.

10. Steve Saklad interview with the author, 8/17/04, Silverlake, CA.

CHAPTER 2

The Responsibilities, The Relationships, and the Setup

HIERARCHY OF RESPONSIBILITIES

First Responsibilities

An art director's initial relationship to the production designer is as intense and short-lived as most film project relationships. Anyone who has experienced summer camp as a child understands this dynamic. First encounters on a new film project are driven by the personal need to establish a sense of belonging to a special group, your department, and a political need to define one's place in the psychological hierarchy of the film. The bond between the prime art department figureheads—the PD and the AD—is forged by these human forces and compels the art director to fulfill first responsibilities.

How does an art director repay the favor of being hired by the PD? The art director begins by acting as a credible emissary for the partnership. By being responsible to the production designer, you are also being responsible to yourself. As codependent as this might sound, it remains as a key factor contributing to the effectiveness of the position. First, the art department budget demands this. The set budget, linked to the visual shopping list of the script, is an outline of how the funds to realize the visual concept will be spent. A good art director defends a PD's vision by managing the budget with the indispensable help of the construction coordinator by strategizing how the funds are dispersed over the set list (see "The Relationships," this chapter.) The unit production manager or **UPM**, the producer, and the head accountant are also an integral part of this process. They are given copies of the set list and budget, and they are constantly kept within the loop of set changes and developments. The ultimate goal here is to preserve the visual concept as much as possible without going over budget or relinquishing the PD's original ideas in the process.

Second, your production designer also relies on your support as an ally. Most situations will demand this: you are on location in Europe, and you are presented with conflicting information regarding the exact placement of an exterior, wooded escarpment for shooting a series of important script shots. This specific location had been decided on after a full day's worth of scouting similar locations several weeks before. Even the location manager's photos look very much alike; the truth is, no one remembers or is really sure. Essentially, this quickly escalating argument is between the PD and the director. You are in the middle, and it is time for you to speak. What do you do? You do what is expected. You take the side of your designer. And you do this diplomatically with logic. You refer back to your scout notes, you present quick plan sketches you made during the original scouting of the location in question, you recall specific conversation at the time of the decision, and you smile. Politically, you cannot afford to offend anyone. Morally, your duty is to your designer. Bonding through these kinds of experiences on a film crew is legendary. In the process, first responsibilities are fulfilled and lifelong working relationships are assured.

Third, being an effective art director demands that you are always ready. The brief scenario described previously illustrates this. Always carry a sketch pad and a PDA and learn how to scribble or enter data while you are talking. You are always relied upon to have exactly the right information at hand for precision decision-making. Readiness also includes knowing every aspect of the script well, reading every page of script changes and memorizing the most recent, staying close to the events in the production office and on set, and having set expense data always at your fingertips. The PD is doing the same thing, but expects you to close the gaps whenever necessary. This is the only way to market yourselves as the "Dynamic Duo" you truly are.

Christa Munro, art director (*Erin Brockovich, Forces of Nature, Hope Floats*), and **Gae Buckley**, art director (*The Sisterhood of the Traveling Pants, Coyote Ugly, What Women Want*), recently shared similar thoughts:

☐ *Christa, what do you require from a production designer to make your relationship work well—is communication the core?*
A dialogue based on trust, a mutual acknowledgement of strengths and weaknesses and things we mutually like/don't like to do. That way you can really help one another out. It should be kind of fun.

☐ *What quality separates a great art director from a good art director?*
Someone who can create a really strong partnership with the production designer is most effective. Of course, it depends on your designer wanting the same type of relationship.[1]

☐ *Gae, what separates a great art director from a good art director?*
I think of a great art director as a clear conduit of information both within the art department and with all other related departments. Ideally, it is someone who possesses an extensive background in art, architecture, design, theater, and film. Aside from talent, skill, and experience, an even-keeled and respectful personality enables you to get people to do their best work for you. It's extremely important, especially in Hollywood. Regarding the

expression of personality, it's also necessary to sublimate your personality and taste to some degree to get into the head and vision of the designer. Ultimately, you're facilitating someone else's vision. Realistically, I would have to say that a great art director must be able to graciously defer to the designer while still managing the art and craft of the film.[2]

Second Responsibilities

The art department is home away from home, 12 to 18 hours a day, six days a week, for a duration of anywhere from three to six months a year. The art department place and people become primary family while primary family often take on a secondary, surrogate role to our professional lives. So, responsibility to the art department is another fundamental concern. As formal head of the department, the art director is its leader-protector. As such, exercising the power to hire only the best crewmembers available reinforces core competencies for the art department. The art department coordinator (see "The Setup," this chapter) is the AD's inter- and intra-organizational interface and most valuable player. Both of you work diligently to keep the machine well-oiled and running smoothly. On *Vanilla Sky* (2001), key staff from all departments at the Paramount lot had walkie-talkie cell phones, making up-to-the-second changes and instant interface effortless. Comfortable working conditions, excellent office equipment, and connection to an Intranet server, if the project warrants it, make daily life workable. At times your tenacity will be necessary to convince the UPM to install an art department server to assist the archivist's task in organizing thousands of digital images for a larger show. Of course, this kind of equipment requires full time IT care, but will benefit everyone on the production. It is only your persuasiveness that will make the difference for the success of your department. Once again, **Christa Munro** shares her observations:

☐ *How can the art department operate more smoothly?*
My primary thought about that right now is about expanding my staff with an assistant art director and possibly two. Part of that completes the archiving question, and the other part addresses the fact that the "paperless office" isn't a reality. We generate a much larger paper trail now with our technology than we ever have, and it needs constant attention. Something you said to me a long time ago comes to mind—you were actually describing what an art director really is in six words or less—"a glorified, middle management executive secretary." The funny thing is we need secretarial backup more now because we need that support just to stay on top of it through the entire show. With that established, I'm more readily available to make changes and also it makes wrap a lot easier.

☐ *Are you a hands-on art department manager, or do you tend to delegate tasks?*
I'm a delegater. In order to do that well, you have to read the person as well as the situation. Personally, I like to get someone directed and then let them take it and build on it. You see very quickly if they'll rise to the occasion or

not. You know, some people are lost without some direction—they need clearly defined parameters. Lately, I find myself double-checking my delegating decisions and re-evaluating midstream as required. The fact is, people get tired after four months on a film going full speed, day in and out. The evaluation check allows me to see how everyone's holding up and where s/he might need to go in order that the project can easily complete itself.

☐ *How wired is your art department?*
It's totally wired. On *The Ring 2* and *Confessions of a Dangerous Mind*, we upload stuff to an online server, EStudioNetwork, at https://www.estudionetwork.com/ESN/welcome.jsp. They were very helpful, had good tech support, and it was pretty easy for all of us to learn how to use. On *Confessions* when we were in so many different locations, combining all of the location photos in the same place with the production info and schedules was a beautiful thing. Although we generally hire great art department coordinators, I can see the need for an archivist in an ideal world. That person would solely handle the images and perhaps also manage clearances but mainly trafficking the images. The documentation aspect of it alone is a huge amount of work. The server issue we've already discussed, and the computer rental issues, i.e., jurisdictional conflicts regarding large format printers, are two small tasks I've been investigating lately so I can fully address them on my next project.

☐ *I suppose your digital camera is always on hand, then?*
It has become indispensable. For instance, on a recent project we had to break apart an ambulance and re-create it as a stage set. We could rapidly document every detail required—or, simply use a digital camera phone for a quick shot of the perfect door pull—snap the item, send it, and then leave a message at the office, "When the boss comes in, let him know he's got some images on email."[3]

Third Responsibilities

The director is an art director's other boss, wielding the primary vision for the look of the film. Reading the director correctly is just as important as an AD's regard for the vision of the production designer. For example, most directors are purely verbal, translating the words of a screenplay, and in most cases, the rewriting of the script. Most likely labeled "an actor's director," they entrust the visual responsibility of the script to the design team. Other directors are exceedingly visual, spending a vast amount of time in the art department during the pre-production phase of moviemaking; they speak the same visual language as the art folks creating the imagery. As a result, the visual information plastering the walls of the art department and PD's office is welcomed and easily digested by visual directors. Concept sketches or ideas scribbled on napkins at mealtime become an overriding form of this shorthand communication. Drafted ground plans, elevations, and details with supporting white models and computer previz presentations easily exist as understandable, workable tools for further debate and

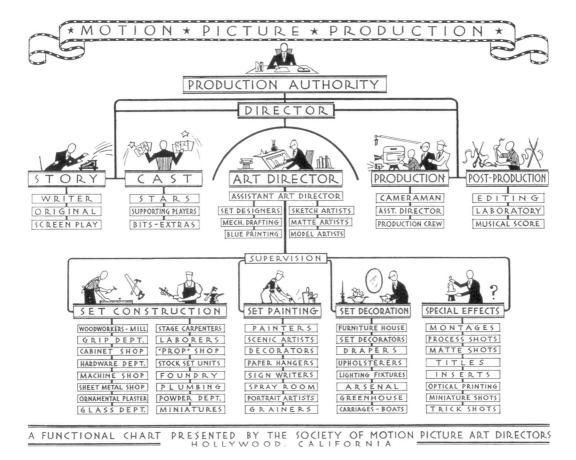

Figure 2-1 Art Department hierarchy: A functional chart. Courtesy of ADG—Local 800 IATSE.

change in the process of nailing the look of the film. We in the art department like this breed of director because they make our lives easier. One favorite champion of the art department is John Gray (*Helter Skelter, Martin and Lewis, The Seventh Stream, The Hunley*). Early in the process, he entered the workspace with a palpable enthusiasm that never diminished and left us with a visual concept. During the prep for *The Day Lincoln Was Shot* (1998), he simply said he was going against the expectations of a sepia-toned vision of the past by shooting the film in blues and gray tonalities as a premonition of the Civil War. Holding fast to that notion throughout, such a salient visual metaphor became our design beacon, inspiring countless choices and clearly answering many questions that would inevitably arise.

Amalgamating the visions of a director and PD is the obvious challenge. Just because the visual concept for a film project arises out of similar conversations does not translate into unanimous agreement. A third-party interpretation on top of those of each of your bosses can easily become a Gordian knot. Care must be taken to maintain a keen sense of neutrality and objectivity, in addition to a well-honed ability for active listening. In most cases, although your input might be brilliant, your goal is to stead-fastly translate and maintain the unity of both visions at all costs. Again, the art director is an enabler of other wishes, points-of-view, and demands—a servant to many masters.

Fourth Responsibilities

The final reporting relationship discussed here is with the studio, its representative the UPM, and the film project in general. It tends to be a more straightforward relationship because it is a business relationship; the super-imposed layers of creativity and artifice do not as easily compound the business of making art as do previously discussed responsibilities. The UPM and the studio are interested in film as product. As a commodity, a project's focus is about getting the best quality product for the least amount of money spent. Taking this a step further, it is about economies of scale, a basic concept that states that the average unit cost of a good or service can be reduced by increasing its output rate.[4] Although we are not producing donuts or widgets, this formula works especially well in terms of the ratio of added crew numbers and production of finished sets per week on a heavy film schedule or crisis schedule. On this level, the art director is operating for the company, or studio, on an efficiency level of most operations managers. Avoiding bottlenecks within the art department, as well as how it effectively functions with all other departments, is the goal. Optimizing division of labor and corresponding labor costs directly relates to economies of scale. On a union film, supervising the management of the construction crew, for example, to work efficiently by steering away from working on days off, unless absolutely necessary, i.e., a crisis schedule, would automatically boost production level but keep down inflated labor costs, correctly supporting economies of scale. On a low budget film, achieving economies of scale, especially in terms of increasing output rate, becomes a challenge considering the smaller size of the labor pool and how thinly everyone's efforts are already stretched. All of this directly relates to the management of the art department budget.

The UPM demands the fiscal loyalty of each department head by requiring strict adherence to the allocated budget figures. Inevitably, changes on both sides of the equation demand a constant adjustment to the numbers. Sometime during the mid-point of the production phase, the once rigid budget brick more closely resembles an overworked wad of Silly Putty. Again, the ability to roll with the punches acts as a release valve for the pressures of handling someone else's money.

A last consideration as a major footnote is the art director's responsibility to the guild and other brother/sister unions also collaborating on a film. All deal memos, contracts, and paperwork must be in order, to satisfy union quotas and requirements. By default, the AD is the union watchdog also responsible to the vigilant union reps waiting like referees at a sporting event to spot a foul. If such a call is made and is in turn ignored by production, the union can, and often does, shut down the film. This happened in the mid-nineties in New Mexico on the Morgan Creek production, *White Sands*, early on in the pre-production process. When the lead actors of the film stood in solidarity with the rest of us on strike, the slowdown was more quickly resolved than if they had not given their support, and production resumed as if nothing had happened. On non-union films, allegiance to the art department crew tends to be fierce and solidarity more unshakable because of the lack of union support and intervention. Typically, events like this catapult non-union people into the various guilds and film craft unions, thereby bestowing union status. My title changed to union art director during that summer. It was an experience where I also learned invaluable lessons on being a union activist before I had legitimate union membership.

The constant "push-me-pull-you" allegiance to the financial, political, and creative forces playing on the art director is extreme in both union and non-union scenarios. Successfully working in a highly collaborative industry like the movie business reinforces fast thinking, self-confidence, action, creativity, and negotiating large egos. It is not for the thin-skinned or weak-minded. It tests every fiber of a personality, as well as one's mental acuity and determination. By relentlessly testing one's social skills as well as inner strengths, art directing presents a range of challenges in the professional film arena bar none.

THE RELATIONSHIPS

Developing relationships in Hollywood translates to cowboy work. From the first moment a tenderfoot steps out of the creaky stagecoach onto the dusty dude ranch dirt, that neophyte is looking for a leg up. Throughout the process of mucking stalls, splitting rails to put up and tear down corrals, learning how to chew tobacco and win spitting contests, tying a proper lariat knot or choking on round-up dust, getting a hand with the hard work and patting other cowpokes on the back, the journey continues from cattle drive to cattle drive. What could be more classically American Western film? Learning the ropes by giving a hand and getting a hand—shorthand for basic film etiquette—is just as critical as understanding the motion capture process. Remember, filmmaking is a collaborative endeavor. One person with a Mac and Final Cut Pro just cannot do it in a vacuum. This next section will explore fundamental relationships and their reciprocal implications.

Art Department

Historically, the art department is seen as the imagery hub of film production (see Fig. 2-2). More than this, it also exists as the central department providing a strategic guide for all crewmembers in their respective departments. As keeper of the visual concept, the art department has creatively inspired and monitored all related activities for decades.

Relationship marketing is transacted in the art department—more specifically, an exchange process of services, support, ideas, options, and

Figure 2-2   Wheel of art department influence.

value for energy expended. The buzzword is show business—emphasis on the word "business." The aim of this creative, relationship marketing is to build long-term, mutually satisfying interactions between players, suppliers, and even vendors outside the film circle, in order to develop and retain lifelong preference and business acumen. Life and work continue beyond any particular film project, so short-sightedness will not do if a productive network of business relations if can exist in the future. Whether one is working on a studio picture or just getting started as an art director on a low budget **Indie**, promising and delivering high-quality service and product at reasonable prices to your immediate customers, the director, UPM, and producers are your main goals especially in non-union projects. The relationships established with other department heads and vendors on a current project had better be extendable into the next project, or you're just spinning your wheels. Why not develop proper etiquette and business form from the onset of your career? It's certainly the best way to give *yourself* a leg up.

Interdepartmental PR

Head Accountant and Staff

Before I begin my first day of work on a film, usually on the same day I interview with the UPM to set up my deal memo and corresponding perk package, I make a beeline to the head accountant's office. This is a vital PR stop more than anything else. Making friends with the head accountant beforehand positively ensures that payroll will happen effortlessly—that vendor checks might be assured to happen within a 24-hour turnaround and that a healthy communication channel is established. Nurturing this relationship is the key to money flow. Once in the Schiphol International Airport, Amsterdam, I boarded a crowded terminal-to-plane shuttle and freely offered my seat to a weary, raven-haired woman who quietly said, "Thank you" in an unmistakably Midwestern American accent. Our first paragraph of conversation revealed that we were both headed for the same 16-seater jet to Luxembourg City, Luxembourg to begin work on a TV film. She was our head accountant, Dana Bolla (*With or Without You, The Naked Man, The Lost Battalion*). Being the first of a handful of arrivals to set up our respective departments, we became fast friends, exploring the local restaurants for dinner and creating a unilateral offensive to the many challenges we would encounter during the course of the film. In this case, it is important to mention that having her as a solid ally was a significant plus in getting anything and everything done with the parent studio being 5,318 miles away. On this same film, the UPM and Dana were old war buddies and were determined to deliver the studio's financial and contractual agenda to the local film company. Befriending the head accountant and UPM extended my own political invincibility and helped ease the demands of my daily tactical tasks.

Locations Manager and Staff

Another early arrival in the pre-production phase is the locations manager. Logistics is what cements your relationship: the locations finally chosen to satisfy the design concept, the schedule of in-and-out movement at a location, access and parking, and strict adherence to what can and cannot be physically done are some of the issues you will face together. Much like the art director, the locations manager is the first to arrive and the last to leave any and all given locations. An emissary for the production itself, the locations manager is the ultimate PR agent for the film company. Together, as external marketing managers, your combined efforts need to be direct and credible to people or companies in the community where you happen to be shooting, in Los Angeles or elsewhere. Although the actual location deals and contracts are the responsibility of the locations manager, an art director's presence and support is fully expected.

This relationship is unique in terms of interdepartmental PR, but it is more client oriented outside of the film project. In this situation, you are actively working to combine the brand images of the art department, the locations department, and the larger film. On the Warner Bros. film *My Fellow Americans* (1996), I was the North Carolina art director and Ned Shapiro (*Intolerable Cruelty, Identity, Legally Blonde, Bulworth, Apollo 13*) was the location manager for the entire film, both in L.A. and Asheville. Our biggest challenges were to convince the Biltmore Estate to allow us to build the south façade of the White House on their pristine grounds for the course of two months; to land a Secourski helicopter in a mountain glen and then explode it on takeoff; and also, to stage a Gay Pride parade in downtown Asheville. Literally, the first two people to arrive in the on-location production office, Ned and I carefully established solid, trusting community relationships by laying pre-film crew groundwork. Without a well-conceived strategy, our efforts could not have been as persuasive. This combined with the right amounts of goodwill and location rental cash will always get the job done.

UPM, Production Supervisor, and Production Office Staff

The bulk of your interdepartmental marketing efforts are exercised with the production office, the other nerve center of film production. All final decisions are made in this office. Your goal as an effective art department manager with the UPM, production supervisor, and production office coordinator is to provide good offensive support. For instance, pretend you are working on a marine movie like *Titanic*. In addition to the normal requirements like building the ship and getting the sets ready, there are special considerations that demand specific attention like building the entire studio: soundstages, office buildings, facilities for art department, construction, props, wardrobe, dressing rooms, etc. At the last minute, production receives its **green light** for this film in June and is expected to be ready for shooting **hero** sets in September. Simple issues like arranging the paperwork, regulations, and permit processes, as well as getting the materials and supplies for scenery building, become somewhat challenging in Rosarita Beach, Mexico because of tariff and tactical considerations. Forcing an elephant of expectation through this keyhole of reality within such a narrow window of time demands flawless strategy and coordination. Without proper art department PR, willingness to cooperate, and a great deal of experience and common sense, the odds of success are minimized.

It would not be practical for the art director to get in the way of such a challenging process. Instead, establishing and telegraphing the benefits of cooperation, flexibility, and anticipation to the production office serve the art department in the long run. Staying in front of paperwork, scheduling, and being ready for every obstacle that will arise, positively projects reliability and instills mutual respect. Admittedly, the *Titanic* scenario is exceptional and true. Nevertheless, the same concept applies to an Indie. Budgetary and staff restraints on a low-budget feature can just as seriously undermine the reliability of strategy and scheduling as much as tariff and border restrictions on an international blockbuster. The key to overcoming obstacles like this is to consider a coin: be flexible enough to compromise on one hand, but be uncompromising about letting go of your initial strategy on the other hand. Playing win-win politics in typical issues like this can mean the difference between good managing tactics and lousy PR.

Indie work is most challenging in this way. When I designed *Notes from Underground* (1995), an adaptation of the Fyodor Dostoevsky novel set, for our purposes, in downtown Los Angeles, I was already an art director with a considerable track record. The budgetary restrictions for our small art department were not an obstacle as much as maintaining a steadfast commitment to what I wanted to see on the screen. Director Gary Walkow (*The Trouble with Dick*, *Beat*) and I discussed our joint effort to maintain realism and faithfulness to the original text. For the kind of control the typical low budget location work doesn't allow, we opted to design six small sets into 9,000 square feet of the smallest of the Delfino Stages in Sylmar, California. By figuring the costs of **retrofitting** available **flattage** and other pre-existing scenery, repainting, and dressing against the costs of location rentals and lack of noise and traffic control, our decision to set up and work in that small soundstage not only benefited the producers but secured my visual control needs. Plus, we came in under budget at $14,600 with benefits far outweighing costs.

First Assistant Director and Staff

The influence of a good art director should be felt everywhere at once. Unfortunately, the shooting crew and its activity on a **hot set** are not an art director's legitimate domain; the first assistant director, the second assistant director, and the second-second assistant director will continuously remind you of that fact. Regardless, you need to do your job despite any restrictions; acknowledging the domain status of the 1st AD is key to working within those restrictions.

What is the job of an art director on set during shooting? Members of the extended art department: the on-set dresser, the on-set prop person, on-set carpenter, and on-set scenic artist require supervision, especially when key scenes in hero sets are being shot. Daily visits to the set just before **call time** allow enough time to chat and clarify what is put in front of the camera for a certain shot, or for an art director to provide moral and political support at a specified time. Suppose there is some confusion about whether a foldable, cloth battle map, requested at the last minute, is right for a close-up shot in a pivotal scene scheduled for shooting later in the day. Ideally, a prop's importance demands attention days before it will actually be used in a scene. Having gotten the information about the hand prop in question at **wrap time** at the end of the previous day, there is now little time to act. Organizing a brief fact-finding meeting at call time with the 1st AD, director and on-set prop assistant might determine that the map, quickly crafted in the art department from 6:00 PM to 6:00 AM that morning, is too large, too rectangular and needs to be more squarish, looks too new, and must easily fit into the character's upper coat pocket. That's a lot of new information to receive, demanding fast work that needs to be done back at the art department, and be ready for shooting in six hours. Because the prop assistant must remain on set, the art director is obliged to make this directorial request his/her prime task until it is completed exactly to specification. Handing the task off to someone else will not insure exactness or speed, but supervising the task yourself will. Necessary calls are made to reschedule other morning and afternoon meetings, and to notify everyone who must be involved in the current emergency. When the task is completed, it is rushed to the set before lunch. Another brief meeting with the 1st AD and director informs you of additional changes to the prop, but more importantly that the scene has been cut from the day's shooting schedule and will be added to other **insert shots** to be gotten later in the schedule that week.

This scenario is typical. Enrolling the power of the 1ˢᵗ AD in any shooting crew or scheduling decision is a smart move. Working respectfully with a first assistant director is like working with an on-set version of yourself. Drew Rosenberg (*Helter Skelter, Stealing Harvard, Alex in Wonder*), 1ˢᵗ AD for *The Hunley*, comes to mind as one who exerted her influence consistently and judiciously. Fighting natural disasters, changing weather conditions, and temperamental actors in order to keep production on schedule, she strove to make my challenges with her all win-win experiences within reason, or the dictates of any given situation. Realistically, this could not have happened without my strength as an equal management agent providing alliance, mutual respect, and support.

Previsualization Supervisor and Staff

The advent of 3D animation and how it has affected the design landscape has forced film designers to rethink the process of matching human and animation film elements seamlessly into the visual fabric of filmmaking. A reluctant respect now governs this young relationship between the art department and visual effects folks. It cannot properly function as an adversarial one because our quickly advancing technology is forcing a paradigm shift. The marriage of minds to create a singular vision has arrived and with it, a rethinking of boundaries.

The relationship between the art department and the visual effects department is obliged to merge as hands connected to arms belonging to the same creative body. Fulltime cooperation has already begun to happen out of necessity. The art department has doubled its size by embracing digital subdepartments and creating 3D templates modeled in Form-Z and Rhino by digital set designers for 3D animators in the visual effects department. The process of previsualization before any scenery is built is an ongoing expectation of the director. All digital images are currently catalogued and transmitted to other department computer screens by the art department server and maintained by an archivist. No longer a question of when but to what degree is now the challenge.

In the final analysis, the art director as marketing manager currently has the task to promote the new and improved brand of the digital art department. Within this constantly evolving relationship, the focus has shifted from interdepartmental to intradepartmental, mixed media to merged media. Effectively marrying two peripherally related departments must be accomplished much like the merger of two corporate cultures. The art director at this point must wear yet another hat as "the human relations director" to effectively assist the smooth transition of both worlds.

ART DEPARTMENT SETUP

The art director contributes to the physical and political setup of the art department by interviewing and hiring the art department coordinator, the set designers, model makers, the archivist, previz illustrators, graphic designer, computer graphic artists, set decorator, mechanical effects coordinator, and prop master, as well as overseeing the selection of the respective set dressers, set buyers, on-set decorators, prop makers, mechanical effect makers, carpenters, welders, plasterers, foam sculptors, set painters and scenic artists, aircraft pilots, marine coordinator, and art department PAs.

When I worked on low budget films, I got to do the jobs of 65 percent of all those people and be paid the salary of one. It was certainly worth the effort of all the sleepless weeks as I gathered the firsthand knowledge of my new experiences as a creative in the art department. While navigating the world of Indies or rappeling the canyons of Hollywood, we hire our friends and tap into our carefully constructed networks. Pre-production is a time to carefully create the comfort zone that will enable us to easily outperform ourselves.

Even on the smallest staffed films, the art department tends to be the most densely populated working area of a movie. The physical, creative process of filmmaking requires so much expertise that it would be exhausting even for a single creative genius to effectively handle every aspect of the task. The head positions for the subdepartments described next provide an outline of a larger scope of involvement. The physical setting up of respective department spaces during the first weeks of pre-production can be assigned to an assistant while various department heads drop in on one another and the art director for regular, informally scheduled daily meetings. The art director is the managing director of this intradepartmental event (see Fig. 2-3). Please also see Fig. 2-3 in color between pages 142 and 143.

Art Department Coordinator

An art department coordinator is a logistical angel in situations that can financially support this position. They are represented by Local 871, Script Supervisors, Continuity & Allied Production Specialists Guild. This is shorthand for an efficiency expert who helps establish the tone of the department through common sense organizational skills and friendly coercion.

First duties include the mutual planning of the physical space, defined by a section of an office suite in any of the Hollywood studios, or the dispersal of trailers-on-wheels or warehouse space at base camp on location. Given the limits of the existing space, the art department takes physical form. Art director and production designer ideally occupy adjoining rooms or share an office with a door and a bulletproof window. The bullpen is supervised by the coordinator and contains various production assistants, PAs. It is the nerve center of the department containing the color printer, preferably Canon, capable of 11×17 size option, 50–200 percent magnification, and job memory. Accept no less. Before settling in with furniture, DSL connectivity on top of a normal phone extension, and routing system is mandatory. (This is particularly important for the archivist's basic needs.)

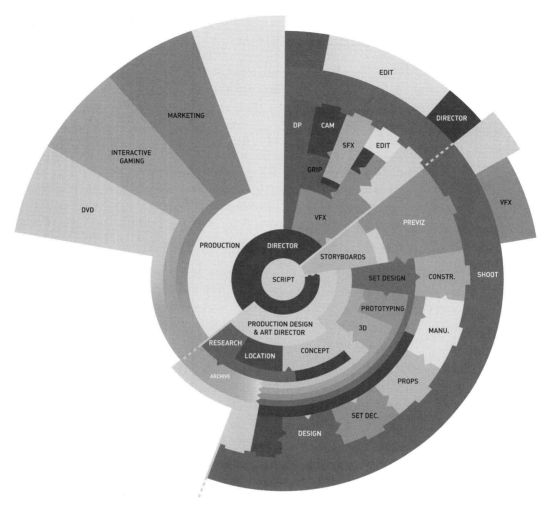

Figure 2-3   The revised art department. Courtesy of Alex McDowell © 2002.

Believe it or not, lighting requirements can also enhance creative performance. A quick purchase of a dozen clip-on lamps that can be directed to a wall or the ceiling easily combat the flicker of ubiquitous fluorescent lighting, visually competing with PC screens. Indirect, subdued lighting psychologically establishes a calmer, more inviting environment.

Beyond providing the physical comforts for the art department crew, functional and political skills are also necessary. A coordinator should be computer literate and comfortable with the Microsoft office suite and Adobe products to ensure the quick creation of word processing or image-making tasks. I suggest the Microsoft platform because it is the standard of business software. No doubt many of the folks in the art department will be creating Mac files to be shared with people outside the art department. In that case, it is necessary to be well versed in negotiating both platforms.

In addition to basic organizational ability, a coordinator's most hirable skill is the ability to research. Even a contemporary film will require Web research for specific visual information and also mining hard-to-find data. When I was working in Luxembourg as my own coordinator, reliable Web connectivity provided most of the visual data on WWI research for France, Belgium, and the surrounding area despite the fact that the data was extracted from the University of Kansas historical archives. Once within the www.ukans.edu site, I simply typed in search words for specific images I needed, and the server's search engine did the rest. Without it, even the small library of reference books we amassed before leaving for Europe would not have given us the depth and range of visual and text data the project required.

Archivist

Archiving is a new concept borne out of technological necessity. The paradigm shift from traditional to digital filmmaking combined with the ubiquitous use of laptops in the workplace has reinforced our daily reliance on computers. In fact, the movie business is populated with first adopters with regard to new technology gadgets. We, in the art department, learned that the collecting and cataloguing of imagery was a specific skill necessitating a fulltime position in order to satisfy the needs of the digital art department. So the digital station of the archivist was born.

Created as a practical job to handle the load of thousands of images created and shared in the art department, the need quickly arose in other related departments on larger, well-funded films—now every size film can use the skills of an archivist. This digital station, available to all departments, needs a computer server, to be maintained either by the archivist or a designated IT person, either physically in the same room or via an online service. A highly skilled PA would normally be employed as an assistant to the archivist and savvy computer techie for the art department. If a server is a budgetary impossibility, then a DSL line or greater would be an acceptable option—only a high-speed, designated line could handle the upload/download volumes and size of documents relayed during the course of a busy day. It's much more cost effective to email images than physically messenger them. In most cases, an archivist's box rental might include a top-of-the-line oversize scanner and inkjet color printer in addition to the typical list of required gear: laptop and inkjet printer. If not, the production should consider these technical purchases for communal use in the art department. This team member needs to have impeccable imaging and technical skills, as the art coordinator needs similar troubleshooting familiarity with the copy machine and fax machine. Without an archivist, the speed of visual exchange is extremely hampered.

From a recent interview, **J. Andre Chaintreuil**, digital set designer (*Spiderman 2*, *The Terminal*, *Minority Report*), recalls his experience on *Minority Report* (2002):

Alex McDowell, production designer of *Minority Report*, understands the computer and how to take advantage of it in a modern art department. He did an incredible setup for the production, one I'd only seen at that level in his art departments. He had a server set up for the show that everyone could access with his/her own drop box on the server and there was a fulltime archivist/IT person to maintain the system. Our PA, Sam Page, now a digital set designer, had those incredible skills. We were encouraged to use the server to archive, share key images, drop and pick up files from one another, and collaborate on designs within the department. It was also great for passing jokes and mp3 files. Another fabulous aspect of the server was watching the progress of the construction as it unfolded through digital set photographs. Other departments were tying into the server with data-bases, making everyone's process with the art department a lot smoother. Basically, Alex was imitating a modern architectural office by setting up an infrastructure that allowed all involved to share access to top-of-the-line color laser printers, plotters, and of course, file sharing. The server helped the flow of information in the department a great deal.

☐   *"How do you casually give someone a file if you're not using the server?"* Sneakernet. (Big laugh.) Burning a CD and walking it to the next person, or by using email, Instant Messaging, or a USB thumb drive, especially if there is no local server available.[5]

Digital Artists

It's no longer enough for an art director to solely be an arbiter of good taste. Lack of digital skills or at least a surface understanding of basic digital concepts will disqualify potential art directors from the running, especially on an animated flick. An intermediate skill set helps determine what is technically feasible with a specific software, and enables easy expression of ideas between an AD and the digital staff. In most cases, every new digital feature starting pre-production signifies an improvement in this new art form. Consequently, this filmmaking challenge requires the advanced skills of your computer artists as either digital set designers, using Adobe Photoshop to tweak 2D and 3D imagery for **keyframe** shots, or enhancing images modeled in Rhinoceros and AutoCAD for digital drafting of scenery. From the perspective of digital artist and set designer, Luke Freeborn (*Lemony Snicket's A Series of Unfortunate Events, Terminal, Chronicles of Riddick, Van Helsing*), "Now, getting ideas out quickly is very important because you have much less time to do more work. As a tool, the computer only assists the workload. It will not magically make a bad designer a good designer, but it could make a bad designer a faster designer."[6]

On the TNT movie-of-the-week, *The Hunley*, the Civil War submarine of the same name was drafted by our set designers in Charleston, South Carolina and transferred to the visual effects group, Station X Studios, in Santa Monica, California. They animated its submersion and underwater travel. Our draftsmen's skills combined with the animation skills of the visual effects department created 3–5 second sequences of uncompromising reality. Ability to speak the language of Lightwave or VectorWorks made my presence more credible to the digital artists.

Set Designers

Digital or traditional patience is a virtue, especially in set designers. Draftsmen constantly redraw whatever they have already drawn. With the assistance of the archivist, every Rhino and CAD document fragment, or drafted scrap of tracing paper, or napkin scribble can be scanned and saved to help ensure that erasures and revisions can happen a lot easier. Draftsmen who are manually and digitally adept are very desirable—this double indemnity insures performance whether the power is on or off (see Chapter 3: The Design Process, for additional information).

Set Decorator

The set decorator is the most valuable player in the art department. The production designer and art director create the structure for a film by defining its concept parameters. The set decorator provides context, subtext, and texture. In a recent Film Society tribute to Bob Boyle (*It Came From Outer Space, Saboteur, Cape Fear, The Shootist, The Birds*), a Universal Studios design legend at 94, he clearly defines the camera as a stand-in for the audience in terms of point of view. Taking this concept he learned from Alfred Hitchcock a step further, he suggested that subtext, "the underlying personality of a dramatic character as implied by a script or text and interpreted by an actor in performance"[7] can be implied in scenic terms and interpreted by the set decorator. Bob Boyle also reminded us that, "Visual narrative supports the storytelling. A jail cell can telegraph volumes of information; it can be blatant or whisper in subtle undertones. Without this vital information present to visually guide us, the most well articulated design spaces remain as impressive but empty icons. Cloudia Rebar (*Vanilla Sky, Without Limits, Mr. Wrong*) sees set decorating like skydiving, "Working in film is like jumping out of an airplane twelve hours a day—striving to get it right and constantly realizing you've just pulled off another miracle is exhilarating. Being on that edge and riding that adrenaline rush keeps my attention sharp, keeps me going."

Greensman

A set decorator's domain extends beyond the interior confines of built scenery *onstage* to the great outdoors. A greensman and crew exist as an extension of the set-dressing department. The scope of a film determines just how involved an art director is in the process of greens dressing, especially if the location is a sensitive one in terms of contract stipulations. Otherwise, the set decorator will supervise the detailing of landscaped exterior sets according to the specifications of the script and the production designer or the director. The greensman is available to the set decorator and art director as an expert botanist and landscape architect.

Prop Master

This is the realm of cinematic detail both literally and figuratively. In general, the broad strokes of the set decorator are distilled into minutiae in this position. Specifically, whatever an actor touches as a hand prop in the blocking of a scene becomes the focus of a prop master. An ancient coin or a cell phone can be fabricated or real, and is either found on the prop man's truck or procured by the prop man. If it's a hero prop, it must be run by the scrutiny of the art director before it is used in an ECU or extreme closeup shot. Mediating the efforts of the prop man and the final decision-making process of the director illustrates how the art director controls the visual concept of the film down to the design of a matchbook.

Construction Coordinator

Before the stateroom of the Titanic is painted and dressed, the literal framework of that set contained within the larger boat must have a solid, shootable structure. Every construction coordinator is a practical expert in answering questions of physical and structural problem solving. For example, is it more efficient to build a three-story shooting platform out of steel tubing or standard wood construction? Given the material, what is the maximum weight, including the camera, the platform will support? Translating that figure into people, what crew size can easily be supported? Can the same platform be built in modules so it can be reused for other scenes and be durable enough to transport and reassemble? Despite the fact that construction reference guides like "Architectural Graphics Standards" or Sequoia Publisher's "Pocket Ref" can help an art director determine the answers to those questions, it's always best to compare notes before making these decisions.

As an operations manager, the head carpenter's domain includes his immediate staff of foremen and gang bosses, and then scores of laborers and painters as support crew. A labor force this size requires close daily scrutiny of man-hours worked and materials used. These budget items are the direct responsibility of the construction coordinator, although the art director is ultimately responsible for potential budget increases and modifications.

It is also important to mention that the detailing work of the lead scenic artist, who operates under the aegis of the construction coordinator, conveys subtext for the visual narrative of set dressing. The literal application of paint color, wallpaper, texture, aging, and surface sealing complete whatever "local reality" is necessary to properly finish the look of the set. Contrary to what one might guess, this is the responsibility of the on-set scenic artist and not the set decorator regarding the fabrication of mechanical and handwritten signage, for example, used ultimately as on-set dressing. Working with the shooting crew, this specialist's scenic skills provide on-set solutions for on-the-spot signage, scenery touch-up, and aging of vehicles.

Mechanical Special Effects

There is a significant amount of overlap between this subdepartment and construction. Generally, the fabrication of any special piece of mechanical scenery used in a scene is the responsibility of the mechanical effects coordinator. The rotating, interior module of a Mars shuttle for the Disney comedy, *Rocketman* (1997), is a perfect example of this shared responsibility because there was a safety factor involved in the flawless operation of the **gimbaled**, revolving set. The welded steel construction of this human-size hamster wheel was finished by the carpenters and scenic artists to match the rest of the space shuttle interior set. On the same project, Jeff Jarvis, the mechanical effects coordinator (*Cast Away, Always, Firestarter, Poltergeist*), also supervised the design and functioning of a full-scale centrifuge with a locked-off camera mount, allowing the director to shoot the effects of g-force at variable speeds. Live action sequences like these support script requirements for most action films and utilize the expertise of such specialty artists (see Chapter 7: Mechanical Effects: A Practical Guide).

Stunts

Traditionally connected to the mechanical effects department, stuntmen straddle both **the below-the-line** section of the film crew and the directing department, as physical effects consultants and second unit assistant directors. Although not necessarily connected to the art department, their active participation in the mechanical effects department requires close scrutiny of how a certain stunt will impact the look of a film and consequently will need to be art directed.

This sub-subdepartment is an exceptional case, requiring the attention given to hero hand props, for instance. In most cases, the lead stuntman will most likely request **breakaway** scenery (shatterable plate glass) or breakaway props (shatterable bottles, glasses, etc.) for action scenes and fight scenes from the art department. An art director's only significant responsibility here is to insure that whatever is requested by the stunt coordinator makes its way to the set for shooting.

Visual Effects and Previsualization

This subject has been briefly addressed earlier in this chapter ("The Relationships"). Victor Martinez, a digital set designer and concept modeler for *The Cat in the Hat* (2003), shares some additional observations.

Alex McDowell, production designer, typically includes the previz department within the art department. He doesn't use previz as a conceptual
design tool as much as a device for dealing with more pragmatic issues. A
previz environment will tell him if a camera will be able to fit into a small set,
or whether we might consider shrinking the size of a set or enlarging it,
depending on the needs of shot. This aspect of our new technology
encourages directors particularly to make those decisions confidently way
ahead of time. A PD like Alex can more easily help inform his director and
then inform me, someone who is involved in more conceptual set designing,
of my direction. As the boundaries between the art and previz departments
get more blurred, our definitions become less clearly defined. On *The Cat in
the Hat*, I routinely exported previz digital models of the sets I was working
on, so that they could be used as models in their proprietary 3D modeling
environments (see Chapter 5: CGI and Digital Filmmaking).

Transportation

Picture vehicles, or hero cars, are shot in just about every film and this subdepartment provides them. In addition to its appropriate historical period, a
vehicle might need to be found in triplicate or quadruplicate for work in
mechanical effects scenes or simply be dusted down with **Movie Dirt** by
the on-set scenic artist to suggest aging and passage of time. Inevitably,
"Transpo" deals with every department because it is responsible for parking
caravans of talent trailers, five-ton trucks, production trailers, and crew
vehicles on all off-studio location sites. This department is directly related
to the locations department.

At this point, it should be abundantly clear that the influence of an art
director's supervision and management skills extends consistently into
many creative areas. Lists and schedules help keep us organized, consistent
decision-making skills help keep us focused on the designer and director's
visual concept, and hiring the best talent available ensures the best quality
of the art department product. One department, not yet described in this
chapter, is the locations department, which shares a unique relationship
with the art department. It qualifies for being included in the next chapter
because of the extensive role it plays in assisting to establish all locations
outside of the controlled studio soundstage environment.

ENDNOTES

1. Christa Munro interview, 9/11/04, Flintridge, CA.
2. Gae Buckley interview, 9/11/0, Studio City, CA.
3. Op. cit., Christa Munro interview.
4. "There are four principal reasons why this operates: construction costs are reduced, costs of
   purchased materials are also cut, fixed costs are spread over many units, and process advantages are found by avoiding bottlenecks as much as possible." Krajewski, L. [1999]. *Operations
   Management: Strategy and Analysis*. New York: Addison-Wesley Publishing Company, 5th
   edition, page 304.

5. J. Andre Chaintreuil Interview, 4/28/04, N. Hollywood, CA.

6. Luke Freeborn Interview, 5/06/04, West Los Angeles, CA.

7. *Webster's II New College Dictionary*. New York: Houghton-Mifflin Company, 2001, page 1100.

□ □ □
□ □ □
□ □ □

CHAPTER 3

The Design Process

Cinema design essentially comes from two sources: the creative efforts of the art department design team and from the well-informed searching of the locations department. Both sources take their direction from the screenplay; both resulting "shopping lists" are compared and finally become the first set list for a film project. That's it in a nutshell. The remainder of this chapter will explain and expand on these activities.

LOCATIONS DEPARTMENT AND SCOUTING

Sometimes it's easier and less expensive to **retrofit** an existing location than to build it onstage. This determination is an ongoing discussion between the locations manager and the production designer—the final decision is made by the latter. Several steps are undertaken in order to distill a set list into locations and onstage scenery to be shot. The first location scout between the locations manager and designer begins this involved process.

First Scouts

Within my first hour of my first day in the production office, the locations manager is one of the first people I am most likely to meet. He and the production designer, among the first arrivals, have already begun the locations search. Their first series of scouts take them out of the production offices to check out several location set possibilities for initial presentation to the director. This process must start early and happen quickly because it can be a long, intensive one—typically running the course of pre-production and part of production time if necessary. During this process, many extraneous options are culled from the prime choice list and tossed into the seconds pile. Winning the director's confidence and enthusiasm is the first goal. Once the director has made decisions about specific locations he is comfortable to shoot, the final goal of obtaining neighborhood permissions and signing contracts begins.

While I am guiding the art department coordinator through our office setup and initial search for scenery reference material, I am also viewing laminated sequences of interior and exterior locations and corresponding details (see Fig. 3-1). What makes this moment significant is that these

Figure 3-1 Typical locations folder: Left: Bradford Building, L.A., Top panorama: Ford Theatre, D.C., Middle panorama: Farmhouse, Luxembourg, Bottom panorama: Moab, UT.

Figure 3-1 *Continued*

montages are the first step in translating the text of the screenplay into tangible shooting realities. Together, the locations manager and designer have seriously begun the visualization process of the art department. Their first efforts are color copied and taped into legal-size manila folders and passed among the designer, director, UPM, producer, art director, and locations department. In most cases, I have already seen digital versions of these initial locations' images via the Web on the art department server if I am working on a film that has provided one. Mine is not the only preview available on the server as it is at the disposal of the digital designers, graphic artists, set designers, model makers coming aboard, as well as whoever else is working during the early phases of film production. Digital artwork overlaid onto location images is next presented to the director, alongside research and concept art. Even with our active sharing of digital images, the instinctive process continues to be primarily hand-to-hand in the initial throes of our collective, creative bonding experience. Please see Fig. 3-1 in color between pages 142 and 143.

Once the ongoing process of location finding is underway, logistical concerns like location base camp setup, caravan setup (crew parking and production vehicle parking), getting in and out of locations, and logical placement of the staging of scenery are addressed. As project manager for the art department, my concerns parallel those of the locations manager in terms of practicality and operations management. For example, cover sets, especially those outside of the studio, are insurance that shooting will continue despite the prevailing weather conditions. Successful location manager/art director teams will always include cover sets within the logistics of location scheduling.

Second Scouts

The initial round of scouting completed, a second series of scouts begins between the production designer and art director. Second scouts serve two purposes by allowing the production designer to confirm the quality of choices made with the locations manager and by providing bonding time between the designer and art director. Physically visiting the locations and sharing their possible shooting potential also transfers creative and managerial responsibility from the designer to the art director. From this point onward, whatever changes happen will be handled by the art director, including interfacing with the locations manager and agents outside of the film, retrofitting physical location changes in preparation for shooting, organizing the logistics of getting into the location site, staying and working there, getting out with little difficulty, and most importantly, the return of the location to its original state after shooting.

In the example shown (Fig. 3-2), scout notes can be copious but are always detailed. Location managers would rather have too much detail than too little for the benefit of the agent renting the location to the production. Scout notes are most likely retyped by the art department coordinator from the art director's handwritten notes into a simple, readable text document

			"My Fellow Americans" Location Information	last modified: 3/20/96

"My Fellow Americans" Location Information   last modified: 3/20/96

Script Date: March, 1996	Director: Peter Segal	Production Designer: Jim Bissell
Producer: Warner Brothers	Michael Ewing / Jean Higgins	Production number: / Page number: 8

Set #:	Loc:	Type:	Set Description:	Location Notes:
435	Asheville	Int	Hollis Horsebarn-night	~~Biltmore Estate~~ *TBD.*
			scenenumbers: 195,196,222 → *NOT A DAIRYBARN*	*SAME AS 447*
436	Asheville	Ext	Maryland Road-Day	TBD-Schedule Driven
			scenenumbers: 199	
438	Asheville	Ext	White House Kennedy Garden	Build at Biltmore
			scenenumbers: 237,243	
439	Wash	Ext	White House N.E. Gate	TBD *?*
			scenenumbers: 248	
441	Asheville	Int	Witnaur's bedroom	Biltmore Forest *GINGER 2744768*
			scenenumbers: 145	*25 → S. FOREST MALL, JUST PAST BROWNTOWN RD, RT 2ND LEFT, 9 DEERFIELD.*
443	L.A. Loc	Ext	Highway/Helicopter duel/culvert	TBD *LA*
			scenenumbers: 106,107,108,109,110,111,112,113	
444	Asheville	Int	Wayne & Genny's Trailer-night	Cover Set-Find location for Factory Lunchroom and build in space nearby
			scenenumbers: 128	*DRAW.*
445	Asheville	Ext	White House S.W. lawn	Construct -Biltmore
			scenenumbers: 214-228,232,233	
445	Asheville	Ext	White House Southwest Lawn	White House
			scenenumbers: 238,239,240,241	
446	Asheville	Int	Factory Lunchroom-Cleveland	Asheville Warehouse
			scenenumbers: 252	*DRAW.*
447	Asheville	Int/Ext	Hollis Kitch/Ext Barn	TBD *?*
			scenenumbers: 221	*SAME AS 445.*
701	2nd Unit	Ext	Sky/Airforce 2	Stock footage?
			scenenumbers: 18	

Figure 3-2   Scout notes for N. Carolina locations on *My Fellow Americans.*

and then distributed to the following departments: Locations, Set Decorating, Construction, Paint, Special Effects, and Props. Combined with the preliminary script, this list becomes the basis of the preliminary set list, compiled and distributed by the art department coordinator (see Fig. 3-3).

Third Scouts

The third series of **rekkies** during pre-production are fact-finding missions. They occur for the benefit of the set designers during a full day visit to all existing locations. By and large, most locations are retrofitted, temporary sets that must be carefully analyzed. Specific measurements of loading docks, elevators, and similar building entrances or egresses are recorded to determine the size of scenery modules to be designed to load easily in and out of the building. Width, length, and height dimensions of rooms including doors and windows, hallways, stairwells, and other shootable areas of location spaces are also recorded for retrofitted scenery.

With necessary gear in hand, accuracy for drawing ground plans, elevations, and construction details can easily happen (see Fig. 3-4). Planning several trips to a location is a realistic consideration; not everything can be thought of for a single comprehensive trip. If a specific location requires a great deal of time-intensive detailing, then arrangements must be coordinated with the locations department for access and additional measuring time (see "Fifth Scouts").

Fourth Scouts

The last formal scout happens before the final production meeting and commencement of principal photography. During this scout all production heads including the director, the director's personal assistant, 1st AD, producer, UPM, head accountant, production designer, art director, set decorator, cinematographer, 1st assistant cameraman, gaffer, key grip, visual effects coordinator, construction coordinator, mechanical effects coordinator, Transpo captain, the location manager, and assistant location managers are assembled for several daylong rekkies. Scheduling this event is comparable to organizing a mini-production meeting-on-wheels in two production vans with scheduled lunch and dinner stops. Seating in the vans reflects each work-related group, positioned within earshot so that logistical questions that arise can be solved during the course of the day. As problems are solved and other considerations arise, mobile phones are in constant use for ordering equipment and supplies, rescheduling dinner, making logistical changes, calling vendors, and updating assistants and department coordinators. Laptops are lit and functioning, organizing timelines, filling in forms, and checking email. The production designer and I are usually found explaining and simultaneously sketching concept ideas or working through foreseeable problems. All in all, this last series of scouts codifies the final onstage and locations set list and the shooting schedule (see Chapter 8: Paperwork and Production Tasks, for additional details).

Fifth Scouts

For one reason or another, locations change at the last minute. In terms of scenery, this can pose a problem because much of it is retrofitted for a particular location. Practicality dictates that whatever can be salvaged from scenery already designed and completed is used in the new location; new retrofits are discussed as additional budget items and are always approved by the UPM as overages in golden time man-hours in order to get the new scenery done on time. In addition, directorial changes regarding aspects of locations originally considered alter how locations are re-retrofitted and consequently require another visit. Subsequent scouts to and from contracted locations are arranged through the locations department, as are changes and revisions that occur during the final production meeting.

Within the preceding few pages, we have seen how vital the affiliation of the art director and the location manager and his/her department is in terms of how the scout list, master set list, and set construction budget emerge out of the first levels of location scouting. This initial, physical work, i.e., scouting, measuring, and photographing architectural and location detail, provides a counterpoint to the development of the design concept and research explored in the remainder of this chapter.

BEGINNING THE DESIGN PROCESS

As locations are being photographed, the designer, storyboard artists, concept illustrators, concept modelers, and physical model makers are rapidly producing sketch ideas and 3D models in order to distill a visual concept. Computer generated imagery, CGI, has accelerated this process of visualization. As newer technology tools become available to creative artists, the design process will become redefined as it has within the past decade. The following pages will demonstrate that both traditional and digital aspects of visualization grow out of different expressions of the same creative impulse. Sharing a brief section of conversation with **Christa Munro** provides a relevant overview of how the design process is a personal one, as unique as anyone who employs it:

☐ *Christa, you were raised in a family of architects giving you a basis in architectural language even though you didn't attend architecture school. Tell me how that influenced you as an art director.*
I explored the more painterly aspects of my creativity early on in my development. What's interesting though is when I showed my drafting from a period film I had done to my sister, a very accomplished architect, she silently went through the huge stack of bluelines and said, "You just get to do the fun stuff." (Chuckle.) And, she had a point—with few code considerations, we just get to reference the real world without having to comply with it. The premise we have to consider when approaching the structure of scenery without the functionality of a family or office suite of people is about telling a story. What I've always liked about working in a

RED DRAGON ART DEPARTMENT, SET BREAKDOWN, 4TH REVISION - AS OF JANUARY 3, 2002

<u>LA LOCATIONS</u>

1.	INT	Concert Hall	No tie-in. No EXT.	N	sc 2
2.	INT	Lecter's Dining Room, Entry	Ties in to EXT Townhouse Location(MD)	N	sc 3, 5
3.	INT	Lecter's Study, as LA Location	Ties into Lecter Dining Rm. Location	N	sc 5, 6
4.	OMIT				
5.	EXT/INT	Leeds House, incl. Kitchen, Stairs, Den, Hall, Master Bedrm., Bath (video:Kitchen -D-sc 35,136)	Bare-tree look is all Night. Summer look on video is all Day. Ties in to Leeds Bathroom Studio Set Note: Lattice outside Kitchen door.	N	sc 11, 12, 16, 34
6.	EXT/INT	Sherman House video, incl. Backyard, Den	No tie-in. Summer look only. Note Rain outside Den windows.	N	sc 114
7.	INT	Reba's Apartment, incl. Living Rm., Kitchen	Ties in to EXT Reba's Apt.Location (MD) Note Rain outside windows.	N	sc 62, 63
8.	INT	Crawford Bedroom and Den	No tie-in.	N	sc 83, 87
9.	EXT	Omni Hotel, Atlanta, estab.	Tie in to INT Hotel Rm. Studio Set.	N	sc 17
10.	INT	Coffee Shop	No tie-in.	D	sc 24
11.	INT	Bookstore	No tie-in.	D	sc 53, 55
12.	INT	FBI Apartment	Tie in to EXT FBI Apt. DC	D	sc 98
13.	INT	Atlanta Police Squad Rm., incl. Springfield's Office.	Tie in to EXT Atlanta Police Station (MD).	D	sc 21, 22
14.	INT	Asylum, Chilten's Office, Corridor, Staircase	Tie in to EXT Asylum (MD), & tie in to Lecter's Cell	D	sc 26, 27 sc 28
15.	INT	Asylum Exercise Pen	Tie in to EXT Asylum (MD).	D	sc 51
16.	EXT	Chroma-Lux Inc., include. estab., parking lot, loading dock, bus stop	Tie in to INT Chroma-Lux Locations (LA). Note Rain for 1st parking lot night scene.	D N N	sc 56 sc 59, 60 sc 142
17.	INT	Chroma-Lux, incl. machinery maze, Personnel Office, Corridor:	Tie in to EXT Chroma-Lux (LA). Tie in to INT Reba's Darkroom Studio Set	D N	sc 57 sc 141, 144, 148
18.	INT	Law Office (Birmingham) No tie-in.		D	sc 66
19.	INT	FBI Offices, including Task Force Office sc 65, 69 Interrogation Rm. sc 96, Conference Rm. 122,136,128 Crawford Office -N- 161,162	Tie in to EXT FBI Headquarters Location (DC)	D D	sc 65, 69 sc 107
20.	INT	FBI Labs, including Hair & Fiber Lab sc 72 Latent Fingerprints Lab 74,162 Document Lab sc 76	No tie-in.	D	sc 72, 74, 76
21.	INT	Library Study Carrell	No tie-in.	N	sc 84
22.	INT	Tattler Printing/Bundling Room	No tie-in. Papers loaded onto trucks.	D	sc 82
23.	INT	Tattler Garage	Tie in to EXT Tattler Street (MD).	D	sc 101
24.	INT	Zoo Infirmary	No tie-in.	D	sc 110
25.					
26.					
27.	EXT	St. Louis Newsstand	No tie-in.	N	sc 100
28.	EXT	Rooftop Helipad w/ Helicopter	Tie in to INT FBI Helicopter (DC)	D	sc 71
29.	EXT	Dolarhyde Mansion, include. Garret POV to Garden: (-D- sc 120)	Tie in to EXT Dolarhyde Grounds (MD), & INT Dolarhyde Mansion Studio Set Note Fire.	D N N	sc 45 sc 104 sc 157
30.	EXT	Dolarhyde Roadwork			

(continued)

Figure 3-3   Preliminary set breakdown for *Red Dragon*.

BALTIMORE LOCATIONS

66.	EXT	Brooklyn Museum of Art	Tie in to INT Brooklyn Museum	D	sc 124
67.	EXT	FBI Apt. (establishing)	Tie in to INT FBI Apt. (L.A.)	D	sc 97
68.	EXT	Reba's Apartment	Tie in to INT Reba's Apt. Studio Set	N	sc 61
			Note Rain falling in first scene.	D	sc 121
			Note front door double-blind for pg 103.	N	145, 147
69.	EXT/INT	Chesapeake Safehouse, incl.Josh's Rm.	No tie in.	D	sc 93, 94
				N	sc 95
70.	INT	Brooklyn Museum, Corridor, Painting Storage	Tie in to INT Brooklyn Museum	D	sc 126,129 132, 133
71.	EXT	Tattler Garage, incl. Street	Tie in to INT Tattler Garage Location (LA)	D	102, 106
72.	EXT	St. Louis Streets (INT Van to Zoo, to Reba's)	No tie in.	D	109, 121
73.	EXT	State Road (Police Caravan)	Possible tie in to EXT Dolarhyde Grounds Location (MD). Note Fire in distance.	N	sc 150
				N	sc 154
74.	EXT	Atlanta Police HQ, establishing facade and Sidestreet	Tie in to INT Atl. Police Squad Rm.	D	sc 20, 23
75.	EXT	Airport Tarmac, DC	No tie-in.	Dawn	sc 91
76.		Shop Setup			
77.		Scaffolding, Lifts			
78.		Fire and Safety			
79.		Expendables			
80.		Signs and Graphics			
81.		Heavy Equipment			
82.		Strike and Restoration			
83.		Hauling, Waste Disposal			
84.		Greens			

FLORIDA LOCATIONS

85.	EXT	Beach/Boatyard/Greens	Tie in to EXT Graham Hse.	D	sc 8, 9
				D	sc 158
				N	sc 159
86.	EXT/INT	Graham House, 1st Floor	Tie in to 2nd Floor Graham Hse Studio Set.	D	sc 9
				D	sc 158
				N	sc 159
				N	sc 163
87.	EXT	Florida Highway	No tie in.	N	sc 88
88.	EXT	Ocean w/ Customs Launch	No tie in.	N	sc 89
89.	EXT	Sailboat at Sea	No tie in	D	sc 172

D.C. LOCATIONS

90.	EXT	FBI Headquarters (establishing)	Tie in to INT FBI Offices Location(LA).	D	sc 64
91.	EXT	FBI Helicopter over Potomac	Tie in to INT FBI Helicopter (DC)	D	sc 70
92.	INT	FBI Helicopter	Tie in to EXT Helipad Location (LA)	D	sc 77
93.	EXT	JW Marriott (establishing)	Tie in to INT Marriott Hotel Rm. Studio Set.	N	sc 85

Figure 3-3 *Continued*

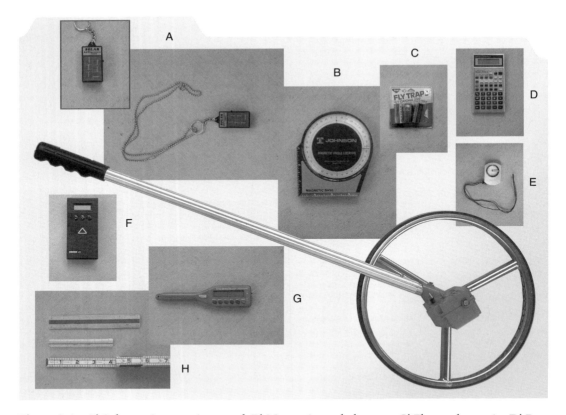

Figure 3-4   A) Solar anti-mosquito guard, **B)** Magnetic angle locator, **C)** Fly catcher strip, **D)** Professional Measure Master II™, **E)** Suunto inclination device, **F)** Digital distance indicator, **G)** Scale Master Classic™ digital plan measure, **H)** Rulers: flat architectural scale ruler, three-sided architectural scale ruler, and a wooden scissor-extension ruler (diagonal). A 12"-diameter measuring wheelie with an extendable tube makes measuring over terrain easy up to 999' without the use of a 500' cloth tape measure (not pictured).

theatrical environment is that it's basically about an illusion of form and space. When you finally get that, the rest of it neatly falls into place.

☐   *Does an art director at this point in time need to know how to draft?*
Yes. (Adamantly.) I've been having so many conversations about this in two worlds: one in the digital design world and the other in just the workplace. I have heard some production designers claim there is no need to draw. Regardless, there's something about laying those lines on paper and understanding their translation into the finished product that's really important and is being missed. And, if you skip that part of the process, then you are relinquishing your design's integrity to somebody else. Why would you do that? There is something intimate and immediate on a creative level about scribbling your idea or explanation on a napkin during a conversation with a director that helps you communicate your ideas. Then, if the director is capable of doing the same thing—I mean to say, "draw"—then you're onto something really good. That's your initial bonding process happening in real time.

After having made the first pass through the script, the creative process begins in your imagination. At this point, how do you begin to translate the text into imagery? I have a little trick I learned from Gene Rudolf (*Raging Bull, The Right Stuff, Diner*). I re-punch the holes so that the backs of the script pages are on the left side of my binder when the book is open. When I read through the script on my first pass, I can scribble my first impressions on the clean backside of the next page. That way, the script, my initial ideas, and my notes are all in the same binder. The first pass is just "my dreaming." I realize the production designer might have something completely different in mind, but this will contribute somewhere down the line and also helps me know if I'm on the right track. After that, I do my set breakdown, and then I keep distilling it. That completes the first set breakdown. I add other elements later on. This is the best way I know to organize my thoughts.[1]

RESEARCH

Research reveals additional information to the designer and art director as they refine the film's **visual concept**. OK, but what *is* a visual concept? It is shorthand for a longer explanation; it abbreviates words into symbols, metaphors, or indexes; it is an image that defines the central idea of a movie. Do all films have a central idea? They should and they are presented in **iconic** terms. Why do you do this? Core images provide coherence and continuity for a film. It is the aesthetic glue that optically binds all sections of the movie, and it defines why the production designer, art director, and art department exist in the first place. What is an example of thematic manipulation? An older example is the idea of depicting "the past" in sepia tones—mimicking an earlier photographic process—not a very good example because it is expected and overused. A better example is found later in this chapter. It is the metaphor of an egg used as the basic shape of the interior Pre-Cog chamber of *Minority Report*. As you read the text and view the images of that particular set, you might consider why an ovoid is a better shape than a pyramid for the "idea" of this interior set within this movie.

Gathering visual research is a powerful way to define the concept. Within the first several weeks of pre-production, the walls of the art department quickly become plastered as a repository of photocopied and color printed images: icons, **indexes**, symbols, and metaphors of the visual concept for the film. We surround ourselves with these images and live within them while we design. The Internet and public libraries are inexpensive ways to accumulate data, and are also more visually comprehensive for research data and imagery than one might guess. Most of the research done for the TV movie, *The Lost Battalion* (2001), was downloaded from the World War I archives of the University of Kansas to my PC terminal on location in Luxembourg City, Luxembourg.

Rare portraits of Cher Ami, a carrier pigeon and First World War hero, and specific photographic references to his carrying cages, and a typical message tube strapped to his ankle, were pulled from the www.ukans.edu

site (see Fig. 3-5A). No book was able to provide this kind of indispensable, arcane information. Most research is found through the normal channels mentioned and can also be bought from private photographic collections (see Fig. 3-5B) showing several images taken in San Francisco in the 1940's.

If actual video and DVD rental for hard-to-locate film research is required, Eddie Brandt's Saturday Matinee located in North Hollywood is available for a nominal fee. Its catalogue of films includes animation, film noir, sci-fi, exploitation, documentary, live entertainment, foreign, silents, serials, and black films—titles and genres not available at Blockbuster Video. As the front page of its catalogue boasts, "We've acquired three centuries of movies in 33 years!"

A designated research budget can buy 30-minute increments of research time at the 20th Century Fox Studios Research Library, Warner Bros. Research Collection in Burbank, the Lillian Michelson Research Library now located at DreamWorks, and the Dorothy Herricks Research Library at the Motion Picture Academy of Arts and Sciences in Los Angeles. These research facilities tend to be expensive, but they are also extraordinary source centers of rare, well-archived images either custom-burned onto CD or beautifully photocopied at the customer's request. Several of the images used for this book came from those collections.

The Fox Studio Research Library is unique among the studios and popular with art department research teams for the scope of its available material. For example, it provides assistance for all types of projects throughout the production process, features a collection of over 40,000 non-fiction books on all topics, over 100 current periodical subscriptions, computer workstations with high-speed Internet access and powerful graphics capabilities including color copier/printer/scanner/CDRW, online services including Nexis, Reader's Guide, and NY Times Archives, and supplies creatives with 2D and moving picture, visual reference materials. Like most research libraries you can also phone or email your research requests.

During the earliest stages of pre-production, the art department by default becomes the center of visual source materials for the entire production. Gathering research during pre-production is a time to steep your psyche into the era presented within the pages of the script, and it is a time to become as deeply knowledgeable about the historical context of your film to help resolve whatever questions that might arise for the director. In the case of Cher Ami, the World War I hero pigeon, several downloaded photos in-hand were undisputed evidence for which pigeon to cast in the starring role based on the original bird's feather markings. Our relentless drive to produce critical data and visual information makes the art department the premier place to answer these questions. Historical dramas, in particular, demand tremendous detail and scrutiny through research sourcing and data gathering. **Linda Berger**, assistant art director and key art department researcher for *Forrest Gump*, recalls a landmark experience in her early career:

Figure 3-5A　Cher Ami, pigeon carrier cages, and message tube—examples of research images captured from the World Wide Web.

☐　*Linda, on Forrest Gump you were the assistant art director and managed the research for the film. Would you tell us a little bit about that?*

I was one of the first people hired onto pre-production. The vision of Rick Carter, the production designer, was very clear and straightforward: the film was a character-driven piece and needed to feel real and human, not like a documentary, though the fictional story clearly had its basis in historical events. It needed to be infused with the humanity of the time we were portraying—meaning, because we were creating history that was relatively recent, we needed to be true not only to that history as it truly was, but to history as people who actually experienced it or remembered it in their mind's eye. With that concept in mind, I built the beginnings of a huge research library. It was truly exciting for me. Kacy Magedman, art department coordinator, and assistant coordinator Anna Hayward did a great deal of footwork for us all along the way. And we kept adding to it, and it eventually filled a room with file cabinets and stacks of information. I focused on sources of recent history like prominent newspapers and *Life, Look, Time,* and *Better Homes and Gardens* magazines. *Time* was a great source for Vietnam research, and the others provided a rich diversity of pop-cultural images. And, of course, Lillian Michelson was a tremendous help to me.[2]

In Washington, D.C., I also found police newsreels about the 60's anti-war demonstrations and other rallies that had taken place at the Lincoln

Figure 3-5B   Typical research images for a 1940's period film.

Figure 3-5B   *Continued*

Memorial where our staged film rally would take place. Also, at hippie campsites in and around D.C. and the Jefferson Memorial where the protestors had stayed overnight, I learned about the kinds of buses that had come from all over the country to bring protesters to the capitol city. Period newsreels were a wealth of information showing signage, buttons, graphics, and banners, as well as style of dress. There was also loads of information to be found about TV trucks and cars, sound and TV equipment, TV cameras' scaffolding and staging, as well as research on police cars and equipment; a lot of it very surprising and sobering. Every image was used as a "true image"—we didn't guess about what we would see—down to creating signs, for example, and we tried to re-create them in their original materials such as cardboard from the backs of cardboard boxes with the folds still attached and poster paints or canvas. Paramount Sign Shop was tremendously helpful. They did the bulk of the work preparing the signage. They reserved a whole crew of sign writers to work on well over 1,700 images including signs, banners, and so on. Robin Miller, prop master, created armbands, buttons, and many of the bumper stickers—all based on much of the research we did together.

Much additional info in D.C. came from tech people I talked to at the networks who did on-the-spot reporting at the time. We were also able to track down some of the original photographers who had gone to some of the actual rallies and were able to purchase their personal photos of the events. These were extremely valuable. Other research came from the Library of Congress, which helped us understand the importance of getting it all historically correct. I was able to hire a great researcher in Washington, who culled through all kinds of police reports and records to help me find information that shed light on a lot of historical background information about the Viet Nam era as well as Watergate. And, Rick Porras and Steven Boyd, working then in Bob Zemekis' office, spent weeks during pre-production in Washington going through film archives for images that would be seen in the film, such as the images of Kennedy, Johnson, and many others. They brought back many clips that were also of great use to me for research as well.

With all of those wonderful places as a springboard, we began to create an outline marrying our historical and current events timelines with the one emerging for Forrest and Jenny, the two main characters. Their childhood and adulthood events needed to mirror or coincide with cultural history in order to remain true to Rick's visual concept of "real and human." Rick loved collages as a way to find the essence of character and asked me to create a visual timeline for Jenny's character, for example. It took up one entire wall in the art department. It was dedicated to everything that might have been present in her daily life and overall life history like magazine ads, book images reflecting the lifestyle of the 50's thru the 80's, and even her route through her drug use, reflected in her character in terms of the times in which the story was being told. Along the top of her personal historical timeline were the years broken down into months of the year and decades; along the side of the chart, there was a section designed for specifics such as hair, dress, school, entertainment, furnishings, cultural interests, etc. Everyone used the wall containing the story of Jenny's life. Joanna Johnston, costume designer, in particular found it very valuable. Once I had collected enough information, I began to make large books, and these were available for everyone to look through and use as research. There was a Washington history Vietnam War Rally research book, the largest and heaviest of all of them, and others ranging from the Southern U.S., the Vietnam War, to the strip clubs and discos, and the New York City of the 70's. Art directors, Jim Teegarden in L.A. and Leslie McDonald down in Beaufort, South Carolina and Savannah, Georgia used these books and added even more research.

I had the great good fortune to go to Washington and supervise the creation of the Lincoln Memorial Rally and campsites and Watergate events with Robin Miller, our brilliant prop master. I'll never forget it. It was such a wonderful and inspiring creative experience. The day we shot the Rally at the Lincoln Memorial, Eric Roth, the screenwriter, remarked to me—and I'll never forget it—that the way it all looked and felt that day was as he had imagined it in his mind's eye. That was a truly gratifying moment for both Rick and me. I'm very proud of what we were all able to accomplish there.[3]

STORYBOARDING

Although there is no specific outline available for a designer's visualization process, some are inclined to rely on storyboards as an effective shorthand method of visually communicating with the director and cinematographer. What we now refer to as "animatics," has its roots in storyboard sketching. Harold Michelson's boards for *The Ten Commandments* (1956) and *The Cotton Club* (1984), Fig. 3-6A and Fig. 3-6B respectively, are extraordinary examples of previsualizing the shooting sequence of a motion picture.[4]

Even though digital tools exist to perform the same tasks as hand-drawn storyboards and concept sketching, both forms of storytelling continue to be used because they are immediate and also explore idea possibilities in a way that **CGI** cannot. Most often, the storyboard artist and concept modeler on computer are working simultaneously on different aspects of the same visual concept. The storyboard artist is drawing two-dimensionally, bound by the rectangular **aspect ratio** of the actual movie screen and filling in the boxes with the continuity of images, while the concept modeler/digital set designer is sculpting digital space to present a different angle of the same ideas presented in the storyboard sketches. Both paths eventually lead to the same place and both descriptions of the journey help to create a richer design.

ANIMATICS

In comparison, the animatics image pages shown in Fig. 3-7A, Fig. 3-7B, Fig. 3-7C, and Fig. 3-7D are fully self-explanatory. Each cell or window of the typical storyboard page sequence is expanded onto its own page. As you can see, each page of the previsualized, computer-generated sketch indicates plan, elevation, isometric sketches for specific scenes, set info, camera info, and additional equipment info, e.g., use of a Techno crane as well as camera blocking data.

The term animatics and Pixel Front Liberation are synonymous. PLF (*Fight Club, Starship Troopers, The Matrix Reloaded*) is located in Venice, CA and provides computer graphic imagery (CGI) and other special effects services for clients in the film, TV, advertising, music videos, and interactive games industries. The company also creates 3D computer animation software that helps movie directors plan film shoots, indicated in the pages for *Panic Room*. The first section of a recent interview with PLF founder and Creative Director **Colin Green** explains the vital contribution of storyboarding on the previs process and how a design resolves itself through animatics:

☐ *Did you work alongside a storyboard artist on Panic Room?*

Peter Ramsey was the storyboard artist on our team. He would sit with us and spend a lot of time tweaking and finessing the camera angles and the blocking as a filter on David Fincher's direction. Peter was able to scribble all of his thumbnails down and digest David's stream of directorese as he quickly and carefully laid out his initial shooting sequence to both of us. Peter was instrumental in getting us oriented; as computer animators, we had had little exposure to that much information, that fast. Our first pass found us compiling our shot list. The secondary pass focused on finessing and refining the composition.

One of the main reasons David wanted us to participate in that film is because of the unique way that set was built with all four floors of that brownstone built within their proper relationship. All floors were set up in the new Raleigh Studios in Manhattan Beach, CA as they would be in reality. As you know, you would normally split the levels of the house into separate floors onto a sound stage **spotting plan** with the ability to **wild** rooms for shooting easy access. All four walls of all rooms on all four floors were built and set in place, as they would be on a location. So there was a lot of sharing of blueline drawings back and forth. Paul Westcott was the draftsperson liaison for both departments.

We were doing shots with motion control that initially required precise grip participation. David did many takes he wasn't happy about. You can't look at a single shot and say, "That's right or wrong." You have to look at it in sequence. In the film there was the Big Shot running about four minutes, tracking along the staircase, through a keyhole and up through the ceiling. That shot was scheduled originally to be a Techno crane shot segment. Because the gripology involved in hitting the mark or getting the shot as smooth as David would've preferred was not being accomplished, we collectively decided to build the shot in the computer and then feed that data to the motion control camera where the shot would be executed pixel by pixel. In that way, the camera would do exactly what David had approved in terms of certain speed changes and framing relationships he wanted. The tricky thing was finding that single piece of equipment that was available and could reach all those spots that needed to be reached. Of course, the boom had to be long enough but agile enough not to bump into scenery

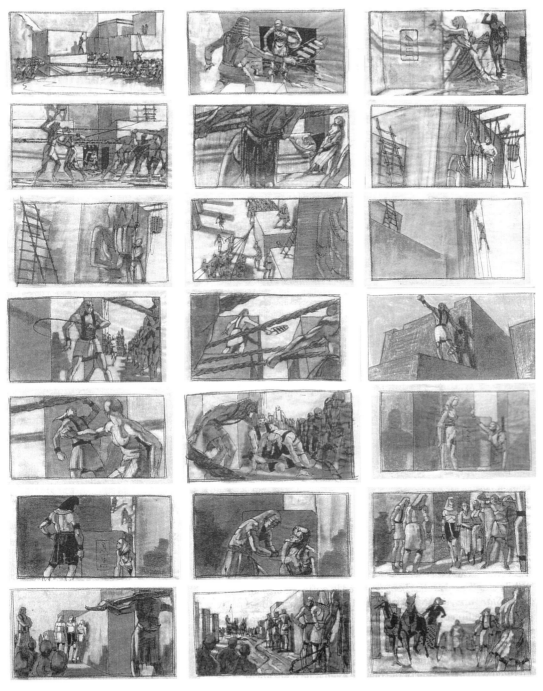

Figure 3-6A Storyboards for *The Ten Commandments* (1956) drawn by Harold Michelson. (The boards read from L to R across the page.) Courtesy of Paramount Studios.

Figure 3-6B Storyboards for the "Prohibition sequence" from *The Cotton Club* (1984) drawn by Harold Michelson. (The boards read from L to R across both pages.) THE COTTON CLUB™ & © 1984 Totally Independent, Ltd. All Rights Reserved.

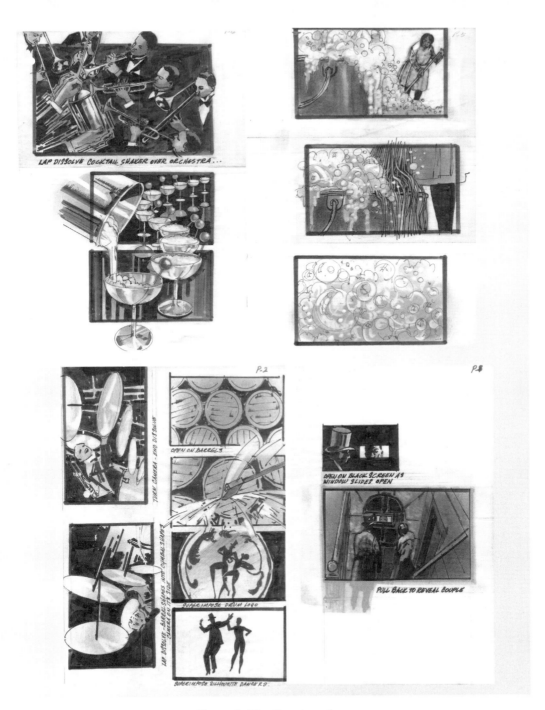

Figure 3-6B *Continued*

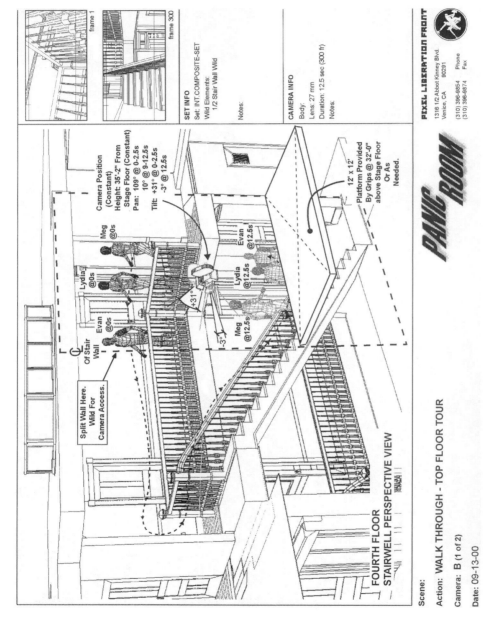

frame 1

frame 300

SET INFO
Set: INT.COMPOSITE-SET
Wild Elements:
 1/2 Stair Wall Wild

Notes:

CAMERA INFO
Body:
Lens: 27 mm
Duration: 12.5 sec (300 ft)
Notes:

Camera Position
(Constant)
Height: 35'-2" From
Stage Floor (Constant)
Pan: 109° @ 0-2.5s
 10° @ 9-12.5s
Tilt: +31° @ 0-2.5s
 -3° @ 12.5s

Meg
@0s

Lydia
@0s

Evan
@0s

+31°

-3°

Lydia
@12.5s

Meg
@12.5s

Evan
@12.5s

12' x 12'
Platform Provided
By Grips @ 32'-0"
above Stage Floor
Or As
Needed.

Split Wall Here.
Wild For
Camera Access.

CL
Of Stair
Wall

FOURTH FLOOR
STAIRWELL PERSPECTIVE VIEW

Scene:

Action: **WALK THROUGH - TOP FLOOR TOUR**

Camera: **B (1 of 2)**

Date: 09-13-00

PANIC ROOM

PIXEL LIBERATION FRONT
1316 1/2 Abbot Kinney Blvd.
Venice, CA   90291
(310) 396-9854   Phone
(310) 396-9874   Fax

Figure 3-7A Walk through—Top Floor Tour animatic, created by Pixel Liberation Front © 2000. PANIC ROOM
© 2002 Columbia Pictures Industries, Inc. All Rights Reserved—Courtesy of Columbia Pictures.

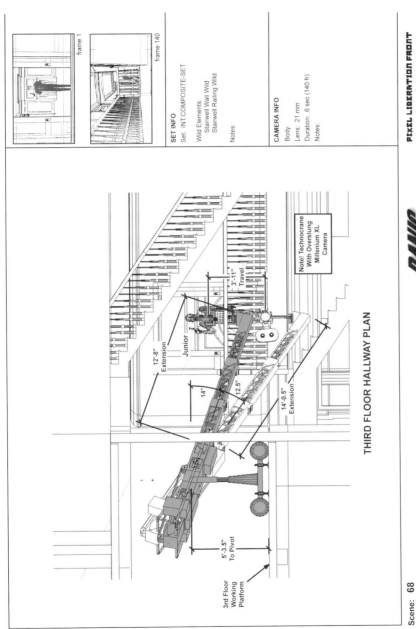

THIRD FLOOR HALLWAY PLAN

12'-8"
Extension

Junior

3'-11"
Travel

14°

12.5°

14'-0.5"
Extension

5'-3.5"
To Pivot

3rd Floor
Working
Platform

Note! Technocrane
With Overslung
Millenium XL
Camera

frame 1

frame 140

SET INFO
Set: INT COMPOSITE-SET

Wild Elements:
Stairwell Wall Wild
Stairwell Railing Wild

Notes:

CAMERA INFO
Body:
Lens: 21 mm
Duration: 6 sec (140 fr)
Notes:

PIXEL LIBERATION FRONT
1316 1/2 Abbot Kinney Blvd
Venice, CA   90291
(310) 396-9854   Phone
(310) 396-9874   Fax

Scene: 68

Action: ELEVATOR CHASE - GET EM

Camera: B (2 of 2)

Date: 10-23-00

Figure 3-7B Elevator chase—Get 'em animatic, created by Pixel Liberation Front © 2000. PANIC ROOM © 2002 Columbia Pictures Industries, Inc. All Rights Reserved—Courtesy of Columbia Pictures.

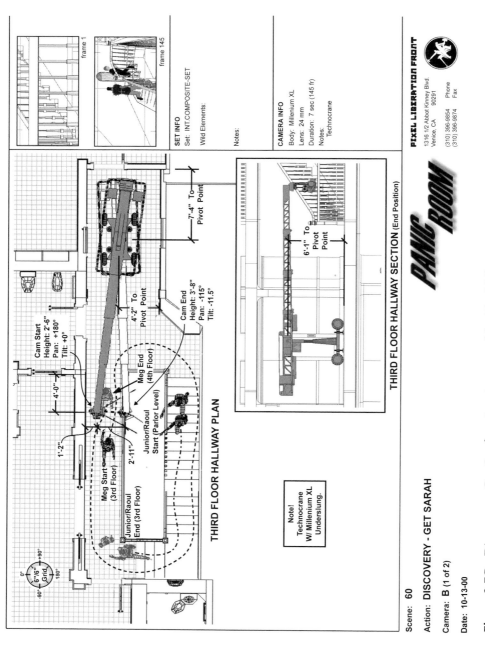

frame 1

frame 145

SET INFO
Set: INT.COMPOSITE-SET

Wild Elements:

Notes:

CAMERA INFO
Body: Millenium XL
Lens: 24 mm
Duration: 7 sec (145 fr)
Notes:
    Technocrane

PIXEL LIBERATION FRONT
1316 1/2 Abbot Kinney Blvd.
Venice, CA   90291
(310) 396-9854   Phone
(310) 396-9874   Fax

PANIC ROOM

Cam Start
Height: 2'-6"
Pan: +180°
Tilt: +0°

4'-0"

1'-2"

Meg Start
(3rd Floor)

Junior/Raoul
End (3rd Floor)

2'-11"

4'-2" To
Pivot Point

Meg End
(4th Floor)

Junior/Raoul
Start (Parlor Level)

Cam End
Height: 3'-8"
Pan: -115°
Tilt: -11.5°

7'-4" To
Pivot Point

6'-1" To
Pivot
Point

THIRD FLOOR HALLWAY SECTION (End Position)

THIRD FLOOR HALLWAY PLAN

Note!
Technocrane
W/ Millenium XL
Underslung.

0°
-90°   +90°
6"/6" Grid
180°

Scene: **60**

Action: **DISCOVERY - GET SARAH**

Camera: **B (1 of 2)**

Date: **10-13-00**

Figure 3-7C Discovery—Get Sarah animatic, created by Pixel Liberation Front © 2000. PANIC ROOM © 2002 Columbia Pictures Industries, Inc. All Rights Reserved—Courtesy of Columbia Pictures.

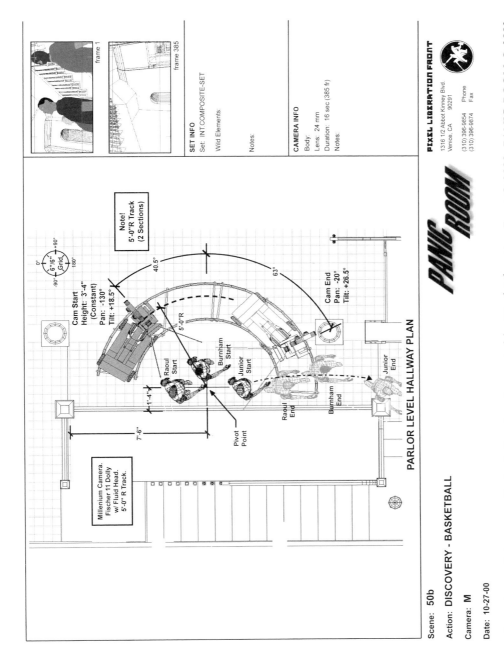

frame 1

frame 385

SET INFO
Set: INT COMPOSITE-SET

Wild Elements

Notes:

CAMERA INFO
Body:
Lens: 24 mm
Duration: 16 sec (385 fr)
Notes:

Note!
5'-0"R Track
(2 Sections)

Cam Start
Height: 3'-4"
(Constant)
Pan: -130°
Tilt: +18.5°

40.5°

5'-0"R

Raoul
Start

Burnham
Start

Junior
Start

Cam End
Pan: -20°
Tilt: +26.5°

63°

Raoul
End

Burnham
End

Junior
End

Pivot
Point

7'-6"

4'-4"

Millenium Camera.
Fischer 11 Dolly
w/ Fluid Head.
5'-0" R Track.

PARLOR LEVEL HALLWAY PLAN

Scene: **50b**

Action: **DISCOVERY - BASKETBALL**

Camera: **M**

Date: **10-27-00**

PANIC ROOM

PIXEL LIBERATION FRONT
1316 1/2 Abbot Kinney Blvd
Venice, CA   90291
(310) 396-9854   Phone
(310) 396-9874   Fax

Figure 3-7D Discovery—Basketball animatic, created by Pixel Liberation Front © 2000. PANIC ROOM © 2002 Columbia Pictures Industries, Inc. All Rights Reserved. Courtesy of Columbia Pictures.

architecture, and the track needed to fit on the staircase but not be in the shot. The Gazelle camera system is the one that fulfilled all of those restrictions.[5]

The balance of the Colin Green interview concludes in Chapter 5 and provides some insight on integrating art department imagery into the animatic process, the intimacy of the director-previz working relationship, and the expectations of previsualization.

CONCEPT ILLUSTRATING

The work of James Clyne, concept illustrator (*The Polar Express, Troy, Minority Report, Bicentennial Man*), presented in Fig. 3-8, underlines the importance of previsualization in sketching and drawing. In essence, a concept sketch can be a single frame plucked from a continuity storyboard, or it can represent a visual concept for a set, a scene, or an entire film. A concept illustrator, whose skills are often shared between a designer and director, is a fundamental interpreter of ideas in an ongoing creative dialogue. In many **high concept** films, the participation of a metaphors illustrator must forward the development of a designer's visual concept. Often, the inherent imagery of an illustrator's productivity is a strong factor in the final design concept and realization of physical scenery. **James Clyne** reinforces this fact (please see Fig. 3-8 in color between pages 142 and 143):

☐ *James, do most directors give you an indication of their vision for a particular*
sequence, or are you expected to generate conceptual options in order to begin
your working relationship?
It varies from director to director. Everyone has a different style of working. Most directors will come to me with very specific ideas and very few will be able to draw them. After our first meeting, I usually have a pretty good idea of where someone is going and what is necessary to see so we can really begin the process. Every director relies on me to interpret ideas quickly like a storyboard artist. I'm good at thinking on my feet and can come up with something that gets a strong response.

If an image I create is strong enough, then sometimes a conceptual sketch can define the look of an entire film. One image that quickly comes to mind is a sketch I did for *Tron 2* for Disney (see Fig. 3-8). We explored a few ways to define the world inside the computer environment. The sketch idea is a powerful example of how the concept of a world we've never seen but only can imagine can exist first on a piece of paper.[6]

COMPUTER MODELING

Architecture has traditionally provided the original source for visualizing the constructed form through the disciplines of model making and drafting to the film industry. It has taken the lead in its use of the most sophisticated software now available to the individual designer. The film industry has quickly adopted its previsualization methods by empowering the art

A

B

Figure 3-8   Concept sketches drawn by James Clyne for **A**) *Tron 2*. **B**) *Instinct*.

department's ability to explore the structural possibilities of sets before they are built. What was once only achievable in post-production, can now happen in real time from the earliest stages of visual previz throughout the fullest range of the complete process of digital and physical scenery production. Currently, no stone remains unturned. In addition to developing a previz vocabulary for motion picture design, we are also providing accurate visual data to many departments, particularly visual effects. A sophisticated understanding of digital technology and a networked team of people using digital tools places the designer and art department back at the center of the generation of information that will determine and control the look of a film. Evidence of this is showcased in images from *The Terminal* (see color insert, Figs. 3-9 through 3-11). Except for the photograph of *The Terminal* set shot, Fig. 3-9B, the remaining five images are digitally derived or enhanced. These images particularly, exemplify commonplace uses of state-of-the-art cinema software. Advances in this technology multiply the possibility of creative cinematic vision and also ensure the delivery of specific storytelling elements of all creative participants.

More specific updates in digital modeling are explained by the rapid prototyping process used on *Reign of Fire* (2002) in a brief section from a longer interview with concept artist and digital set designer **Victor Martinez**:

☐   *Victor, is NURBS modeling directly related to rapid prototyping used in Reign of Fire, for example?*
The rapid prototyping done on *Reign of Fire* involved a process called stereolithography requiring .STL files (stereolithography files). These files are polygonal not NURBS, Non-Uniform Rational Bezier Splines, and require solid modeling, or totally closed volumes, versus surface modeling. All the modeling had to be done as solids and converted to polygonal objects. There are other types of rapid prototyping techniques that favor NURBS surfaces rather than solid polygonal objects. It all depends on the type of fabrication technique being used.

On that show, I was solely in the VFX department doing rapid prototyping modeling. It's a different ball game from traditional set design modeling in that we were creating pieces that would be grown out of wax. We had manageable, miniature model pieces capable of being casted off and fabricated in multiple. Our main project was a miniature of the House of Parliament in quarter-inch scale that ended up being twenty feet long. It took 6–8 weeks to get the modeling and fabricating ready for 2–3 weeks of painting and detailing. The model shop supervisor mentioned that by utilizing digital modeling and rapid prototyping in the fabrication of the miniature model, we were able to expedite that process, and in the end, save money on the total cost of its production rather than make the model entirely by hand.

☐   *When you're rapid prototyping aren't you modeling in full scale?*
Yes, I worked in real scale where a foot is a foot. When I exported it out to the fabricators, it was in quarter-inch scale, so it's much like printing a page from 11 × 17 to 8.5 × 11. The wax is "printed" in layers on top of a base sheet

A

B

Figure 3-9 **A)** CG model of interior newsstand set for *The Terminal.* **B)** Set shot of interior set for *The Terminal* showing elliptical backing and reflective ceiling. Courtesy of Alex McDowell. Photograph by Merrick Morton for the motion picture *The Terminal*™ © 2004 DreamWorks L.L.C., reprinted with permission by DreamWorks L.L.C.

A

B

Figure 3-10 **A)** CG model of the exterior of the terminal set for *The Terminal.* **B)** Aerial view of JFK airport showing CG addition (circled) for *The Terminal.* Courtesy of Alex McDowell. Photograph by Merrick Morton for the motion picture *The Terminal*™ © 2004 DreamWorks L.L.C., reprinted with permission by DreamWorks L.L.C.

as opposed to other types of prototyping where you can do undercuts from full 3D blocks of material. As you might guess, this finished wax model in its many pieces acts as a positive mold for the final model measuring 20 feet in length. An advantage to this was that we had unlimited pieces that could be generated from the original and used for creating other models. It was used as a composite matte shot with live action in the foreground and the miniature in background, essentially like any other miniature matte shot would've been.[7]

What Victor has described is a physical form of miniature model making derived from digital modeling. In simple terms, the architecture of the House of Parliament was drawn on a computer screen and then that digital information was fed into the machine that sculpted the wax model as it interpreted the digital data. That remarkable process was borrowed from the automobile industry that needs to prototype original drawings before making full-scale multiples en masse.

There are two 3D modeling software packages used in set designing. Form Z (Auto-des-sys Inc.) is both Mac and PC compatible, and Rhinoceros (Robert McNeel & Associates) is only compatible with PCs. And AutoCAD (Autodesk Inc.) and VectorWorks (Nemetschek) are now widely used by set designers and art directors in the realm of 2D scenery drafting. These software packages not only allow set designers to elevate the walls of a set from a ground plan but also quickly enable the set to be extruded as a three-dimensional model. There are a number of services teaching computer assisted drawing and drafting, **CADD**, in the Los Angeles area that are directly connected to the Set Designers Local 847 and the Art Directors Guild Local 800. Among them are Gnomon in Hollywood, concentrating on visual effects and animation, and Digital Media Exchange (DMe) in Burbank, focusing primarily on film production previsualization. The latter is run by Don Jordan, well known to art department folks for his comprehensive classes in the basics: Adobe Photoshop and Illustrator; the CADD softwares, AutoCAD and VectorWorks, bridging the 2D to 3D gap; and basic Maya for 3D animation and modeling needs. All digital tools assist the previsualization process necessary for making movies.

Although Don's instruction through DMe is geared for working film professionals, classes are open to anyone interested in gaining skill. In his perception of teaching, a student needs to understand animatics, combining storyboarding, previsualization, and camera movement, in order to effectively participate in the filmmaking process. His patient, thorough, and soft-spoken manner describes an easy-to-digest teaching style that comes highly recommended for a beginner.

WHITE MODELS

Sometimes, it is actually easier to physically build a white model than to take the time to generate a digital concept model on a computer screen. **Luke Freeborn**, digital set designer and modeler (*The Terminal, The Chronicles of Riddick, Van Helsing*) supports this:

A major portion of what we do has to be done by pencil and paper or a model because it can be faster, given where you are in the process. So, a napkin and a pen can be a stronger tool than anything else.[8]

With its origins in architecture, a white model is not as developed as an architectural model of a building—it acts as a 3D sketch of a scenery volume, representing a set or a full-scale scenic object like the oversized kitchen table in *The Eternal Sunshine of the Spotless Mind* (2004). A white model happens quickly. Drafting for interior sets, for instance, is photocopied and then spray mounted onto $^3/_{16}$" fomecore. The set walls are cut out of the fomecore as individual pieces, then glued or t-pinned together as rough $^1/_4$" model sketches. Like computer-generated concept models, white models allow the viewer to analyze the structure and make appropriate changes to the evolving design. This small, easily handled, physical replica of a set or scenic piece then underlines the value of constructing a quick and dirty white model from $^1/_4$" scale drafting to support the visual understanding of a set for the director and cinematographer (see Fig. 3-11). Looking into a white model and studying its volumetric relationships can easily determine restrictions and the need for **wild walls**, for example, where none had originally been indicated. As integral as CG modeling has become in the previsualization process, there are instances when a physical model is more dynamic in its ability to reveal the potential of built scenery.

HAND DRAFTING

Set designers, or draftsmen, are the unsung heroes of the art department. They are responsible for the actual design of the film because they are the most intimate with the drawn details. The adage, "God is in the details," can be conveniently modified to suit our needs by realizing that "The details are in the set design." And those details are most typically found in one-quarter scale (3" = 1') or in full-scale (1' = 1') as architecturally drawn detail for all scenery, although other scales are used as required. What the full-scale detail (see Fig. 6-5 or Fig. 6-6) does is to act as an interpreter of specific information when a set designer or art director cannot be present in the woodshop as construction questions arise. Details also insure the preferred but sometimes counterintuitive look of how scenery is built. A good example of this is obvious in any of the *Star Trek* films—in the pneumatically driven double sliding doors of the Enterprise spacecraft—they are not typical doors so they need to be articulated by drafted, full-scale details.

In more general terms, a draftsperson is actually designing within the strict parameters of the production designer's conception of the film's visual requirements. These limitations are not as confining as one might think; the set designer is well paid to have the time to work out the details of how the scenery will physically be constructed. Consequently, set designing provides the necessary nuts-and-bolts pragmatism in the overall design process. The draft person's drawing table is a place where the realities of the physical world meet the vagaries of the realm of concept and ideas. **Barbara Mesney,**

A

B

Figure 3-11 **A)** White model of *The Terminal* set. **B)** Finished CG model of the exterior detail of *The Terminal* set. Courtesy of Alex McDowell. Photograph by Merrick Morton for the motion picture *The Terminal*™ © 2004 DreamWorks L.L.C., reprinted with permission by DreamWorks L.L.C.

a senior level, union set designer, shared thoughts and facts about her work as a film design professional:

☐   *Is draftsperson the politically correct term for your title?*
Draftsperson is a valid title. I prefer the term set designer. Interestingly, the nomenclature was a great part of the negotiations when the Hollywood set designers' union was started. Basically, what a set designer is doing all day *is* designing; we are not just drafting someone else's scenery.

☐   *That's certainly true from my perspective as an art director. Barbara, your passion for drawing is obvious in your drafting. It's beautifully rendered, has just enough detail, and shows significant info for the carpenters. How would you rate yourself as a set designer?*
Thank you. Well, I know what I want to be. I currently work at selling myself as a first-rate set designer. My goal is to become the Reginald Breem (most sought-after English draftsman) of Hollywood. The point of this is not to price myself out of the market, but rather to make myself so indispensable and invaluable that I'll always be employed. Basically, no one wants to do this job. It requires intense focus and a lot of mental concentration. It requires sitting in one room for the sole purpose of doing math and art all day long. Most people don't want that much focus, you know, especially in a world like theater or film where it's more social. I emerge from my cocoon, make a cup of tea, say some friendly words in the art department bullpen, and then disappear back into the drafting vortex. It's exactly what I did as a child in my basement studio by focusing creatively in solitude. This suits me perfectly.

Comparatively, most people in this business need more social interaction than I do. It's understandable why there are more art directors than set designers; it's not that it's particularly an easier job. From my point of view, as an art director you're on call 24–7, you're married to the project, and your butt is constantly on the line. Too many drawbacks to consider for the trade-off of better pay for the personal toll it demands. That's much too extreme. Because producers don't like paying overtime, the set designer's hourly contract is much more manageable. You put your pencil down, and you are off for the day. I go home and have a life. In film terms, having a life is gold. My art director friends never sleep.

☐   *Aside from speed, how much about being a set designer is about patience?*
[Chuckles.] Patience, first, and lack of noticeable ego, second. Because you're designing all day long, you know a particular set more than anyone else in terms of what it can or can't be, and what it can or can't do. Any number of people will come into my cocoon and ask me to change any and every aspect of what I'm drafting. This happens all day long. Every day. You simply say, "OK" and make the changes knowing full well that everything you've just done for hours becomes obsolete and all that info goes into the delete file. So there can't be any ego involvement, per se. Also, the ultimate end of the project is not yours despite the fact that you've invested time and creative effort.

What I've found to be the most fascinating aspect of this dance is the fact that in my experience, at least 50 percent of the time we always come full circle. There's a moral here that cautions to never toss away the first drawings in a series of changes. So, I have to qualify that delete file I just mentioned—it's actually a *faux* delete file that might be filled, but never gets emptied. Putting it aside for future reference is always the best recourse.

☐ *Resigned or not, this caprice must take a toll. How do you balance yourself?*
My own art—the fine art painting I do on a regular basis—is what saves me. In that world, I have the final say-so; all the decisions are mine alone. My painting is totally gratifying.

☐ *When is a set design finished? There are instances when even after the drawings are signed and built, change is still in play, isn't it?*
The nature of the business dictates this. Everything moves at lightning speed with little time to do anything properly, right? People on the front end, namely the production designer and art director with the director and cinematographer, are doing their damnedest to think things through, but inevitably something will slip between the cracks and changes will have to happen. This doesn't happen through any direct fault of theirs, especially when some of the most important decisions are made in the scouting van in-between looking at locations for the film with little reflection. Given all this, where mistakes and subsequent changes can be made, it's my job as a methodical set designer to check the details and communicate any discrepancies to the AD and construction coordinator.

☐ *Given the trend toward technology, are you now pressured to be adept at CAD programs?*
I'm not using CAD 14 because it's more suited to architecture where many revisions and overlays are required; CAD hasn't adapted as well to our uses for it in Hollywood. VectorWorks, formerly known as *MiniCAD*, has been adopted by television designing more in Hollywood as the drafting software of choice. It's a highly intuitive and remarkable program, and yes, I am studying it to stay competitive.

I was talking recently with my current AD about how ill-suited VectorWorks can be for film. Film is so variable compared to TV, which deals more with stock flattage, more like theater. In terms of organic drawing, it's also less effective. Several months ago I was drawing an African spirit hut. Even though it's possible, it's not practical to do it effectively in any form of CAD, including Vector Works. The truth is a great deal of what I do is to make organically designed scenery forms work. Contrary to popular belief, there are fewer straight lines and a lot more freehand drawing in film than you can imagine.[9]

Injecting the visual concept into the design of the physical scenery is an involved task. The art director, via his/her activity and communication skills, performs the injection for the production designer. And, it requires Job-like patience on the part of the set designer, who interprets that information and then designs and draws it. According to digital set designer **J. Andre Chaintreuil** (*Spiderman 2, The Terminal, Minority Report*):

> From a digital set designer's point of view, the idea of timing and pacing is slightly different than an ordinary set designer. I find it's easiest to model even the simplest set in 3D because of the way I can analyze and troubleshoot in 3D. I ultimately learn, for example, two planar surfaces might collide in a specific corner and will not work. These decisions can be discovered faster and influence a design. Some other advantages of a digital set designer are when a set has a complex shape or a lot of repetition such as a bank of lights or a colonnade. Revisions also go quickly in a digital format. Once a 3D model has reached a satisfactory level of design, it can be translated into drawings very quickly, and the model can be easily shared with other departments.[10]

This technology in current digital designing has become a necessity and the working knowledge of how to manipulate the software, a prerequisite for any aspiring digital concept modeler, draftsperson, or art director. The quixotic nature of film design, especially at this stage, is critical in budgetary terms. With the PD's permission, a good rule of thumb is to make it a regular practice to provide a space on the title block of every drafting plate, hand-drawn or otherwise, for the signature of the director. This reinforces active participation in the design process and ensures the maintenance of the scenic budget. Any further changes can be attributed to a directorial decision and not creative caprice on the part of the art department. The key is to reinforce this simple ritual with the perseverance of a terrier. The challenge is to present the idea of committing a signature to a document as an assurance that the built design will exactly follow the drawing. It is a good practice for the director, the set designer, and the art director.

As we have worked our way backwards from computer models to hand-built models to computer drafting, we arrive full circle at the final point where scenery continues to be hand drafted with a parallel, adjustable triangle and mechanical pencil. Archaic or not, it's really important to know how to do this, especially in case of a power failure or loss of generator power on location. When fast changes need to happen, no production designer or director in the world has the patience to wait for the power to resume before seeing new pages of drafted scenery. Knowing how to draft traditionally as a set designer or art director is the surest way to cover all your bases and make sure you are that more marketable.

DESIGNING FOR THE LENS

Nothing we do can happen without light; it enables the entire operation of the motion picture process. Insufficient light compels the **gaffers** to make it adequate and operable for the cinematographer. Sufficient light showcases the scenery, the costumes, and actors wearing them. Light is also the critical element driving movie cameras, theater projectors, and computer monitors. The entire movie industry is built around light as a stimulus, the manipulation of light, and light as the delivery system for our well-crafted images. In the art department, we design for the audience through the camera lens. As cinematography is basically a photographic medium, those same principles apply for our purposes as designers. Table 3-1 introduces the basic effect of light on lens systems.

Lenses 101

An aperture is the hole through which light passes into a human eyeball or camera. Light is focused through a lens and is captured and fixed on film emulsion creating an image. Cine lenses are made of glass elements and are grouped into three commonly used types of wide (<10 mm, 10 mm to 35 mm), medium (35 mm to 100 mm), and narrow (100 mm to 1,000 mm, >1,000 mm) fields of view. Lenses have two names, e.g., 50 mm f1.4: the first name tells us the focal length of the lens in millimeters, and the second name indicates the maximum aperture opening of that lens. The focal length is the measurable distance from the optical center of a lens, focused at infinity, to the film emulsion where an image is recorded. The depth of field is the area between the nearest point and infinity that an object in front of a lens will be in acceptable focus.

In cinematic terms, the area in front of the lens system is referred to as the *object space*; the area behind the lens system, the *image space*. Similarly, the object space is described in terms of depth of field, and the image space in terms of focal length. The light that passes through a lens system is captured or stored on an area of a given size called the *film format* in the back of the image space. A film format is based on the physical size of the film stock being used to capture an image through the lens system attached to the camera. (Film format and aspect ratio are discussed later.) The aperture is adjustable within fixed intervals for a specific lens and is given prescribed numeric values of 1.4, 2, 2.8, 4, 5.6, 8, 11, 16, and 22—largest opening to smallest. F-stops are mathematical ratios between the size of the hole and the focal length of the lens. To go a step further, if the amount of light allowed to pass through the lens is measured, a T-stop value has been recorded. Both F- and T-stops are used interchangeably in cinematography to describe the change of the amount of light from one stop to the next. Depending on the direction you are going, each stop either halves or doubles the amount of light with relation to the next stop. These numbers are so reliable that they have been etched onto the focus rings of all cine lenses.

Aspect Ratio

Three elements—depth of field, aperture, and aspect ratio—must be considered when referring to cinematic images. The first two, depth of field and aperture, have been briefly discussed. The third, aspect ratio, is synonymous

MODERN APPLICATIONS OF THE CAMERA OBSCURA	
OUTSIDE—IN	<u>Concept</u>: An exterior light source passes through an adjustable opening and falls on a "receiving" surface, inverted and reversed. In the case of the inside of the human eyeball, the brain flips and reverses the image so we can make sense of the world around us. This process reproduces a smaller image from the original, real image on the retina but retains the integrity of the original image in our mind's eye.
A > Light source B >> Adjustment* C >>> Image capture	> Aperture >> Pupil** >> Shutter >> Iris** >>> Emulsion >>> Retina
INSIDE—OUT	<u>Concept</u>: A powerful interior light source, e.g, xenon bulb or carbon arc, passes through the film strip at the gate of the projector and translates the moving image through the lens system, to a size a hundred times larger, on a movie screen. This reverse process magnifies the original image, presenting what exists in the collective imaginations of all involved.
A > Light source B >> Imaging device C >>> Image capture	> Film strip >> Projector lens >>> Movie screen
	* Adjustment refers to the lens as a collecting or imaging device. ** Pupil and iris are elements of the human lens system.

Table 3-1 Linking the *camera obscura*, the human eye, photography, and cinematography.

with image format or the frame through which a film is viewed. What a lens "sees" is the angle of view, referring to both the horizontal angle of sight and the vertical angle of sight—together they create an aspect ratio, the numerical relationship of the width and height, respectively, of image formats used in film and television. There are several standard image formats used internationally, e.g., 16 mm, Super 16 mm, 1.33:1 [TV] 35 mm, 1.85:1 35 mm or Normal Academy aperture, 2.40:1 [anamorphic] 35 mm,[11] 8-perforation VistaVision® 35 mm, 65 mm, 15-perforation IMAX 65 mm. The most common aspect ratio found through the 1950's was called *Academy Aperture*, at a ratio of 1.33:1—the same as 4:3 on a TV screen. New widescreen formats and aspect ratios were introduced in the 1950's, from 1.66:1 and higher. CinemaScope® was a widescreen movie format used in the US from 1953 to 1967, and other anamorphic systems such as Panavision® or Technovision® have a 2.40:1 AR, while 70 mm formats have an AR of 2.2:1. Cinerama® had a 2.77:1 AR; letterboxed videos for widescreen TVs are frequently in 16:9 or 1.77:1 AR. The cinematographer determines which type of lens and format (AR) to use based on script indications, technical considerations, and creative collaboration of the director-design team.

The *American Cinematographer Manual* not only contains an All Format Depth of Field Table, but more importantly, a Field of View Table for 8 mm to 400 mm lenses. How does all of this relate to scenery? The latter table, especially, is helpful during the initial stages of scenery design. If an art director knows that the cinematographer will be shooting an interior set with a 35 mm lens in 1.85:1 format, Normal Academy aperture, then Fig. 3-12 provides valuable design parameters. The Field of View table for a 35 mm lens displays a black horizontal row named, Angle of View. For each format listed in the row below, it assigns a horizontal (H) and vertical (V) angle of vision for each dimension of the aspect ratio: 33.3° and 18.4°, respectively. If an art director also knows that the camera will be placed 18 feet from a dining table sitting in the middle of the set, then the vertical angle of the frame can be checked to know how much ceiling above the shot might be seen. Why is ceiling a consideration? Ceilings are more prone to being photographed because of the greater height of the 1.85:1 aspect ratio, see Fig. 3-13A. In order to properly check this, a quick section view of the set should be drawn including the position of the camera, and most importantly, the height of the center of the lens at 4'6" from the floor. Using the 18.4° vertical angle of vision found in the Field of View Table, we know that a portion of the ceiling will not be seen, see Fig. 3-13B. Set pieces like ceilings restrict the lighting crew; removable ceiling pieces should be considered whenever possible. The Field of View table is indispensable in resolving these questions, and it should be referred to continuously throughout the designing process.

An art director should also be aware of the opinion that sets can be less wide if a 1.85:1 format is used instead of 2.40:1. Is this fact or myth? Fig. 3-13A, clearly shows two very important aspects of a 1.85:1 AR: 1) the vertical value is greater than its 2.40:1 counterpart, but 2) it shares the same

35mm FIELD OF VIEW

SETUPS (Approximate Distance)	Full Aperture	Academy 1.33:1	Academy 1.66:1	Academy 1.85:1	Anamorphic 2.40:1	Super 35 1.85:1	Super 35 2.40:1	VistaVision	VistaVision 1.85:1	VistaVision 2.40:1	65mm
Ext Close Up	1' 5"	1' 8"	2' 0"	2' 2"	1' 5"	2' 0"	2' 7"	1' 1"	1' 3"	1' 8"	1' 2"
Close Up	2' 2"	2' 7"	3' 1"	3' 5"	2' 2"	3' 2"	4' 1"	1' 8"	2' 0"	2' 7"	1' 9"
Medium Shot	4' 1"	4' 9"	5' 9"	6' 5"	4' 1"	5' 10"	7' 7"	3' 1"	3' 9"	4' 10"	3' 4"
Full Figure	11' 3"	13' 1"	15' 10"	17' 8"	11' 4"	16' 2"	21' 0"	8' 5"	10' 4"	13' 4"	9' 2"
Angle of View	H 39.2° V 29.9°	H 33.3° V 24.6°	H 33.3° V 20.4°	H 33.3° V 18.4°	H 62.7° V 28.5°	H 37.9° V 21.0°	H 37.9° V 16.3°	H 56.6° V 39.6°	H 56.6° V 32.5°	H 56.6° V 25.4°	H 73.9° V 36.4°
2	1' 1" / 1' 5"	0' 11" / 1' 3"	0' 9" / 1' 3"	0' 8" / 1' 3"	1' 1" / 2' 6"	0' 9" / 1' 4"	0' 7" / 1' 4"	1' 5" / 2' 2"	1' 2" / 2' 2"	0' 11" / 2' 2"	1' 4" / 3' 0"
2½	1' 4" / 1' 9"	1' 2" / 1' 7"	0' 11" / 1' 7"	0' 10" / 1' 7"	1' 4" / 3' 2"	0' 11" / 1' 9"	0' 9" / 1' 9"	1' 9" / 2' 8"	1' 5" / 2' 8"	1' 2" / 2' 8"	1' 8" / 3' 9"
3	1' 7" / 2' 2"	1' 4" / 1' 11"	1' 2" / 1' 11"	1' 0" / 1' 11"	1' 7" / 3' 9"	1' 1" / 2' 1"	0' 10" / 2' 1"	2' 2" / 3' 3"	1' 9" / 3' 3"	1' 4" / 3' 3"	2' 0" / 4' 6"
3½	1' 10" / 2' 6"	1' 7" / 2' 2"	1' 4" / 2' 2"	1' 2" / 2' 2"	1' 10" / 4' 5"	1' 4" / 2' 5"	1' 0" / 2' 5"	2' 6" / 3' 9"	2' 0" / 3' 9"	1' 7" / 3' 9"	2' 4" / 5' 3"
4	2' 2" / 2' 10"	1' 10" / 2' 6"	1' 6" / 2' 6"	1' 4" / 2' 6"	2' 1" / 5' 0"	1' 6" / 2' 9"	1' 2" / 2' 9"	2' 10" / 4' 4"	2' 4" / 4' 4"	1' 10" / 4' 4"	2' 8" / 6' 0"
4½	2' 5" / 3' 2"	2' 1" / 2' 10"	1' 8" / 2' 10"	1' 6" / 2' 10"	2' 5" / 5' 8"	1' 8" / 3' 1"	1' 3" / 3' 1"	3' 2" / 4' 10"	2' 7" / 4' 10"	2' 0" / 4' 10"	3' 0" / 6' 9"
5	2' 8" / 3' 7"	2' 3" / 3' 2"	1' 11" / 3' 2"	1' 8" / 3' 2"	2' 8" / 6' 3"	1' 10" / 3' 5"	1' 5" / 3' 5"	3' 7" / 5' 5"	2' 11" / 5' 5"	2' 3" / 5' 5"	3' 3" / 7' 6"
5½	2' 11" / 3' 11"	2' 6" / 3' 5"	2' 1" / 3' 5"	1' 10" / 3' 5"	2' 11" / 6' 11"	2' 0" / 3' 9"	1' 7" / 3' 9"	3' 11" / 5' 11"	3' 2" / 5' 11"	2' 6" / 5' 11"	3' 7" / 8' 3"
6	3' 2" / 4' 3"	2' 9" / 3' 9"	2' 3" / 3' 9"	2' 0" / 3' 9"	3' 2" / 7' 6"	2' 3" / 4' 1"	1' 9" / 4' 1"	4' 3" / 6' 6"	3' 6" / 6' 6"	2' 8" / 6' 6"	3' 11" / 9' 0"
6½	3' 6" / 4' 8"	3' 0" / 4' 1"	2' 6" / 4' 1"	2' 2" / 4' 1"	3' 5" / 8' 2"	2' 5" / 4' 5"	1' 10" / 4' 5"	4' 8" / 7' 0"	3' 9" / 7' 0"	2' 11" / 7' 0"	4' 3" / 9' 9"
7	3' 9" / 5' 0"	3' 2" / 4' 5"	2' 8" / 4' 5"	2' 5" / 4' 5"	3' 9" / 8' 10"	2' 7" / 4' 10"	2' 0" / 4' 10"	5' 0" / 7' 7"	4' 1" / 7' 7"	3' 2" / 7' 7"	4' 7" / 10' 6"
8	4' 3" / 5' 8"	3' 8" / 5' 0"	3' 0" / 5' 0"	2' 9" / 5' 0"	4' 3" / 10' 1"	3' 0" / 5' 6"	2' 3" / 5' 6"	5' 8" / 8' 7"	4' 8" / 8' 7"	3' 7" / 8' 7"	5' 3" / 12' 0"
9	4' 10" / 6' 5"	4' 1" / 5' 8"	3' 5" / 5' 8"	3' 1" / 5' 8"	4' 9" / 11' 4"	3' 4" / 6' 2"	2' 7" / 6' 2"	6' 5" / 9' 8"	5' 3" / 9' 8"	4' 1" / 9' 8"	5' 11" / 13' 6"
10	5' 4" / 7' 1"	4' 7" / 6' 3"	3' 9" / 6' 3"	3' 5" / 6' 3"	5' 4" / 12' 7"	3' 9" / 6' 10"	2' 10" / 6' 10"	7' 1" / 10' 9"	5' 10" / 10' 9"	4' 6" / 10' 9"	6' 7" / 15' 0"
12	6' 5" / 8' 7"	5' 6" / 7' 6"	4' 7" / 7' 6"	4' 1" / 7' 6"	6' 4" / 15' 1"	4' 5" / 8' 3"	3' 5" / 8' 3"	8' 7" / 12' 11"	7' 0" / 12' 11"	5' 5" / 12' 11"	7' 11" / 18' 1"
14	7' 6" / 10' 0"	6' 5" / 8' 10"	5' 4" / 8' 10"	4' 9" / 8' 10"	7' 5" / 17' 7"	5' 2" / 9' 7"	4' 0" / 9' 7"	10' 0" / 15' 1"	8' 2" / 15' 1"	6' 4" / 15' 1"	9' 2" / 21' 1"
16	8' 6" / 11' 5"	7' 4" / 10' 1"	6' 1" / 10' 1"	5' 5" / 10' 1"	8' 6" / 20' 1"	5' 11" / 11' 0"	4' 7" / 11' 0"	11' 5" / 17' 3"	9' 4" / 17' 3"	7' 3" / 17' 3"	10' 6" / 24' 1"
18	9' 7" / 12' 10"	8' 3" / 11' 4"	6' 10" / 11' 4"	6' 1" / 11' 4"	9' 7" / 22' 7"	6' 8" / 12' 4"	5' 2" / 12' 4"	12' 10" / 19' 5"	10' 6" / 19' 5"	8' 1" / 19' 5"	11' 10" / 27' 1"
20	10' 8" / 14' 3"	9' 2" / 12' 7"	7' 7" / 12' 7"	6' 10" / 12' 7"	10' 7" / 25' 2"	7' 5" / 13' 9"	5' 9" / 13' 9"	14' 3" / 21' 7"	11' 8" / 21' 7"	9' 0" / 21' 7"	13' 2" / 30' 1"
25	13' 4" / 17' 10"	11' 5" / 15' 9"	9' 6" / 15' 9"	8' 6" / 15' 9"	13' 3" / 31' 5"	9' 3" / 17' 2"	7' 2" / 17' 2"	17' 10" / 26' 11"	14' 7" / 26' 11"	11' 3" / 26' 11"	16' 5" / 37' 7"
50	26' 8" / 35' 7"	22' 11" / 31' 5"	18' 11" / 31' 5"	17' 0" / 31' 5"	26' 7" / 62' 10"	18' 7" / 34' 3"	14' 4" / 34' 3"	35' 7" / 53' 11"	29' 2" / 53' 11"	22' 6" / 53' 11"	32' 10" / 75' 2"

Figure 3-12 35 mm Field of View. American Cinematographer Manual, 8th Edition—Courtesy of the American Society of Cinematographers.

A

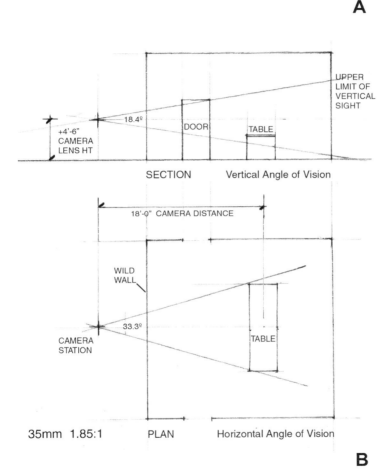

B

Figure 3-13 A) *Aspect Ratio 1.85:1.* The larger and smaller rectangles shown here refer to the width and height, respectively, of the 1.85:1 AR as equal to the 2.40:1 AR. Depending on framing, the Normal Academy aperture will always show the same width but considerably more height than its 2.40:1 counterpart. For this reason, some cinematographers see it as a preferable lens choice in some situations. AMERICAN CINEMATOGRAPHER MANUAL, 8th Edition—Courtesy of the American Society of Cinematographers. **B)** *Vertical field of view for a 35mm lens* showing the plan and corresponding section. Using both horizontal and vertical angle of view shown in the Field of View Tables contained in the ASC Manual is always helpful in determining wall heights, ceiling coverage, and height of translites and greenscreens.

horizontal value as the 2.40:1 AR. Obviously, format doesn't necessarily dictate the width of a set—a Normal Academy aperture might require as wide a set, depending on the design and composition required by the cinematographer and director.

Perspective 101

This final application of depth of field, aperture, and aspect ratio can now be explained in graphic terms. One-point perspective tells us that all outlines of object surfaces in the picture plane converge to the same vanishing point on the horizon—this is called *convergence*. From this we can draw a parallel in terms of how the focal length of a lens determines the degree of convergence in a photographic image. An art director can use the angle of view for a lens to determine graphically the degree of convergence in a perspective set drawing. Any perspective drawing can be made to represent what any given lens would see in terms of its focal length and its degree of convergence.

Harold Michelson, the storyboard artist represented in Figs. 3-6A and 3-6B, clearly saw this relationship and devised a system of perspective drawing for cinematography called **camera angle projection**.[12] At first glance, this process seems complicated and overwhelming, but once the fundamental concept of the system is understood, it is logical, methodical, and foolproof. A working knowledge of drafting and a basic understanding of cinematography (briefly presented here) will enable anyone's skill at this kind of informative perspective drawing. Since Harold devised this system, its concept has been translated into the 3D modeling programs we use in the art department today, e.g., 3D Studio Max, Maya, SoftImage, etc.—animatic programs use the concept of this system as well, as shown in Figs. 3-7A through 3-7D.

Lens Test

Fig. 3-14 displays a series of lens tests taken to determine the best establishing shot for the scenery elevation photographed in the example. A previously drawn landscape plan was used to reference general distances from the front porch overhang. Subsequent lens tests were taken at 18 mm at 120', 25 mm at 130', 35 mm at 190', and 50 mm at 284'. Close inspection of the photo samples reveal more foreground detail with the widest lens shown, although there is greater background detail and texture in the photo shot with the 50 mm lens. The director-design team made an appropriate decision based on this information and what would best forward the storytelling.

The journey from hand-drawn to digital model design and how it becomes physical and digitally derived scenery will continue to be the focus of the next few chapters. It will draw on modes of motion picture production in-studio and in-camera through basic concepts of optical lab processes, and by doing so, will connect us to twenty-first century film design.

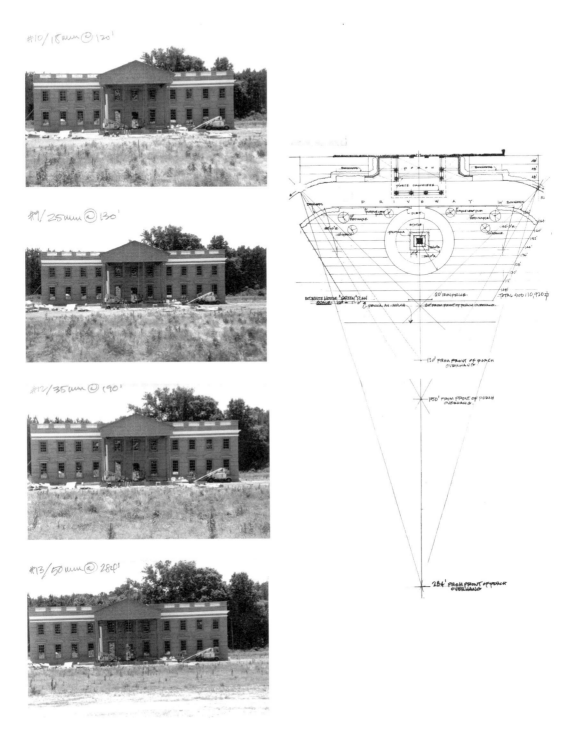

Figure 3-14 Lens test.

ENDNOTES

1. Christa Munro interview, 9/11/04, Flintridge, CA.

2. "Lillian is considered to be the dean of motion picture research. Thirty-three years ago she founded the Lillian Michelson Research Library, which contains 7,000 books, 100,000 periodicals, and 1,500,000 clippings, stills, and photographs. She was asked to join DreamWorks in 1995 and is presently located at its studio in Glendale." Internet article: *6th Annual Hollywood Film Festival®, October 1–8, 2002 Hollywood Richard Sylbert Outstanding Achievement in Production Design Award™ Honoree Harold Michelson* retrieved from the World Wide Web at http://www.hollywoodawards.com/michelson/

3. Linda Berger interview, 8/16/04, Studio City, CA.

4. The Art Directors Guild selected Harold Michelson for a lifetime achievement award in 1999. He was nominated for an art direction Oscar for *Star Trek: The Motion Picture*. Other art direction credits include *Dick Tracy, Spaceballs, Terms of Endearment, Mame, Johnny Got His Gun*, and *Catch 22*. Credits as an illustrator include *Cotton Club, Hair, Day of the Locust, Fiddler on the Roof, Ship of Fools, The Birds*.

5. Colin Green interview, 9/13/04, Burbank, CA.

6. James Clyne interview, 5/17/04, Santa Monica, CA.

7. Victor Martinez interview, 4/21/04, N. Hollywood, CA.

8. Luke Freeborn interview, 5/06/04, West Los Angeles, CA.

9. Barbara Mesney interview, 11/13/03, Venice Beach, CA.

10. J. Andre Chaintreuil interview, 4/28/04, N. Hollywood, CA.

11. "It must be unequivocally stated that the anamorphic format is defined at 2.40 : 1 not 2.35 : 1, which has been popularized by well meaning but incorrect individuals or companies. To be exact, the universally used anamorphic film format is 2.39 : 1 at the film, which translates to 2.40 : 1. This anamorphic ratio has been around for nearly 30 years, and it is remarkable that other format ratios like 2.35 : 1 keep popping up to describe widescreen anamorphic movies."

    Neil, Iain A. *American Cinematographer Manual*, 8th Edition, "Formats and Lenses." Hollywood: The ASC Press, 2001, pages 164–165.

12. A detailed explanation of camera angle projection is presented in the following book:

    Katz, Steven D. *Film Directing Shot by Shot: Visualizing from Concept to Screen*. Boston: Focal Press, 1991, pages 337–356.

CHAPTER 4

A Legacy of Historical Techniques

The mirror represents the objects faithfully but retains them not; our canvas shows them with the same exactness and retains them all.[1]

Tiphaigne de la Roche

Leonardo da Vinci first advocated the use of the *Camera Obscura*, or dark room, as an aid to drawing. It wasn't until 1827, a little over three hundred years, that Niépce in France produced the first successful picture image created from chemical materials that hardened after an eight-hour exposure to light. Just fifty years beyond that time in 1878, *Scientific American* published an article on Eadward Muybridge's animal and locomotion photographic sequences, and then a few years later in 1884 when George Eastman introduced flexible, photographic film for his box cameras at the turn of the century, photography become available to the masses. The still image rapidly became a moving image in America as early as 1908 at Black Maria, Edison's revolving film studio built around the turn of the century in Orange, New Jersey. There he experimented with short films such as *Boxing Cats* or *A Kinetoscope Record of a Sneeze* (1894), freeing artists to create moving images "without the aid of a pencil or brush." This new medium was by no means an American invention—it was European: originally developed by the French, then adapted by the early American entrepreneurs in New York City like William Fox. Americans saw its value as a product by developing and marketing it as the Nickelodeon—a customer paid a nickel to watch a minute-long movie in a box. Soon after that, film production was established in Los Angeles in the early teens of the twentieth century by Thomas Ince, Joseph Brandt, Jack and Harry Cohn, Carl Laemmle, William Fox, Marcus Loew, the Warner Brothers and Adolph Zukor, making the rest film history. We will investigate the legacy of both manual and digital modes of cinematic image making, respectively, within the following two chapters, beginning with the historical techniques used by the art department.

Figure 4-1 The earliest known photograph of the glass shot setup pioneered by Norman Dawn. Courtesy of Dr. Raymond Fielding.

PAINTED GLASS

Australian filmmaker, Norman Dawn, while working as a still photographer circa 1905 used the glass matte process, and later translated its use into film-making technique in his films *For the Term of His Natural Life* (1927) and his chef d'oeuvre, *Tundra* (1936). A photograph (see Fig. 4-1) documenting one such photographic project where he shot footage in Tasmania in 1908 reveals a platform covered by a canvas cover supporting his camera rig. If you look carefully, the painted element is visible on a sheet of glass. It is a replica of the roof of a historically important building partially destroyed, then restored in the accompanying composite below. Later on, the "Dawn Process" created a matte box that could be mounted on the camera for

Glass paintings can be mounted either on separate stands or on supports
attached to the camera for glass, transparency and mirror-shots.

Figure 4-2   A modern example of the Dawn process camera and glass rig. Courtesy
of Dr. Raymond Fielding.

steadier glass-shot photography (Fig. 4-2). It's interesting to see how these
techniques cross-pollinated from Europe to Australia to America in the earliest years of the twentieth century and vigorously developed in precision and
quality. What is even more remarkable is the fact that the simplicity of techniques like the glass shot hasn't lost its effectiveness almost a century later.

The glass painting technique is one of the earliest techniques used to
combine, or **composite**, additional visual information onto action footage.
It is one of several foundations of the compositing process to be explored
here. This technique was perfected by mid-twentieth century and was in use
worldwide. Graphic examples of the work of John Graysmark, designer
of *Courage Under Fire* (1996), *Blown Away* (1994), *So I Married an Axe
Murderer* (1993), *White Sands* (1992), *Robin Hood: Prince of Thieves* (1991),
Gorillas in the Mist: The Story of Dian Fossey (1988), *Duet for One* (1986),
The Bounty (1984), *Ragtime* (1981) will serve to expand the text throughout
the rest of this chapter. As my early mentor, his invaluable experience
appropriately illustrates examples of traditional moviemaking techniques
through his early art directing filmography, including *Anastasia* (1956), *Inn
of the Sixth Happiness* (1958), *2001: A Space Odyssey* (1968), and *Young
Winston* (1972). (NOTE: All drawings and sketches were completed by
J. Graysmark in 2005 for this publication.)

Sometimes an exterior location is perfect for shooting except for a
hydroelectric plant looming in the distance. This was a scenario encountered while filming the village of Huang Cheng for *Inn of the Sixth Happiness*. A present-day solution would simply be to shoot the scene digitally
and then erase the unwanted sections. Technology in 1958 provided a solution in glass painting, by using a large piece of glass to act as a mask between
the camera and actors. Categories explaining the shot, the scenery, technique involved, and an explanation are as follows:

Shot: The main characters were filmed crossing the mountainside with a **locked-off**, or stationary camera on a tripod. The shot was **blocked** with actors working behind a large, painted piece of glass to mask out unwanted objects in the distant landscape.

Scenery: A $6' \times 8'$ piece of $\frac{1}{4}''$ tempered glass was used as a transparent canvas between the locked-off camera and actors.

Technique: 1) Several days before the shoot, the camera was set up in exactly the spot where the scene would be shot with exactly the same lens to be used in the action sequence shot. 2) The glass was sturdily set on sandbagged **C-stand frames** and surrounded with a large enough black velour box (the American equivalent would be **duvetyne**), eliminating all ambient light and reflection on the glass, Fig. 4-3. 3) Ideally, it would be best to have two scenic artists working on this step to expedite the work at hand. One scenic artist would draw with a wax pencil on the glass within the area in the landscape needing to be obscured; the other would check through the same lens to be used in the final shot, to see that the masking drawing was on the correct area of the glass. 4) The landscape was painted to "soft mask" the unwanted objects in the distance—in this case, the hydroelectric plant. The position of the sun, i.e., time of day, was noted to insure that real shadows cast in the distant landscape in the final shot would match the painted shadows on the painted mask.

Explanation: "Once the glass was painted, the shot could then include the masking image on the glass. Care had to be taken that the actors would not move any part of their bodies behind the section of masked painting on the glass for fear of spoiling the shot. For that reason the shot had to be carefully orchestrated."[2] Again, two points to remember are for the artists to have the exact lens in the camera for reference while working on the matte painting and for the cinematographer to shoot at the same time of day the painting was completed in order to achieve a perfect match.

GATE MATTING

According to John, this particular technique of matting footage for compositing was originally a French technique where the matting happened within the camera in the matte box at the gate, as opposed to outside of the camera as discussed in the painted glass technique. (Although the schematic below features the interior of a projector and not a film camera, the concept is the same.) Apparently, for Stanley Kubrick, the director of *2001: A Space Odyssey* (1968), the use of the gate matting technique was a quality control decision as well as an aesthetic one.

Shot: The monolith embedded in the archeological pit at Clavius was surrounded by the lunar landscape and deep space.

Scenery: The walkway surrounding the perimeter of the dig site at Clavius and all scenery in the foreground were built on the silent stage at Shepparton Studios, London.

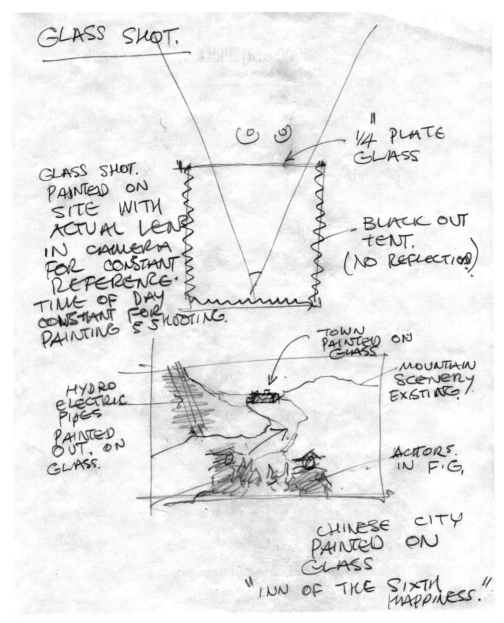

GLASS SHOT.

GLASS SHOT.
PAINTED ON
SITE WITH
ACTUAL LENS
IN CAMERA
FOR CONSTANT
REFERENCE.
TIME OF DAY
CONSTANT FOR
PAINTING & SHOOTING.

1/4 PLATE
GLASS

BLACK OUT
TENT.
(NO REFLECTION)

TOWN
PAINTED ON
GLASS

MOUNTAIN
SCENERY
EXISTING.

HYDRO
ELECTRIC
PIPES
PAINTED
OUT, ON
GLASS.

ACTORS.
IN F.G.

CHINESE CITY
PAINTED ON
GLASS
"INN OF THE SIXTH
HAPPINESS."

Figure 4-3 Sketch of painted glass setup in plan and section by John Graysmark for *Inn of the Sixth Happiness.*

Technique: A grid was drawn to scale over the ground plan (Fig. 4-5), suggesting where and how the silent stage set and model piece, above, would be composited. The Clavius set was shot with the matte—an ultra-thin zinc plate—in place in the camera's matte box, masking out the top of the frame including the area of the lunar landscape and deep space in the background (Fig. 4-6). Please also see Fig. 4-6 in color between pages 142 and 143. On the sketch, it is labeled as "First Pass." The scene was then shot, exposing that half of the film emulsion on every frame. Then a reverse

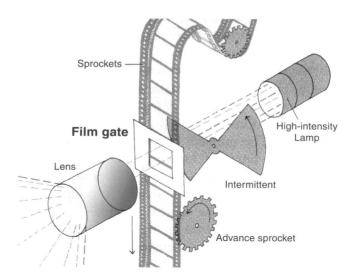

Figure 4-4 Simplified schematic of the interior of a projector showing the location of the "Film Gate."

matte—a precisely cut, opposite puzzle piece of zinc plate—was placed in the matte box masking out the scene previously shot in the set on the bottom half of the frame. (Notice that in the schematic in Fig. 4-4, the film emulsion is just behind the film gate as the filmstrip is pulled down through the intermittent movement.) "The background miniature of the lunar landscape and deep space was then exposed, frame per frame, for "one plus minutes in the camera gate at very slow exposure, to burn the crisp blacks and whites of space without atmosphere."[3] It is important to understand that both top and bottom matte halves were carefully manipulated and shot *within* the camera to insure an exact registration of the foreground action in the studio and the miniature in backgrounds of Fig. 4-6 and Fig. 4-8. This example of precisely planned, double-exposure is typical of the director's obsession for **in-camera** control.

Explanation: Kubrick's reasoning made perfect sense considering the film was being shot as if it were chronicling events in deep space where there was no atmosphere. The exact fit of composited elements had to ensure jigsaw puzzle precision (Fig. 4-7). As you watch the film, all model shots consistently display the deepest blacks and high-key luminous whites in this contrasted image technique (Fig. 4-8).

Kubrick was interested in controlling every aspect of the shooting and editing process. Consequently, the bulk of in-studio shooting he did on *2001* used many miniatures and models. The in-camera techniques he employed also assured the integrity of the 70 mm film stock he used. In other words, every time a strip of film was printed, a generation of clarity or resolution was lost—70 mm film has four times as many frames as 35 mm film, making

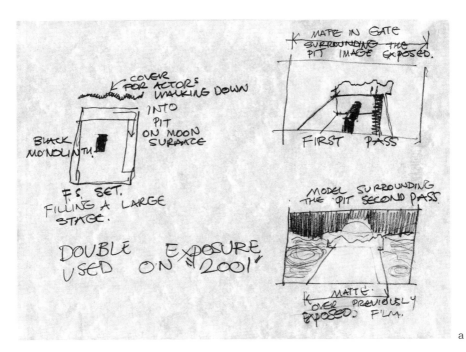

COVER
FOR ACTORS WALKING DOWN
INTO
PIT
ON MOON
SURFACE

BLACK MONOLITH!

F.S. SET.
FILLING A LARGE STAGE.

DOUBLE EXPOSURE
USED ON "2001"

MATTE IN GATE
SURROUNDING THE
PIT IMAGE EXPOSED.

FIRST PASS

MODEL SURROUNDING
THE PIT SECOND PASS

MATTE
OVER PREVIOUSLY
EXPOSED FILM.

a

b

Figure 4-5 A) Sketch of onstage set showing the elevation and plan by John Graysmark of Clavius Lunar Site in *2001: A Space Odyssey*. **B)** Descending into Clavius Lunar Site. Courtesy of Metro-Goldwyn-Mayer/THE KOBAL COLLECTION.

Figure 4-6 Set shot of Clavius lunar site in *2001: A Space Odyssey*. Courtesy of Metro-Goldwyn-Mayer/THE KOBAL COLLECTION. Please also see Fig. 4-6 in color between pages 142 and 143.

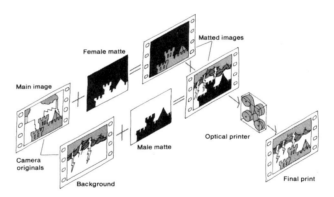

MATTES. Both male and female mattes are derived from the main.
In the stationary matte technique they are drawn; in the travelling matte system, the main image would be backed up by a blue screen (not shown here) and the mattes would be derived optically.

Figure 4-7 Simple schematic showing how a male-female matte works.

Figure 4-8 *2001: A Space Odyssey* miniature shot. Courtesy of Metro-Goldwyn-Mayer/THE KOBAL COLLECTION.

it four times larger. If a single **dupe**, or duplicate, of the originally shot film had to be made, it would degrade to 35 mm status and be acceptable for theatrical viewing.

I have intentionally focused on this film because it is a characteristic example of a contemporary film shot entirely **in-studio** using the most state-of-the-art in-camera techniques at the time. The designer and art director's functions were to design the scenery especially for many of the in-camera sequences to comply with how the film was shot and processed. Obviously, the design team was not just making pretty scenery; process was just as important as production value.

THE PROCESS CAMERA

As we've just seen, in-camera matte shots required successive re-exposure of the original negative. **Optical printing**, another aspect of adding to or subtracting from original film stock footage, concerned itself primarily with master positives and dupe negatives. Bi-pack contact matte printing was a transitional technique that replaced older glass and matte techniques. The term "bi-pack" refers to two **magazines** or spools of film; one spool contained a master positive struck from the original negative and one spool contained a roll of fine-grain, negative raw stock (Fig. 4-9). Negative raw stock (A), emulsion in, was threaded into a process camera with the master positive stock (B), emulsion out. Both strips of film were placed emulsion-to-emulsion just behind the aperture plate in the **intermittent movement** of the process camera. As the filmstrips were pulled together through the

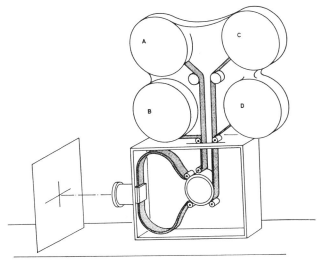

A simplified, cut-away sketch of a process camera, loaded for bi-pack printing. Duplicating negative raw stock is loaded into chamber A, emulsion-in. A master positive is loaded into chamber B, emulsion-out. The exposed dupe negative is taken up into chamber C, the master positive into chamber D. The two strips pass through the intermittent movement, emulsion-to-emulsion, with the raw stock to the rear.

Figure 4-9   The process camera. Courtesy of Dr. Raymond Fielding.

printer, each was recollected into its own receiving spool (A into C) and (B into D). The goal of this setup was to use this **process camera** as a **step printer**. In photographic terms, a step printer is an apparatus that develops film whether it is 35 mm film from a reflex camera or a 35 mm movie camera. (Remember, cinema is fundamentally photography.) Keeping this concept in mind, the master positive was used in the bi-pack process as a "negative," and the raw film stock was used as high quality photographic "paper" to accept a new printed image. Anyone who has spent time in a darkroom is familiar with how film is developed. Early filmmakers realized this and used these fundamental concepts for their new craft. What would the new image be? It would be whatever needed to be added to the master positive to complete the finished image on the filmstrip.

How was a new image added to the master positive? Fig. 4-9 also shows a square of matte board that acted as a rigid easel for holding either matte or counter-matte images like those shown in Figs. 4-10A and 4-10B. As long as the image on the matte board was evenly lit, the light rays bouncing off the board would act as the primary light source in the photographic step printer, etching a new image as it passed through the aperture and the master positive onto the raw film stock behind. The new image would be

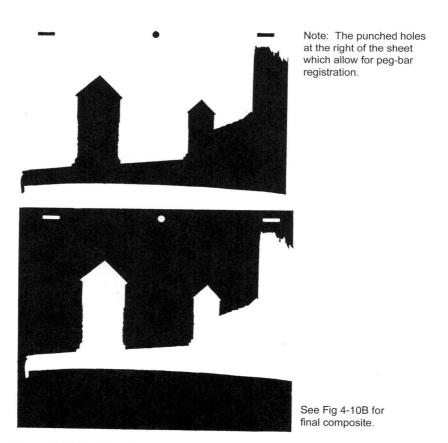

Note: The punched holes at the right of the sheet which allow for peg-bar registration.

See Fig 4-10B for final composite.

Figure 4-10A   Matte/counter matte . . . Courtesy of Dr. Raymond Fielding.

First printing for a bi-pack matte shot combining two live-action scenes.

Second printing, adding background detail photo-graphed from the top of a ten-storey building.

Final composite. See Fig 4-10A for mattes used for this shot.

Figure 4-10B   . . . and resulting composite image. Courtesy of Dr. Raymond Fielding.

a combination of the originally shot footage with the image on the matte board. This technique of manipulating film stock and images was prevalent during the mid-later twentieth century, 1965–1980. Although this information is somewhat technical, the concept is important. Once the range and technique of any of these processes is understood, the concepts can be more confidently applied as the basis for solutions to new problems.

Speed and greater precision are what digital techniques add to the foundation of these concepts.

TRAVELING MATTES

Compositing foreground action with actors and a background shot elsewhere onto the same piece of film has been the concern of filmmakers since the beginning years of the commercial film industry. An original solution to this problem was resolved through rear projection. The translucent projection screen was substituted for the glass (as in the painted glass shot) and a projected photographic film image was applied to the back of the screen instead of paint. The rest is self-explanatory. More complicated compositing processes allowed actors to move about within the frame without disappearing behind matted background areas. The Dunning-Pomeroy self-matting process accomplished this by allowing changes in background position, size, and composition from frame to frame, giving the actor and director free movement within the picture frame. This revolutionized moviemaking but had its drawbacks: it was limited to black-and-white cinematography, and was not flexible in the editing or post-production process. Unfortunately, once the final positive was composited that is how it remained.

Early cinema pioneers continued to learn valuable lessons from color photography and applied this knowledge to the filmmaking process. Each of the primary colors of red, blue, and green (also known as **hues** or **chroma**) could be separated and placed on their own filmstrips. Combining this fact with the need to solve the flexibility problem mentioned above, the traveling matte process improved dramatically. **Chromakeying**, or separating the primary light colors out of the original color image, and using the black-and-white photographic process in conjunction with the color process utilized a more exacting and successful compositing system.

The key steps in contact printing, a conventional traveling matte in popular use during the last quarter of the last century (Fig. 4-11), begin with an actor shot in color negative in front of a **bluescreen** (Step A in Table 4-1). The entire process as seen in steps A to H shows a flip-flopping between color and B/W negatives and positives to arrive at the male and female composite strips to be married onto a single strip of film. Table 4-1 replaces words for images in explaining Fig. 4-11. Hopefully, this will simplify your understanding.

Once these challenging concepts are understood, the reader will be able to easily apply the fundamentals of the traveling matte process to the current applications of this relatively simple technique to digital filmmaking.

Rotoscoping, borrowed from animation, was a technique of tracing each frame of live action and then hand painting in the silhouette (see Fig. 4-7, Figs. 4-10A and 4-10B). The silhouetted artwork was either photographed or used directly to composite the foreground and background with the same camera to create the matte. This technique is still used today with imaging programs like Avid Illusion® or Commotion® (Pinnacle Systems). Although

Figure 4-11 Conventional bluescreen traveling matte. Courtesy of Dr. Raymond Fielding.

Explanation of the **Bluescreen Traveling Matte** Printing Process	
A An actor is photographed with white light on color negative film stock in front of a **bluescreen.**	**B** The resulting color negative is step-printed in contact with a black-and-white master positive of the same scene; this records only the blue chroma component of the scene. The result of this step is a hybrid, B/W color separated positive with a clear background.
C Repeating step B, the color negative is printed onto another B/W master positive, but this time separating out the red chroma component. The resulting background is black. This positive is step-printed to a duplicate on high-contrast film, producing its corresponding negative image with another clear background (as in step B).	**D** In this step, the blue chroma positive and the red chroma duplicate are optically printed using the bi-pack method onto additional high-contrast B/W stock. At this point, A TRAVELING MATTE is the result, showing a black background matte and clear area signifying the actor in the foreground action.
E A corresponding male counter-matte is simply printed from the female traveling matte in step D.	**F** This step shows the male traveling matte (E) of the actor combined with the background master positive.
G This step shows the female traveling matte (D) of the background combined with the actor master positive.	**H** Either a color or B/W composite is produced here from bi-packing the composites in steps F and G.

Table 4-1   A Bluescreen Traveling Matte is achieved through optical printing.

originally a time-consuming process, these software programs produce flawless animation and super-fast results.

At one time a phenomenon, digital compositing is now universally accepted as the norm in the pre- and post-production process. The vivid blue or vivid green backing against which the foreground action is shot becomes a criterion for color difference matching. Digital compositing artists working in VFX film departments must do four things with this digital data: 1) Check the backing screen for irregularities and correct for uniformity—this is also known as *screen correction*, 2) Create an alpha channel or silhouette mask, as the original rotoscope artists once did, 3) Check the foreground for screen reflections and suppress them by giving them a value of black—also known as creating a processed foreground, and 4) Combine the elements into a believable composite. All of this is just an updated version of bluescreen traveling matte work done with an optical printer.

Questions about color remain: Why a bluescreen and not red? The answer lies within the skin tones of any given actor. It's simply easier to separate out the blue tones than the red tones of the skin pigment. Even with the precision of getting down to the pixel in digital film production, the bluescreen has been upgraded to a greenscreen in certain instances but still works exceptionally well. Wardrobe color and exterior location (foliage) also determines the use of either color. One advantage green has over blue is less grain noise in shadows or semi-transparent objects found in foreground action.[4]

MINIATURES

Three types of miniatures have been used in traditional moviemaking: 1) The miniature is used as an element inset, backing through an opening in the set, 2) The model is shot as is, or 3) It is used as a component in image replacement for a composite. By comparison, a miniature is a 3D alternative to a 2D matte image (see "Glass shot" and "Gate matte" discussed previously in this chapter). Where a glass painting incorporates fixed light, shadow, and perspective, these same elements can be varied, making miniatures more versatile. Miniatures can be static as viewed in a long shot, for example, or as moving pieces, increasing the realism and believability of a shot.

Common sense and experience tell us that familiar objects at rest and in motion behave a certain way in the physical world. If they do not or if we perceive the slightest deviation from an expected norm, we become suspicious. We either think about checking our eyesight, or wonder about a psychological aberration. If all else fails, we realize we have been deceived. Deception is what we work at and ultimately do best in the art department. It's our stock-in-trade. Cinematic deception is derived from using the laws of physics to our advantage through a proven formula or by twisting those formulas into desired shapes through trial and error. Insight is an additional ingredient that helps to fill in the gaps.

To be effective, miniatures shot "as is" must be as close to full scale as possible. Remember full scale shows a relationship of $1:1$ or $1' = 1'$. The optimal range from the largest to the smallest models should fall between quarter scale: $1:4$ or $3'' = 1'$ to twelfth scale: $1:12$ or $1'' = 1'$. Comparatively, it costs less to build a larger miniature than a smaller one in terms of detail and time. Mobile models smaller than the range noted require extremely high-speed camera drives to capture movement, increasing time and labor costs. This information should serve only as a guideline. Different projects will dictate requirements and budgets; these variables will affect how problems are solved and how rules are appropriately broken to serve the solutions to those problems.

Combining miniature use with live action lends itself to unquestioning believability. Why? As detailed and realistic as the model might be, the live action playing in front of it is a diversion by pulling enough focus to enroll the audience. If the miniature and live action sequences are to be shot separately, then it would be best to build the miniature and shoot it first, and then shoot the live action footage to work within its parameters. With this information in mind, let's get to some historic examples.

Hanging Foreground Miniature

As a young draughtsman, John Graysmark encountered this simple technique on *Anastasia* (1956). Wallace Smith's drafting was used for the construction of the miniature. Details of the process follow:

> Shot: A Trans Atlantic crane, very high, slowly panned across the nighttime expanse of the city of Paris (circa 1928, during Russian Easter) to the bell tower of the Russian Orthodox Church. The shot was held, faded, and then tilted down below the miniature, hanging piece to the street and church below.
>
> Scenery: An architectural miniature of the bell tower (Fig. 4-12) was suspended in the foreground above, with the nighttime city of Paris in miniature in the background. This hanging miniature was in quarter scale (3:1), corresponding to the full-scale church and street built on the studio lot below. The miniature was bordered on the bottom with a course line of bricks and finishing moulding—this acted as a hard cutting edge for the transition between the miniature bell tower model and full-scale church and tower on the studio lot.
>
> Technique: "There were two issues to consider: the depth of field and the nodal point of the camera lens. The same camera lens was used for shooting both the model miniature in front of its Parisian background miniature and the full-scale church and street scene. By using the same lens but adjusting for focal distance when shooting the miniature tower and full-scale tower, the transition was smooth from the bottom of the suspended tower miniature to the body of the full-scale church." According to Graysmark, "Using a tilting pan head would've been incorrect—the camera must have a nodal head because the center of the lens had to be stationary, acting as a fixed fulcrum point for the movement—in this case, by tilting.[5]
>
> Explanation: The reason for transitioning from the miniature to the full-scale church is to create a believable opening shot for the movie (the skyline of Paris looked different in 1956 when the movie was shot, as opposed to when it was scripted to take place in 1928). "The POV, or the focal distance from the camera lens to the miniature, stayed the same. That way the scale of the miniature didn't distort, and it worked beyond depth of field as the camera refocused on other objects."[6]

The reason why John differentiates between the tilting pan head and nodal head is fundamental (see Fig. 4-13). A nodal head operates much like a human head as it nods up and down "yes" (tilt), or turns left and right "no" (pan) while the body is seated in a fixed position (fixed fulcrum). The tilting pan head works exactly the same way *except* the camera base (body holding the head) rides an arc, much like being on a playground swing (changing fulcrum point). A change in fulcrum, or position, for the camera lens located in the head, also changes the depth of field and focus as it moves along an arc. If the body were sitting still on the swing with no movement at the

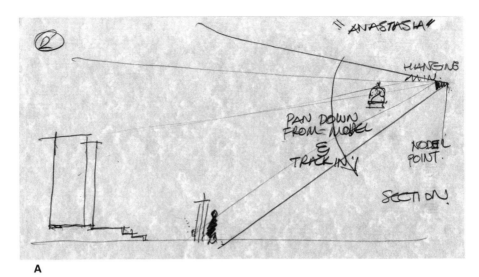

A

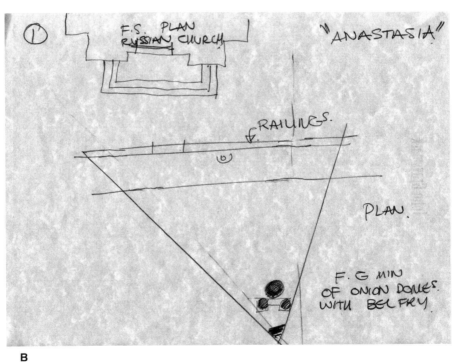

B

Figure 4-12 A) Plan sketch of foreground hanging miniature set by John Graysmark for *Anastasia*. **B)** Elevation sketch of foreground hanging miniature set by John Graysmark for *Anastasia*.

valley of the arc, nodding up and down, then the effect of a nodal head is once again at work. The shot in the scene described previously would have obviously looked very different without the use of the nodal tilting head. This illustrates a critical design point. Without an understanding of basic camera movement, lens choice, and employment of various tricks-of-the-

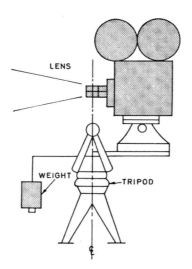

The camera can be panned and tilted across glass-shot paintings, provided that it is mounted with the fulcrum point of the pans and tilts located at the nodal point of the lens. This diagram shows one type of nodal-point mount. Alternatively, adaptor plates are available for some of the studio gear-heads which position the camera in similar fashion.

Figure 4-13 Schematic of a nodal point mount. Courtesy of Dr. Raymond Fielding.

trade to successfully make a shot, any design produced in the art department is incomplete and misinformed.

Foreground Miniature

Escape to Athena (1979) provides a quick and simple example of the use of a foreground miniature (see Fig. 4-14). Before we analyze this, it's important to note that: 1) A 25 mm wide angle lens for best depth of field was used, and 2) The F-stop indicated by the cameraman for this lens provided to the art department with the exact depth of field as an exact reference, e.g., 2" 10" to 5'–2".

> Shot: Climax scene of actors hiding behind protective rocks at the bottom of the frame as the monastery explodes above them at the top of the frame.
>
> Set: The miniature monastery in question was built in 1" = 1' – 0" or 12 : 1 scale on the ground to imitate the look of a mountainous outcropping along the coastline on the Island of Rhodes, matching shots both before and after it.
>
> Technique and explanation: The split matte used for this scene was shot at two different speeds. The miniature, above, was shot at 120 frames per second and slightly beyond proper depth of field at 5'–3" to keep it out of focus and ensure believability. The actors, below, were shot at a normal 24 frames per second. Compositing the images in bi-pack created an acceptable scene of potential danger as a resolution to the movie. Going against logic in terms of keeping the foreground miniature slightly out of proper focus, worked best for the shot and the art department as well as shooting at 120 fps adjusted the speed of the fireball.

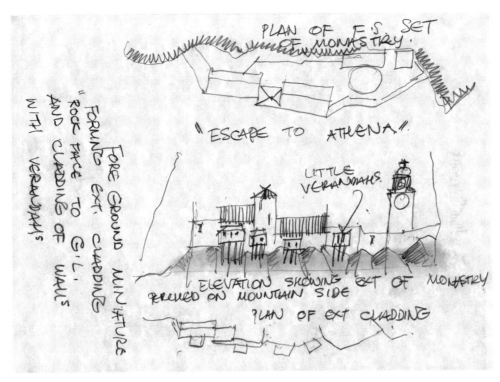

Figure 4-14   Sketch of foreground miniature set up by John Graysmark for *Escape to Athena*.

Cutouts: A Variation on Miniatures

Design work on *White Sands* (1992) filmed in Alamagordo, NM at the National Monument required miniature building and an explosion. The restrictions of this fragile location were: 1) No vehicles allowed on the pristine, white gypsum sand, 2) Wind gusts were a regular, unexpected occurrence, 3) A limited timeframe was strictly enforced to complete our work and leave without a trace, or face stiff penalties.

Shot: An arms-operative fired a shoulder missile at a tank in the near distance to prove the accuracy of his new product.

Set: Quonset huts and a breakaway tank were among other disused military vehicles on an abandoned army base.

Technique: The first part of our solution was photographic. Our set photographer accumulated a variety of both truck and tank views with a 35 mm reflex camera at a nearby military installation. Selected images were mounted to framed lauan and cut cleanly around edges to give us a workable 2D view of the vehicles. The next part of our solution was practical. By combining the front and side views of a typical tank, we created a half-scale model of it that could be easily "destroyed" by the shoulder missile. The mechanical effects department required multiples for three takes. Additional side views or front views were individually mounted on lauan, framed, jacked, and heavily sandbagged into regimented rows in the distance. The mechanical effects department did several tests. The day before the shoot they also cable-rigged the dummy missile just above the actor's shoulder level from the locked-off position to its target at the breakaway tank cutout.

Explanation: The shooting sequence followed this pattern: 1) On cue, the shoulder missile was fired by the effects crew, 2) It "hit" its target by stopping short of the cutout tank model, 3) Cut, 4) A fireball explosion was detonated and filmed, 5) Cut, 6) Explosion debris was prepared by the scenics and scattered by the on-set dressers around the explosion site after the effects crew removed the cutout. We repeated with several takes for assurance.

This scene was filmed at night to accentuate the smoke and fire of the explosion. This technique was easy to pull off and worked, when methodically executed, in a variety of situations (*Tora, Tora, Tora* or *Courage Under Fire*) where it's easier to scenically paint or apply a photograph to a cutout surface than to transport large and expensive pieces of set dressing into a remote and fragile location. It saves money and time, and is very controllable.

Forced Perspective

This is a practical technique for shooting a scene in a studio with less space than might be required. How can that happen? Isn't the size of a studio predetermined by the number of sets scheduled to occupy the space? Initially, it is. Then any number of things could happen: the schedule changes or a critical location is lost or an additional series of shots are added to forward the storytelling. At that point, a forced perspective set might be squeezed into the empty space previously occupied by a set already shot and wrapped.

The 1994 film *Blown Away* provides an example of forced perspective (Fig. 4-15). During the movie's **exposition**, this technique remains onscreen for two seconds before the shot changes. Here is the analysis:

Shot: The hero emerges from an upper floor stair landing as he runs into a hallway junction, pauses a moment to decide where to go, then exits through the door, camera right. The stationary camera pans from right to left, pauses, and pans briefly back to the right.

Scenery: The top section of a stair landing with window and translucent backing beyond leads up into an MIT hallway wall with a practical door leading into an office.

Technique and explanation: In the scene previously described, we are looking through the **picture plane**, noted as "P.P." in the plan drawing to several pair of pilasters and headers diminished in scale toward a back

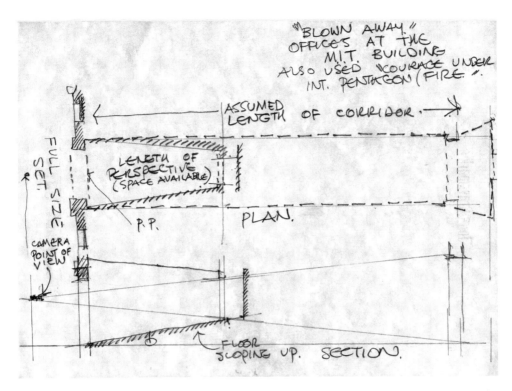

Figure 4-15   Two forced-perspective sketches drawn by John Graysmark for *Blown Away* (2005).

wall that included a door with a translucent glass panel and a translucent transom. This picture plane was physically created by the closest set of pilasters and header to the camera. The floor of the hallway was purposely set on a steep slope, forcing the perspective through exaggeration. The "camera POV" noted in the section sketch below the plan sketch was fixed except for the minimal panning it did—watching this shot several times, one could estimate the fixed height of the camera lens at the same height as the translucent, glass paneled door at the far end of the forced perspective hallway. Lasting just a couple of seconds, this shot forwards the storytelling successfully via this highly believable and compelling technique.

This technique clearly uses forced perspective scenery as a 3D miniature glass painting. Seven decades earlier on a production of *Monte Cristo* (1922), a similar use of this technique extended the believability of a hallway that would otherwise be too costly to build. By forcing the linear perspective, the physical reality of scenery closest to the camera was distorted; the distortion continued rapidly as the distance was compressed. It is important to note from a design point of view that perspective detail on the built scenery tended to fall away as the eye of the viewer moved gradually down the force perspective hallway (Fig. 4-16). To push the illusion even further, an art director could insert a pale gray bobbinette into the width of the hallway somewhere just beyond the first $\frac{1}{3}$ of the distance of the corri-

A hanging miniature is a partially-constructed model which is interposed between a full-scale set and the camera.

The finished composite. Note the false perspective which is produced by continuously varying the scale of the hanging miniature.

Figure 4-16   Hanging miniature built in forced perspective also acts as a 3D glass painting. Courtesy of Dr. Raymond Fielding.

dor. Backlighting a bit more intensely in the remainder of the corridor beyond the fine scrim forces the bobbinette to "go transparent" and creates a visual sense of atmospheric perspective. This technique is borrowed from the theater. Given this example, it is easy to use the phrase "trick-of-the-trade" to explain this and other techniques, but it is a misnomer. There is no trick involved, only careful, collaborative planning—calculated deception based on experience, yes, but no trickery.

Mobile Miniatures

Mobile miniatures demand that attention be paid to time-scale relationships, i.e., the laws of physics, namely gravity, buoyancy, velocity, and friction. *Speed* (1994), a recent, high-concept action-adventure designed by Jackson De Govia, showcased the most excellent use of miniatures as it addressed three laws of inertia, velocity, and friction. This is expressed in two prominent miniature sets: an L.A. skyscraper elevator/shaft and a section of the L.A. Metro/subway train. Once research and fundamental design decisions had been completed and built for onstage shooting, the development and supervision of each miniature set was subcontracted to Grant McCune Design for the elevator/shaft and Sessums Engineering for the L.A. Metro work. Not only is this commonplace in the movie industry but also necessary. Grant McCune Design is a mini-film studio offering the following in-house services: art department, dark room, machine shop, metal fabrication, woodshop, milling, model shop, paint shop, mold shop, production offices, production lot (12,000 sq. ft.), and production motion control/smoke stage (5,000 sq. ft.). GMD offers any level of miniature photographic supervision from storyboarding to prop design and graphic production, as well as providing any three-dimensional object needs: set pieces, sculptures, miniatures, table top props, mechanical props and rigging, theme park models, promotional items, prototypes, replicas, and rentals.[7] Professional studios like this become a temporary arm of the art department by thoroughly assisting production design teams while remaining under strict supervision. The superb craft of Grant McCune's elevator shaft and elevator car miniatures were seen during the opening credits of the film, foreshadowing general clues about the plot and the events of the first near-catastrophe we encounter.

> Shot: A motion control crane descended along the vertical length of a multiple elevator shaft, displaying the opening credits of the film. The camera was angled in a medium close-up on the respective floor numbers, as well as the adjacent shaft showing the intermittent movement of other elevator cars. A horizontal I-beam at the bottom of each floor station cleverly wiped each credit off the screen and revealed the next as the camera slid down the chute. This POV shot began at the 41st floor, paused at the 32nd floor long enough for the film title, *Speed*, to quickly appear and disappear, progressed to the 10th floor, displaying the production design credit, and continued its descent below the first floor lobby to P4 garage. The shot continued, pulling back from the elevator along a short corridor, and rested about 20 feet from a door. Cut to the full scale set and a **CU** of a sign on this door reading, "Caution."

> Scenery: "The entire first shot was a miniature including the shaft and elevator cars, the corridor, the door, and the sign. The details of the miniature set were taken from the full-size set pieces onstage and shot after most of the full-size sets were struck. The miniature set measured $27\frac{1}{2}" \times 57" \times 69'$ in $1/8"$ scale and included 46 floors and 8 elevator bays. It was laid on its back on the stage and shot horizontally."[8]

> Technique and explanation: A motion control crane shot the opening sequence by simply rolling on a dolly trough to the right side of the miniature set. This counterintuitive approach worked with gravity, making the shots easy and practical.

The L.A. Metro sequence used inter-cuts of miniatures and full-size, live action footage. Miniatures of subway tunnel, terminus station, and trains were designed and built by Sessums Engineering, another full-service Hollywood production house. This sequence precedes the end of the film and is analyzed below:

Shot sequence: Three main shots make up this sequence: the first car of the runaway train splits from the second car, the lead car slides into a vertical I-beam and splits in two, and then it continues up a ramp out from the underground.

Scenery: In eighth scale or $1 - \frac{1}{2}" = 1'$, miles of subway track connecting tunnel sections between stations, unfinished North Hollywood terminus station and subterranean model work filled a newly acquired Sony ImageWorks warehouse at the time. Sessums Engineering, headed by Jack Sessums, undertook another, painstaking quest by detailing its train miniatures for the closing scenes of the movie. The miniature production company used two of the four extruded aluminum cars. The super-detailing of the subway cars was specific down to the rubber window gaskets. Allan McFarland, lighting wizard for Sessums, lit the cars with 9" fluorescent tubes imitating that of the full-size cars. Sessums' mechanical effects department carefully constructed one of the breakaway cars to split in two on impact.

Technique and explanation: Anyone who has played with a model train set has a basic idea of the intricacies and patience involved in creating a satisfying fantasy. Choreographing the derailment according to the dictates of the storyboards was Sessums Engineering's biggest challenge. First, the mobile miniatures had to move quickly from inertia to 11–12 m.p.h. A DC motor powered the lead car on its downhill slide. The rest was left to the Sessums' special effects crew and airplane cable working in the Sliding Car miniature set. The derailment and split of the first and second cars were accomplished by pulling each car onto its own train track by guide cables. Once derailed, the same cable rig guided the main car toward the vertical I-beam that splits it in half, much like flying a kite. The cable and pulley system was attached to a longer cable leading outside the warehouse to Jack Sessums driving a Suzuki ATV. The miniature design team cleverly suspended all vertical posts in this set, several inches above the floor so that the cable/pulley kite system could slide beneath without jamming or tangling. A truckload of peat moss covered the floor to aid sliding and to mask the cable rig. "Once cameras were ready to roll, the room was lightly smoked and two, multi-camera takes for each setup went smoothly. Retake setup took 4–5 hours on average. Most of the shots were one-take shots covered by several cameras; there were no problems with dailies, requiring no further retakes."[9]

FRONT PROJECTION

2001: A Space Odyssey was the first motion picture to perfect the technique of front projection. The process was as simple as it looked.

Shot: A stationary camera shot the famous scene of an ape seated on the savanna pounding a small pile of dried bones with a large femur bone.

Scenery: The foreground savanna set—small, **raked**, and rocky—was placed in front of a **highly directional**, front-projection screen acting as background. The curved screen was equidistant at all points from the center of the locked-off camera lens. This assured that there would be no falloff in picture density, thereby retaining full focal distance and focus on any point of the curve.

Technique: The camera shot directly into the center of the set. It employed a projector at a 90-degree angle to the camera lens and a plate of surface-silvered mirror on a 45-degree angle sitting in front of the camera, fully covering the scope of the aperture opening (Fig. 4-17). The projection screen, made of 3M material, was highly-directional meaning it reflected most of the light back to the camera with little ambient light loss; the surface-silvered mirror has a 50/50 reflective/see-through capacity and a perfect ability to both reflect and transmit light. The projector transmitted the background image to the glass, reflecting it onto the screen behind the actor and savanna set placed on the same axis of the camera, as the scene was shot. Very little of the reflected light was lost from the screen as it returned to the camera lens through the mirrored glass and struck the film stock, burning the image onto the film emulsion.

Explanation: Why were there no shadows on the screen behind the actors on the set? There are several reasons for this: 1) The camera was on the same axis as the projected image, 2) As long as the camera remained stationary, the shadows were cast, unseen, directly behind the actor on the screen in background, 3) Fill lights, placed on either side of the set, washed across the center of it erasing any ghost shadows playing on the background screen.[10] All of these factors made the shot perfectly executed.

Another ingenious use of front projection was on the Cannon movie, *Lifeforce* (1985), designed by John Graysmark and shot at the Star Wars stage at Elstree Studios, London.

Shot: A stationary camera photographed actors on top of a crypt in a cathedral apse. From there, an energy field was supposed to stream from the body of one of the actors up through the dome to a craft hovering above the church.

Set: A colonnade of six columns, containing a sarcophagus surrounded by a railing, framed the apse. Tony Reading, John's art director, masterminded the geometric projection sequence for the climax scene set in a cathedral crypt with a front projection screen behind the actors on the tomb (Fig. 4-18).

Technique and explanation: John conceived a simple solution to the required effect by using two pieces of projection screen material. One smaller, jagged piece of 3M material was mounted against black velvet. A crewmember blew cigar smoke from beneath. The projector just behind the mirror placed on a

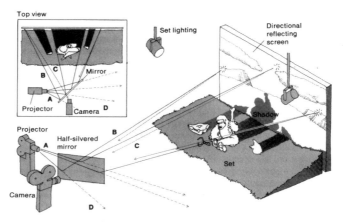

FRONT PROJECTION.   The screen is highly directional, reflecting a great deal more light from the projected image along the axis than off to the side and thus providing a bright enough image. The projected scene travels from the projector (A), is reflected off the half-silvered mirror onto the screen (and set and actor) (B), and then back into the camera, *through* the mirror (C). Some of the light from the projector is also transmitted through the mirror (D).

A

B

Figure 4-17   A) Schematic of front projection using "The Dawn of Man" scene from Stanley Kubrick's *2001: A Space Odyssey*. **B)** Set shot of "The Dawn of Man" scene from Stanley Kubrick's *2001: A Space Odyssey*, Courtesy of THE KOBAL COLLECTION. Used by permission of Oxford University Press, Inc. from HOW TO READ A FILM: THE ART, TECHNOLOGY, LANGUAGE, HISTORY, AND THEORY OF FILM AND MEDIA, 3rd Edition by James Monaco, copyright © 1977, 1981, 2000 by James Monaco.

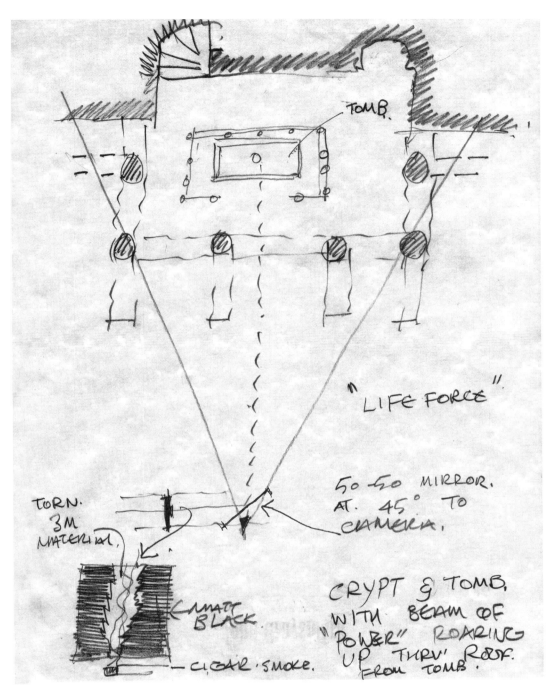

TOMB.

"LIFE FORCE"

50-50 MIRROR.
AT. 45° TO
CAMERA.

TORN.
3M
MATERIAL.

MATT
BLACK.

CLEAR SMOKE.

CRYPT & TOMB.
WITH BEAM OF
"POWER" ROARING
UP THRU' ROOF.
FROM TOMB.

Figure 4-18 Sketch of plan and schematic by John Graysmark for *Lifeforce* Cathedral scene, front projection technique.

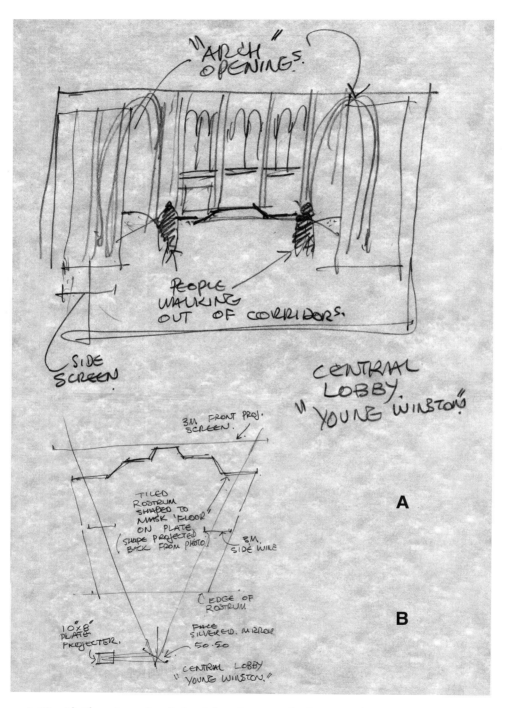

Figure 4-19 **A)** Elevation sketch by John Graysmark showing the onstage, front-projected House of Commons Lobby set (2005). **B)** Plan sketch by John Graysmark showing the onstage, front-projected House of Commons Lobby set (2005). YOUNG WINSTON © 1972, renewed 2000 Columbia Pictures Industries, Inc. All Rights Reserved—Courtesy of Columbia Pictures.

45-degree angle to the camera lens, threw the image of the swirling smoke twenty feet in front of the camera onto a translucent projection screen just beyond the actors on top of the sarcophagus in the crypt area, noted as "tomb" in the sketch. "The effect showed an energy field roaring up to the ceiling and out of the building to a spacecraft above. The visual effect was relatively simple and extremely effective."[11]

A final example of front projection is found in the film *Young Winston* (1972), production designed by Don Ashton, who used front projection technique on a large scale.

Shot: A brief meeting and conversation between two actors takes place in the corridor and is filmed by a stationary camera.

Scenery: The location of the central octagonal lobby of the Palace of Westminster was the design base for an interior set that was too unjustifiably large to build onstage (see Fig. 4-19).

Technique: The designer took multiple exposures in an 8 × 10 plate camera of the actual lobby, much like tiling a montage of images into Photoshop to create a larger image. According to John, this was an intensive, all-night process. Once developed, these large format images were combined, providing a super-size, perspective image of the rear of the octagonal lobby and into the corridors beyond. This giant, composite photo was versatile enough to work for front-projected screen images. A large backing piece of 3M screen material, the same size as the actual lobby, touched down behind the high end of the raked stage floor, exactly matching where the black-and-white tiling of the real set floor would continue back in perspective. Two flats covered with 3M front projection material were also placed each side of the center image closer to the camera, allowing actors to enter the stage floor from behind "the foreground, projected architecture," camera-left and camera-right, and work between the rear backing piece and two front projection panels on the set.

Explanation: This technique, described in each of these three scenarios, was a viable solution to today's greenscreen process by providing a practical alternative to the challenges encountered on this production.

REAR PROJECTION AND MIRRORS

The *2001: A Space Odyssey* art department also employed some good examples of the rear projection technique. All of the graphics displayed in various monitors in the Pod bay of the lunar shuttle set, as well as the activity in the windows of the lunar base miniatures, were mini-movies shot in 16 mm for those smaller screens. The graphic geometry, animated by Doug Trumbull, technical graphic animator, was shot for the 16 mm rear projection monitors in these sets and seen as animations in real time within the larger screen. "And often, if we couldn't get the projectors to do a straight throw, we'd use mirrors to halve the distance and make the images work. The problem then was Stanley's consideration about what percentage of light was lost in the mirror reflection—all that photographic stuff was his game. Of course, he would go to the movie theater and read the light output directly from the projection screen. He was a mad perfectionist."[12]

"Making pictures" as John learned it and refers to it was a total, artistic process from the drafting of Palladian quality plates, to the manipulation and shooting of carefully designed, built scenery. Because every piece of it was an artifact created with sublime effort, the quality of the film as a whole was elevated as an art form. Proper learning of movie craft was essential for the system to operate correctly. "The lords of the industry at the time in Hollywood's Golden Age, namely Alfred Junger who ran MGM-England and Cedric Gibbons who ran MGM-Hollywood, earned the right to occupy their places at the top of these studios. Today, the learning of film craft through a comprehensive guild system is sadly lacking. When you boil it all down, you're given the script and must figure how you present the best solution to tell the story cost effectively. The job of a properly trained art director is to use these tools to make the scenery work to interpret the script so the story can properly be told."[13]

ENDNOTES

1. Tiphaigne de la Roche, *Giphantie*. Paris, 1760 (English translation, Giphantia, London, 1761). Retrieved from the World Wide Web on 10/01/04 at http://www.holonet.khm.de/Antizipation/Tiphaigne_de_la_Roche.html

   The full translation of the book's section follows:

   "That window, that vast horizon, those black clouds, that raging sea are all but a picture. You know that the rays of light, reflected from different bodies, form a picture, and paint the image reflected on all polished surfaces, for instance, on the retina of the eye, on water, and on glass. The elementary spirits have sought to fix these fleeting images; they have composed a subtle matter, very viscous and quick to harden and dry, by means of which a picture is formed in the twinkling of an eye. They coat a piece of glass with this matter and hold it in front of the objects they wish to paint. The first effect of this canvas is similar to that of a mirror; one sees there all objects near and far, the image of which light can transmit. But what a glass cannot do, the canvas by means of its viscous matter, retains the images. The mirror represents the objects faithfully but retains them not; our canvas shows them with the same exactness and retains them all. This impression of the image is instantaneous, and the canvas is immediately carried away into some dark place. An hour later the impression is dry, and you have a picture the more valuable in that it cannot be imitated by art or destroyed by time . . . The correctness of the drawing, the truth of the expression, the stronger or weaker strokes, the gradation of shades, the rules of perspective, all these we leave to nature, who with a sure and never erring hand, draws on our canvasses images which deceive the eye."

2. John Graysmark interview, 4/05/04, Mar Vista, CA.

3. Ibid.

4. Pages 300–360 of the American Cinematographer Manual, 8th edition examines optical printing and traveling mattes in greater detail.

5. John Graysmark interview, 4/05/04, Mar Vista, CA.

6. Retrieved 11/10/04 from the Grant McCune Design Web site on World Wide Web at http://www.gmdfx.com/

7. Quoted from conversation with Smokey Stover of Grant McCune Design, 11/16/04, North Hollywood, CA.

8. Quoted from conversation with Jack Sessums of Sessums Engineering, 11/17/04, North Hollywood, CA.

9. Note: 3M reflective materials are versatile and ubiquitous, seen on every road sign in any given city. This material was also used on the Light-Saber blades for the *Star Wars* films. The facets of three-sided, Light-Saber blades were covered with narrow strips of 3M reflective materials. The blade revolved in its handle at high speed. Once shot on film, the light reflecting off the rotating blades was later enhanced as "glowing" by Frank Van der Veer, rotoscope specialist, optical cinematographer, and photographic effects supervisor, at the ILM Studios for Lucas.

10. Ibid., Graysmark interview, 4/05/04, Mar Vista, CA.

11. Ibid., Graysmark interview, 4/05/04, Mar Vista, CA.

12. Ibid., Graysmark interview, 4/05/04, Mar Vista, CA.

13. Ibid., Graysmark interview, 4/05/04, Mar Vista, CA.

CHAPTER 5

CGI and Digital Filmmaking

If anything can be certain about the future, it is that the influence of technology, especially digital technology, will continue to grow and to profoundly change how we express ourselves, how we communicate with each other and how we perceive, think about and interact with our world. These "mediating technologies" are only in the first stages of their modern evolution; they are still crude, unwieldy, unpersonalized and poorly matched to the human needs of their users. Their fullest development in those terms is emerging as one of the principal technical and design challenges of the emerging information age.[1]

MIT Media Lab Web site

BREAKING GROUND

A lover of cinematic history can easily appreciate the efforts of those early visionaries who contributed to the digital moviemaking tradition now more than 20 years old. Back in the late 70's the Internet was referred to as ARPANET, Microsoft was still a fledgling company, and video games were found in experimental form, offered as Atari VCS and Mattel's Intellivision. In 1981, production designer Dean Mitzner (*1941, Nine to Five, Looker, Princess Daisy, The Man with One Red Shoe, Charmed*) had just begun his contribution to the fledgling visual effects revolution. His participation in *TRON*, an animated/live-action Disney experiment, heralded a creative departure for him by its presentation of a bold design concept. In technical terms, it ventured beyond the marriage of traditional animation techniques and live-action in *Mary Poppins* (1964) by also including backlit animation to the mix. It was the first film to use CGI for its vehicles and in its action sequences, and involved the completion of over 1,000 visual effects shots that required compositing on the average of 12 to 15 layers, or wedges, per frame. Each wedge presented a different light intensity: the background being the least intense and the helmeted faces sitting on the top layer, the most intense. In order to provide the most optimal, physical background for the actors in the live-action sequence shooting, Dean covered every inch of scenery with black-flocked paper, inadvertently giving the film a handmade quality—a cinematic paradox—successfully absorbing all ambient light and providing the perfect, nonreflective palette for director, Steven Lisberger. *TRON* presented a vividly striking, minimalist beauty of its innovative scenic design. Nevertheless, the Academy of Motion Picture Arts and Sciences disqualified the film from being nominated that year for a deserved visual effects Oscar because it "cheated" by using computers. What an amusing thought.

Dean candidly admits to having felt somewhat in the dark at the time by designing scenery for a high-concept film cutting inroads into such uncharted territory.[2] Nevertheless, he can take full comfort in knowing that without his unshakable faith in the vision of his intrepid director and the solidness of his own talent, the success of this technical milestone, and the subsequent trailblazing of other experiments like *Star Wars*, *The Matrix*, *Lord of the Ring* trilogy, and even *Toy Story*, would have never been possible. *TRON*, a precursor of next-generation, animated, live-action motion pictures, clearly predicted the direction of the future.

Merged media converging in the new and improved art department is blurring titles, rewriting job descriptions, and re-establishing it as the crucible of all cinematic imagery. What was once done in optical houses after the fact is now performed as a matter of course by using previz techniques in our computers. Previz and visual effects, now subdepartments of a greater concept dynamic, begin the process of design analysis and proactive certainty much earlier in the pre-production process with the director. Combining all aspects of the analog and digital tools spectrum, they guarantee a richer visual product. The only downside is the length of the credit crawl at the end of today's digital films (Fig. 5-1). Otherwise, what is old is certainly new again. Many of the techniques of the digital cinema process rely on traditional methods of achieving the same effects within a "modern" context. The preceding chapter was methodical in its analysis of the tried-and-true, nuts and bolts techniques discussed. The conceptual ideas in this chapter will be presented in full interview format, either cited by face-to-face interviews when time and space permitted or by Internet interviews where time was short and space nonexistent.

CONVERSATIONS ON THE VISIONARY FRONTIER

Alex McDowell, *Production Designer*
(Charlie and the Chocolate Factory, The Cat in the Hat,
Minority Report, Lawnmower Man)

Film technique is universal and easily applied to an industry operating in any country in the world. The international filmmakers I've had the great pleasure to work with practice their craft just as assiduously as anyone else, and once a film product filters through the Hollywood system in production or distribution, it loses its accent. The expansion of cinema iconography into the digital realm similarly defines no political boundaries. As we continue our discussion, the fact that the following section will focus on another, more recent production designer of English cinema culture, Alex

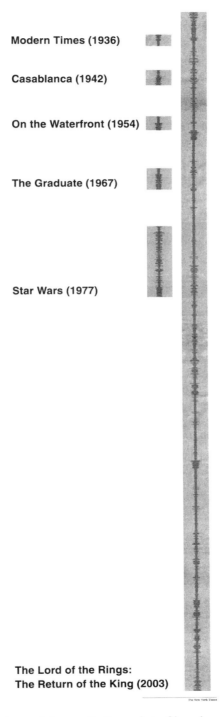

Modern Times (1936)

Casablanca (1942)

On the Waterfront (1954)

The Graduate (1967)

Star Wars (1977)

The Lord of the Rings:
The Return of the King (2003)

The New York Times

Figure 5-1 A comparison of the credit lists of six films from *Modern Times* (1936) to *Lord of the Rings: Return of the King* (2004). Courtesy of the New York Times: Baseline/Filmtracker and New Line Cinema.

McDowell, is purely coincidental. In this case, my connection to Alex is derived through American art department artists who have worked with him on the projects noted, and it exemplifies the organic process of film networking, and ultimately, of how this handbook was written. An ongoing Internet conversation with Alex has produced a continuous dialogue to be shared here. How fitting that data explaining the philosophy of twenty-first century cinema process was exchanged through cyberspace.

☐ *Let's begin with the digital art department: What is your philosophy about it?*
Digital technology is opening up a growing wealth of new design resources for the film art department. Digital tools are more than just an extension of the design toolkit. Because the most sophisticated software is now available to the individual designer, not only is the art department able to explore the possibility of sets before they are built, but we are also providing accurate visual data to many departments, particularly visual effects. The look of sets that will not be fully realized until post-production can now be under discussion with director and cinematographer in enough time to affect the development of the content of a film.

A sophisticated understanding of digital technology and a networked team of people using digital tools places the production designer back at the center of the flow of information that will determine and control the look of a film. For example, a large amount of the output from the *Minority Report* art department was focused on elements that would be built by the VFX houses, particularly ILM. In the past few years, as the idea of VFX really took hold, the designer took a back seat as VFX houses built up their own art department for CGI sequences. In contrast, not only were matte paintings and set extensions conceptualized within the art department, the designers also built all the key 3D elements and designed all the animations of the Hovership, Maglev vehicles, and traffic system, the Spyders, and the Hall of Containment sequence.

☐ *How do you implement the digital art department: the setup, the practical aspects of operation, etc.? What positions have been added/subtracted?*
The digital aspects of the art department should be set up at the beginning of production, so that as the department expands each person plugs directly into the network, connected to one another through the server. This means that tech support from the production and within the art department is essential. I have found that on average it takes three to four weeks to set up the server and network, which means motivating production to set this in motion often before the art director is hired.

The digital art department is essentially straightforward to set up. Most office spaces that are offered up as art department space are already set up with an Ethernet network. A studio that is already using a network for accounting, for example, can assign part of that server space to the art department for archive, drop boxes, etc. Or an external hard drive can be plugged into an Ethernet network as a server.

The researcher and archivist scan images and archive them on the server to be accessible to concept artists as they start work. The locations department downloads all files to the same archive, where stitched images are stored by location and accessible to art directors and concept artists. Digital artwork overlaid onto location images is presented to the director, alongside research and concept art. The department starts to release a growing catalogue of images that portray an accurate picture of the director and designer's vision of the film, long before anything physical exists. The 3D set designers work alongside traditional set designers, often in tag teams. The 3D files are sent through drop boxes on the server to the concept artists, who lay lighting, textures, set dressing, and set extensions over an accurate lens view of a potential set. The 3D files are also sent to the previs artists, who combine the set models with storyboard information to create animated sequences within virtual sets that the director can control.

☐ *Can you recommend the name of a reliable server?*
The make of server itself is unimportant, and for the purposes of a book, any recommendation would soon be outdated. There are some issues with using a PC-based server if the design team is mostly Mac-based, but these problems are regularly overcome. The important thing is to have good IT support within the production, and definitely to have a very savvy computer techie in the art department. Generally, this person is employed as high-tier PA, and will be crucial to the archivist, setting up the digital art department, maintaining the server, and constantly updating all publication of design data and images to the server. That person will be constantly busy.

☐ *On a small film, what's more important—a server or a digital modeler?*
The server. Even if your small film is only using a digital locations department, producing graphics digitally, or distributing storyboards, the server will increase the efficiency of the visual communication.

☐ *Do you consider power backup for your server in case of an emergency?*
Power backup is definitely essential. Also a daily auto backup of the data isn't a bad idea.

☐ *Are online servers useful or not customizable enough?*
There are a couple of problems with online servers. They are likely not to be large enough to support the equipment and data storage that are generated by a department whose stock-in-trade is high-resolution imagery. And there are often security issues—production offices are very reluctant to allow any kind of system that involves an outside agency, or one that can be accessed externally.

☐ *During the Post Digital Workshop hosted by the AD Guild at the Panavision Screening Room on 4:05:03, you used a graphic at the beginning of your PowerPoint presentation depicting the sphere or structure of the digital art department. This image directly corresponds to the paradigm of the "new" art department and how it is being reclaimed through technology.*
Yes. But please note that this is a work in progress, and only hints at the complexity of the film production structure. It is a good way to look at the consolidation of the design departments into all aspects of production, and how new technology can and will alter the structure of production itself. It's already true that previz and VFX are starting much earlier, and that the art

department is actively involved in post-production planning, as well as driving design through to the end of post.

It is not noticeable at the moment that any positions are being dropped in the art department because of the increase in the use of digital technology. Certainly, there is a trend in both set design and concept design toward embracing these new tools, and I no longer work with any concept artist who does not use 2D or 3D software as well as pencil.

In set design, it's important to note, that although film is far behind architecture in its complete embracing of digital tools, there are good reasons for film design not to commit fully to CAD and 3D. The most successful design teams that I've worked with have been a 50/50 split between digital and analog. The traditional or analog draftpersons have a deep knowledge of film and theater craft that is often not reflected in the younger digital designers who are tending to come into the industry from architecture. But more to the point, film is unique in that it deals with the re-creation of history, and where digital tools might be appropriate across the board for a futuristic film, the pencil will probably always be more relevant for the design of period and decay.

The digital archivist is a position that we created and that developed out of the combination of research and the opportunity that a server provides to both store a huge database of images and make those images, including concept art, animation, location images, graphics, etc., accessible and available to all the departments. Currently, our archivist publishes new images and references to the server on a weekly basis where the whole crew can be updated with new material. The side product of this is that the crew is receiving a common set of images, leading to a much greater consistency on the look of the film.

☐ *What's the greatest argument an art director can make about the position of archivist as a vital member of the art department?*
The argument is quite simple. Scanning and inputting research, concept, or location images onto a server that everyone can access saves equipment rental costs and printing costs, provided the server is properly administered by an archivist. Similarly, the digital storage of design imagery, plus data and images from many other departments, gives the producers a readily accessible archive in the post-production and marketing phases of a film. This is a completely new resource that in the past would not have been available, but is only possible if the data is constantly maintained and packaged into an accessible database by the archivist. This position is necessarily one that requires both a good visual background and an excellent knowledge of digital tools and a wide range of software.

☐ *Cite specific instances—with images—where this was clearly the case: Lawnmower Man, Fight Club, Minority Report, or Charlie and the Chocolate Factory?*
I have had the digital archive in place since 1998 when we set up the *Minority Report* art department. At that time I had a computer specialist and a researcher working hand in hand to provide a research/archive/tech

support department that worked well. Since then I have tended to separate research from IT, which works equally well and allows me to use researchers who do not necessarily have extensive computer skills. For *Charlie and the Chocolate Factory*, I have a good system with 1) A researcher inputting to and updating the research archive, 2) All designers networked and constantly downloading new design work to the server where the research processes, prints, and archives, and 3) A locations department with their own digital unit for downloading, stitching, creating presentations, and archiving to the server. These days I show fewer and fewer images to the director, because I can view the selection onscreen before any prints are made, and digitally we can create more easily a few pans at a high resolution that give a clear idea of a location.

It is important to note that, for each show, the art department has to set up and impose a clear file-naming protocol that each designer/user is responsible for maintaining with his own work. Otherwise the network will fall apart. This is as important as correctly labeling and distributing blueprints—an area that could be vastly improved through a digital system.

☐ *Your primary focus, then, is on hiring folks adept both traditionally and digitally to solve problems in both environments?*
The most effective crew I have found is one that balances the traditional skills with those adept at using state-of-the-art technology and tools. The individual draftsperson tends to specialize at one end of the spectrum or the other so the ideal for me is to tag team the pencil designer with the digital designer. The same applies to the combination of 2D and 3D—the 3D designer can be working in a complex, and therefore slower environment, while outputting 2D views that a 2D artist can take to a much higher resolution.

☐ *Are storyboard artists valuable to you?*
I do a great deal of my design work with concept artists. They can render design ideas to a greater degree of accuracy and at a photo-real level. That makes discussion with director and crew much more informative than a rough sketch. Increasingly, the concept artists are either using a combination of 2D and 3D tools themselves, or they are working on top of specific views that are selected by the designer from 3D set design images or 3D files from previz. These views represent a specific camera lens and position and give the director the most accurate view possible of a set not yet built, complete with atmosphere, lighting, color, and set dressing.

Storyboard artists are valuable because they are connected straight into the director's back brain. Storyboards are a very effective way to interpret and break down a script. They tell us a great deal about the reality of shooting any complex sequence. But they are increasingly becoming a vital step toward a previz model which can incorporate a narrative sequence into a 3D environment. Many 3D animation artists are as adept at the storytelling eye that a storyboard artist has traditionally provided. Both *The Terminal* and *Charlie and the Chocolate Factory* were driven by directors who felt constrained by storyboards; previz was able in many sequences to replace a frame-by-frame approach with an environment that reflected the needs of the sequence without pinning the director down to specific action within the space.

☐ *Colin Green, of Pixel Liberation Front, shared the story of the "Big Shot" seen early on in the movie Panic Room where, through the use of animatics, David Fincher & Co. determined that the Gazelle crane would be the most expedient piece of equipment to navigate every aspect of that complicated shot. Is this what you're referring to? Can you cite a similar personal experience?*
There are a number of instances where we have used previz to drive the production and design approach. In *Minority Report*, the scene where the Tom Cruise character is hiding from the Spyders in a seedy hotel was conceived as a single overhead shot from a crane. However, this required a large scope of travel—more than a conventional crane could feasibly handle. By building the imagined environment accurately in previz—including crane, track, and camera body with specific lenses—we found that the shot was feasible using a Super Technocrane. The physical track was laid according to the previz data, the shot rehearsed manually with grips following the previz on a playback screen, and the highly complex sequence was achieved on the shoot day in four takes. This was not a VFX problem, but a physical one solved in camera by using a powerful digital tool.

On *Charlie and the Chocolate Factory*, previz has been used in coordination with director, choreographer, and composer to lay out a complex dance sequence performed by CG characters in a physical set.

The Terminal set was built in previz to allow the director to test the limits of a space that was on camera for 80 percent of the film. The same data was taken to a higher and higher resolution as it was first used as the visual basis of a traditional painted backing, and then for the 3D animated environment as a composited background element.

☐ *Along these more technical lines, would you cite specific projects that clearly translate a historical technique like traveling or working matte processes with a digital solution? Perspective registration? Plate photography? Multi-camera moves?*
I've used a couple of glass mattes and foreground (in-camera) miniatures in the past and enjoyed it. These days it's just not economical to have a camera set up for a couple of days in a setting while these traditional techniques are enacted. Historic theatrical techniques are being updated constantly. Glass mattes developed into RP (rear projection) that transitioned into 2D paintings as composites that are now $2\frac{1}{2}$D and 3D miniatures; rather than disappearing, they are becoming fundamental elements tracked into camera moves or as composites. Still, whenever possible I would use old-fashioned theatrical tricks because the in-camera solution is almost always the most economical.

The most effective VFX work is always that which uses several techniques to solve the inherent problems. Mixing methodologies between sophisticated VFX and in-camera sleight-of-hand within a sequence is the best way to support the gag and impact the audience.

The films I've worked on in the past few years are so strewn with effects solutions of every description that it's hard to pick out specific examples. The plane crash sequence in *Fight Club* is a classic use of combined live action and post effects, with motion-controlled camera, digital actors, live actors, physical set, set extension, and digital matte all combined in one sequence and planned to the millisecond and millimeter in previz. *Charlie and the Chocolate Factory* used every resource—traditional and state-of-the-art digital—in combination to solve a highly complex set of problems involving reduced scale Oompa Loompa characters in a live environment.

☐ *What do you expect from a digital art director?*
I expect from any art director that they be open-minded, hard working, creative, intelligent, and questioning. I do not use an art director specifically for digital elements, because I see it as a disadvantage to make a separation between digital and analog. We use the tools at our disposal, and at any time one tool may be more appropriate than another, even within the same set.

☐ *How can traditional art directors make a successful leap into digital filmmaking?*
There is no such thing as a traditional art director. It is the particular job of an art director to stay current with filmmaking processes. Other designers in the art department can specialize in traditional filmcraft and the production designer can be a curmudgeonly Luddite, but the art director's job is to coordinate all aspects of the filmmaking design process with full peripheral vision. If an art director chooses to stay "traditional," then he or she is in denial of one of the basic truths of filmmaking: that it is an art that is constantly reinventing itself. Film as a young medium does not possess a traditional label at all.

To answer your question more specifically, I think an art director can usefully know the principles of digital technology without needing to use all available software, just as he can direct a construction department without having all the skills of a finish carpenter. By this I mean knowing what 2D and 3D design tools are capable of, and knowing enough of the language of these tools to be able to push their limits. One should always question the self-imposed limits of any technology, traditional or digital.

It is interesting to notice that as the digital tools become more ubiquitous, more universally based in 3D, there is a democratizing of the process that breaks down the artificial divisions between skill sets. When the lit and texture-mapped output from a set designer's 3D model looks just like the output of a concept artist's 3D rendering based on the same data (as was true of the images that we outputted for Steven Spielberg for *The Terminal*), it may be time to start hiring individuals for their specific skills rather than because they are labeled with a certain skill set. My approach now is rather to create interlocking design teams, comprised of a pencil designer, a 3D set designer, and a CAD designer, with a satellite 3D modeler and a 2D or 3D concept artist. This is a structural model closer to VFX than an art department but more appropriate to the tools available.

☐ *So, do you use previz as a design tool or a pragmatic indicator?*

I am the primary interface from my department with previz. It is a design environment that I use more and more frequently to hammer out spatial problems. I'm increasingly comfortable working in a 3D space where the issues of that space are much more clearly defined. It is not only the 3D, but also the added elements of animation and space meeting time that I find liberating as a designer. This is the appropriate testing ground for film language.

I often use previz as a forum for discussion of lighting, visual effects, or special sequences with the appropriate keys. The place where narrative meets environment is a good place to chat with the director. Outside the design process once the previz data is fairly fixed, it becomes an excellent tool to indicate production strategies, and is becoming the tool of choice for several departments.

☐ *How has your process as a designer been changed by comparing* Lawnmower Man *and* Minority Report, *e.g., a significant difference in approach or use of more developed technology to solve similar design problems?*

Basically, the more we experience, the wider the range of tools we stumble across and learn. Of course, the dramatic difference between *Lawnmower Man* and *Minority Report*, other than budget, was the access to affordable digital tools that could be brought into the art department or accessed through outside vendors even in other industries. Seeing CNC tools produce a set like the Pre-Cog Chamber cheaper than it could have been constructed by hand would have been a technology that we would likely have employed on *Lawnmower Man*, had it been available.[3]

Colin Green, *Previsualization Supervisor*
(I Robot, Van Helsing, Elf, The Matrix Revisited, Fight Club)

☐ *After you finished training at MIT, wasn't your early work based on the East coast?*

Starship Troopers (1997) was the contract that brought us out to Los Angeles, while we maintained a base office in New York City. During the course of that project, we realized that computer visualization service was something we could market and sell. A lot of people didn't even know what it was, thinking it was referring to storyboards. They didn't realize that it was three-dimensional, offering specific benefits to the process and saving money. Now we don't have to explain ourselves.

We have to build a digital version of everything you see in the movie in terms of the detail level and what the quality threshold will be. Part of the skill set in being a specialist in previsualization is figuring out what the important details are and then portraying them accurately. Often a director will be right there with us, but he expects what we're doing to be accurate enough for him to focus on other things. In terms of checking the accuracy of what we're showing people, we can usually do that with the art department, specifically the art director. The physical reality also needs to be checked so we will do a site survey and base the detail of our previz on that.

☐ *As an art director, I would insist on providing you with both raw and specific site survey measurements previously taken by the set designers responsible for drawing up the physical scenery. Is that level of participation helpful or a hindrance?*
Integrating set drawings in an efficient and accurate manner is one of the more difficult things to do. It is not a necessarily fast process. In addition, if drawings are coming from a CAD-based art department, the expectation is that the data will be used. The fact is the CAD files are not terribly user-friendly or compatible in our Softimage 3D environment, mainly because the way you might depict things in a CAD file is different from how you structure it in a 3D scene. So there's a good amount of boring legwork that goes into taking that information and turning it into a set. Keeping on top of the most current set of drawings generated in a given art department is slow, time-consuming, and definitely a challenge. We usually require one person from our staff to be focused just on keeping track of the up-to-the-minute changes. Sometimes, our process is generating the revisions. We'll be sitting with a director who is having a sightline problem through a doorway. He requests it to be widened, and we do it instantly. We then note the change and communicate it to the art director who follows through with the physical changes to the set. But once the request is made through our contact with the director, then it is our responsibility to track the change and keep on it until it's completed.

☐ *What do you require from an art director?*
We require ground plans at $\frac{1}{4}''$ scale. After that we give our corresponding sets a simplified color scheme just to give our models a simple aesthetic.

☐ *Can you use photographic references provided by the art department as texture maps?*
It is possible to take location stills and use them as texture maps for our previz set, but often they are not necessary. A good amount of time goes into applying the map and making it work. Usually, it's problematic.

☐ *How are you budgeted?*
On *Panic Room* there was a very long and elaborate previsualization phase that overlapped with the photography. We didn't stay on until the wrap of principal photography, but we did manage to finish sequences we were contracted to complete. After the design was built, we were busy doing what we called "rapid response" to explore requests from the director, such as the removal of a wall and how it affected the sequencing. This impacted the cost, but like most departments, we didn't have a fixed budget. Usually, these are discretionary costs requested by the director making the budget line we fit under, a struggle for the accounting department. Similarly, a production designer might request the previz process to happen, but there is often no money in the art department budget allocated to cover the cost for our services.

☐ *Is the transfer of data from computer hard drive to camera similar to the path from, say, a PC to a printer?*
If only it were that easy. Yes, the digital aspect is flawless; then there are the physical aspects. The lens has to be nodalized and then, once calibrated, the same kind of head has to be used every time. All working parts of the camera have to be physically adjusted to exactly match the digital data fed to the camera. If you think about when, in the early nineties, we first started to explore the idea of doing camera moves on computer, then exporting them was, in a way, revolutionary. No one fully believed it could be possible.

It is interesting to see how the goal of previz has changed over the years. Early on, the goal was to save money and be more efficient with shooting resources. And certainly, we did help with a lot of those things. Now, primarily we gave a director like David Fincher a tool to direct a better film. It was much more in the seminary of the cinematic process where we were able to make a contribution, rather than saving money on stage days, for example. The movie became a much higher expression of the level of directing David wanted from the process. He was able to make decisions with far better knowledge of what the limitations were. He had tried four different versions of it, knew how it fit and cut, and overall, had a total lock on what he was trying to do. We enhanced his ability to do that.

Panic Room was definitely an extreme case of a director being very focused on specific details and wanting to get things exactly right. Usually, there is a car crash or similar stunt problem that needs to be solved; they bring us in to help figure out answers for those questions. It was also an extreme of how much we overlapped into shots that had no technical reason to be previsualized.

☐ *Who are you most likely to hire into your company, Pixel Liberation Front?*
The basic things are solid, fundamental computer skills. A newcomer doesn't necessarily have to know the exact packages we are using. We would expect a person to know what Quick Time movies are, what Premiere does, what Photoshop is, and of course, have a thorough knowledge of the 3D modeling environment. On top of that, knowledge of filmmaking is important: composition and framing, camera moves, etc., that don't look like computer graphics but instead look like filmmaking skills. A lot of computer animating has a very marked aesthetic, but our focus is to simulate as closely as possible the filmmaking vernacular. Communication skills as far as understanding what someone is saying when they are describing a shot sequence are important, as well as being a high level communicator about creative things is also important. Architecture school is good training as it encourages people to talk about the design process, which is vague, unfinished, and evolving. This can be translated into later conversations with a production designer or director. By restating in different words what has just been said, confidence is created about your understanding and ability as a communicator. If you can establish that trust through communication, then you're in good shape.[4]

Doug Chiang, *Director of Concept Design, Visual Effects*
Art Director, Production Designer
(Star Wars: Episode I: The Phantom Menace & Episode
II: Attack of the Clones) (Forrest Gump, Death Becomes Her,
Ghost) (The Polar Express)

This Internet interview reveals the experience and thoughts of a real ground-breaking collaborator. Doug's recent work with Rick Carter, the "other" production designer of *The Polar Express*, brings the art of digitally captured live-action motion movies full circle, as it also explores their successful experimentation with $2\frac{1}{2}$D. Animation links the beginnings of moving picture creation to its most current explorations in the illusion of moviemaking. The work of Doug and Rick signals a new synergy between the director and designer. It will be examined in the dialogue and analysis to follow:

☐ *Do you use previz as a design tool or a pragmatic indicator?*
Both. It's a powerful design tool mainly because of the speed in which you can see, in rough form, what the sets and action will be. It's also a great reality check to make sure that the designs can really work as planned—or not—or in some cases pointing out where we have to cheat to get the set design and shots the director wants. Previz allows us to get this information as early as possible in the design process.

☐ *Have the previz folks been absorbed within your larger art department as a subdepartment?*
The previz artists are integrated into the rest of the art department—at least in the ones I've set up. I think it's important to have lots of crossover so people have multiple jobs and responsibilities. This is essential to make the art department more flexible and efficient. For example, on *The Polar Express*, many of the previz/modelers were also very good designers so it really helped to have them build models while designing them at the same time. And likewise, the 2D designers could take the rough work from the previz team and design right on top of that work. The design process went back and forth, and the lines between 2D and 3D were often blurred. That was the biggest difference between the *Polar* art department versus previous art departments that I've worked with. We were able to merge 2D and 3D design into one streamlined process.

☐ *Would you define "director of concept design?"*
Basically, it's a variation on the production design credit. *Star Wars* was unique in that two distinct art departments were created to design the film. My primary role was to be in charge of the designs for the film including sets, characters, vehicles, environments, storyboards, etc., essentially everything a typical production designer would do with the exception of actually building the sets. My work started long before the production designer came on board and ended long after he left. It was just the nature of that *Star Wars* film, the design work started very early before there was a script and ended just weeks before the film's release.

☐ *How does The Polar Express differ from any movie you've done thus far?*
The main difference for me was primarily in the art department. It was the
first film where Rick Carter and I tried to merge 2D and 3D design, in essence
making the 3D design process as efficient as 2D. This really simplified and
sped up the overall design process, enabling us to integrate set designs with
lighting design at a very early stage so the director, Robert Zemekis, could
see how his film could look even before he finished writing.

☐ *Would you go into some detail about working with another production
designer, Rick Carter, i.e., benefits, strengths, downsides, or weaknesses?*
There were no downsides, only up. On a film like *The Polar Express*, it was
necessary to divide up the work and attack it from our two diverse design
backgrounds. *Polar* was also unique in that going into it, we weren't really
sure how we were going to do the film, both in terms of design and
execution. It really challenged both of us, and I don't think it could've been
designed any other way. We were a great team. We were able to combine
both of our strengths to achieve something that had never been done before.
You can look at the art of *The Polar Express* to get more info if you like. The
book was released November 2004 from Chronicle books.

☐ *How will the art department look in a decade?*
That's a tough question since it's hard to anticipate what technology and
tools will be available by then. One thing that is certain is that the new tools
will definitely make us more efficient. New tools have always allowed us to
try different ideas quickly and modify things more efficiently. For example,
with 3D prototype machines, future art departments will be able to quickly
create 3D models in the computer and make "hard copies" of designs as
quickly and as easily as it is now to make photocopies. That technology is
available today but is very expensive, but in ten years I'm sure it'll be
commonplace.

Technology will always be very liberating and allow us to try more ideas.
This will be the biggest difference—more ideas in a shorter amount of time.
But the bottom line is that it'll still be up to the talent of each individual
artist. They can never be replaced by technology. The positions will remain
the same; only the tools will be different. Even in the past two years, I've
noticed a radical shift from designers doing most of their work on the
computer instead of with pencil and paper. However, what still matters
are the ideas. Future art departments will have the ability to create and
implement more, which will result in a higher level of work. It's always about
the ideas and how we can get them from our mind's eye to the paper in front
of us.

Thinking way out there, wouldn't it be wonderful if some day a tool
could be invented that could take our mental image and put it out there
for everyone else to see? Now that would be the future, since often it's too
hard to depict what we see in our minds. But that's too much sci-fi, of
course!

☐ *What is your philosophy about the digital art department?*
I believe it's the next step. Digital makes sense because filmmaking is changing and art departments need to be on the leading edge of that change. We are often the first people to visualize the written idea, and any tools that make that process more efficient are good. But this doesn't mean that the old tried and true methods will go away. On the contrary, I sincerely hope we never lose that real-world component to design. Nothing can replace a real, physical model. What will change is the process of how that model is made. I like to think that traditional model building will always be an integral part of the art department just as quick sketches on napkins will never disappear. Digital art departments will be hybrids, combining the best of both worlds.

☐ *What positions have been added/subtracted?*
From my perspective, it's more adding instead of subtracting positions. We still need solid set designers and model builders, only now we augment that with artists who are skilled at 3D modeling in the computer.

☐ *How does the digital art department directly borrow from traditional filmmaking?*
The process is similar. The only difference is the tools. Instead of perhaps a traditional modeler, I use a CG Maya modeler to model the sets in the computer. However, I should note that even though we are a digital art department, I still think it's crucial to have practical card models made. Nothing can really replace a physical model that everyone can hold and study. The other advantage of building CG models is that often these sets are being produced digitally in post-production so the various post-production houses can use our models directly without having to completely rebuild them. This is obviously a big-time and cost-saver in addition to insuring that what is finally built remains true to the original vision of the director.

☐ *On a small film what's more important: a server or a digital modeler?*
Digital modeler. I prefer good talent to equipment.

☐ *Do you consider power backup for your server in case of an emergency?*
Not yet. We routinely back up daily and burn CDs. Some day, if we are big enough, a power backup would make sense, but it's not needed now.

☐ *Are online servers useful or not customizable enough?*
We don't use online servers since there are still problems with networking and security. All of which can be overcome, but to keep things simple and efficient, we don't. But that also could change very soon.[5]

THE CUTTING EDGE

What is particularly interesting regarding *The Polar Express* is the fact that there are no prohibitively expensive sets to build, no time-consuming

lighting rigs to consider, or bulky heaps of camera equipment to grip to location. Most importantly, there is no film. There is only the story, the actor,
and the director. Does this concept totally threaten the jobs of the traditional filmmaking population, reducing the size of film crews to a fraction
of their current size? In this world of "No Cinematography," how do we see
the unseen?

MoCap is the solution and threat. Yes, film crews will be impacted, but
not particularly in size. Mocapographers are replacing on-set wardrobe assistants and camera crew, as they will outfit actors in form-fitted body suits
and head caps, much like scuba gear, studded with tiny reflectors. They are
also replacing on-set carpenters and set dressers by preparing and maintaining the "volume," or $10' \times 10' \times 10'$ performance space, with a network of
infrared sensors mounted to the interior surface of its structural, capture
dome. The job titles have changed, but it still takes a small army to create
the product.

All movements of an actor within the parameter of *The Polar Express*
performance space were reflected off the mocap suit and grid of 150-facial
reflectors, and digitally recorded as points of light floating in a black volume
of 3D space. The performance capture infused the digital action with the
believability of humanness. It then became the task of an army of digital
artists to preserve the individuality of the actor, embedded within the cloud
of swirling constellations of the actor's motion, as they painstakingly connected the dots into the fabric of the storyline. The significant contribution
of *The Polar Express* was the development of facial performance capture to
this new paradigm.

The film pays homage to the book of the same name, written and illus-
trated by Chris Van Allsburg. The fundamental premise of the design col-
laborators, Doug and Rick, was to keep visually true to the book by
establishing a template based on the author's pastel and oil painted palette.
Their solution was not about what the PC could do, nor about the best technique to overlay, but it was about seeing the visual template from the inside
out. In other words, could the PC make the story true to itself? Interestingly,
the original presentation of what was possible was grounded more in a tangible, emotional reality than an actual, visual metaphor as the larger picture
of this experiment held "belief" as the nucleus of the story.

Technically, the process was quite simple. It happened in three general
strokes: 1) The performance capture was saved in the computer hard drive,
2) Deconstruction, 3) Presentation of a theater-in-the-round type of experience. In more specific terms, steps 2 and 3 were derived in Maya, where the
3D environment was comprised of three distinctly different scales: the
adultscale, childscale, and elfscale. The 3D volume was quickly modeled
from storyboards in lo-res, structural form and corresponding global lighting, as an underlay for the final painting. Lens choice, focal distance, and
camera angles were determined next. Then set dressing and lighting based
on the camera angles and nighttime light were specified. The final painting
was applied to line up with the 3D image, completing the process all within
a week's time, defining the $2\frac{1}{2}$D landscape. Of course, this was the working

template for the imagery in *every* scene; the final, overall working process totaled two and a half years. This $2\frac{1}{2}$D journey deconstructed the illusion of space and the suspension of disbelief. It forced the participants to re-ask the question, "What is live action?" The answer was found somewhere between mocap and the PC's interpretation of our physical reality.

The greatest difficulties in the creation of *The Polar Express* were not in the technical challenges but "overcoming fear by having fun with doubt," honestly spoken by Rick Carter. In a recent tribute sponsored by the Art Directors' Film Society, Rick also pointed out, "The production designer gets to be the first believer."[6] In his interpretation of his relationship with Bob Zumekis, he asserted that the director was the primary medium of the story being written. As Rick interacted with Bob, he realized he could not get in the way of the vision, but rather be a secondary medium for the story to express itself, unencumbered. In this way, the story pre-exists everything and before we can successfully perform our work, we must believe the reality of that world. The only way to do that is to trust in the truth of creativity and collaboration.

We can now view the art of motion pictures, examined in these last two chapters, as it progresses toward a future that is firmly rooted in and clearly defined by the past. Catapulting from the earliest visual effects attempts in Georges Melies' *Voyage Dans la Lune* (1902) to those of George Lucas' sixth and final installment of the *Star Wars* cycle, moviemaking continues to be the layering of dream upon dream, culminating in our current legacy of technology's digital presence. With our technological tools in hand, the future is only bound by the limits of our imaginations.

ENDNOTES

1. MIT: Media Lab Web site. Online source: *Program in Media Arts and Sciences, Massachusetts Institute of Technology—GENERAL INFORMATION FOR APPLICANTS*. Retrieved from the World Wide Web at http://www.media.mit.edu/mas/index.html

2. Art Directors' Film Society tribute to Dean Mitzner: "TRON: Production Design and the Next Generation of Animated, Live/Action" presented June 6, 2004 at the Directors' Guild, Los Angeles, CA (Linda Berger, chairperson of the Art Directors' Film Society 2003–2004, has been the writer and producer of 11 programs in the last two years. She has been an active member of the Film Society for the past seven years and during that time, a contributing writer and interviewer of oral histories and onstage interviews of many celebrated art directors.)

3. Alex McDowell Internet interview, retrieved from the World Wide Web and completed 10/19/04 from Pinewood Studios, Iver Heath, Bucks, SL0 0NH, UK.

4. Colin Green interview, 9/13/04, Burbank, CA.

5. Doug Chiang interview, retrieved from the World Wide Web on 10/15/04.

6. Art Directors' Film Society tribute to Rick Carter & Doug Chang: "*The Polar Express*: The Production Designer Comes Full Circle" presented December 5, 2004 at the Directors' Guild, Los Angeles, CA.

□ □ □
□ □ □
□ □ □

CHAPTER 6

The Physical Scenery Process: Construction

Once hand-built and digital models are constructed, drafting is detailed and approved, and then blueprints are distributed to the construction coordinator. The design is committed to physical form from that point onward. Changes are expensive. It's wiser to wait a day or two for a firm decision from an indecisive production designer than to rush plans into the shop and literally pay for the consequences. This isn't necessarily a rule-of-thumb, but it is worth considering in the midst of the hundreds of trade-offs having to be weighed every day. Each situation will certainly dictate which realistic options to consider and how important timing or spending is at the moment a decision is made. One point can certainly be stressed, and that is, make your decisions as a manager; ultimately, the artistic decisions are finalized by the designer.

At this point in the process, drafting flows from draftsmen's computers or drafting tables to the wood shop for the duration of pre-production. What is typically built from the blueprinted page for the camera are rooms from bottom to top: floors, then walls containing openings like doors, fireplaces, arches, and windows, staircases, and ceilings fitted with recessed lighting, staircase openings, support beams, trusses, and skylights. Appendix A of this handbook provides current reference and source lists in Los Angeles for most design and construction needs.

What is typically exercised during the building process is total quality management, TQM. This phrase is an American translation from the original Japanese business concept, *kaizen*, or continuous improvement. Construction detail management is an ongoing process. To prevent being overwhelmed by every detail that must be built exactly as drawn, it might be advisable to appoint a trustworthy proxy in the shop to sweat the small stuff, while your sights are focused on the hero items, requiring more intense focus. If your prep work is being done at a studio where the art department and the construction shop are close by, then your senior drafts-man or assistant art director can be supervised to oversee various smaller sets and corresponding details. Delegating the workload advances the concept of continuous improvement and collaboration. TQM applications in art direction find greatest expression in the work of the set designers. On a draftsman's PC screen or drafting tabletop, a benchmark of consistent improvement and high-level design quality is maintained by detailed, accurate construction drawings. Two general categories of interior and exterior sets are where TQM is exercised and will be examined here.

INTERIOR SETS

Interior scenic design problems were resolved clearly and exactly by Maya Shimoguchi (*Terminator 3: Rise of the Machines, The Ring, Minority Report*) in her drafting for interior city jail/Willie's cell, *Murder in the First* (1995). The holding cell Figs. 6-1A and Fig. 6-1B is based on a concept idea created by the production designer, Kirk Petrucelli (*Lara Croft Tomb Raider, The Patriot, Blade*) and director, Mark Rocco (*Where the Day Takes You, Dream a Little Dream, Scenes from the Goldmine*), as to what could be shot for greatest production value as opposed to the reality of where a typical prisoner might have been held.

The holding cell was theatrically placed in the center of the stage space as a cage to scrutinize Willie, the main character. It comprises the largest area of the plan, also including an interview room to its right and an access

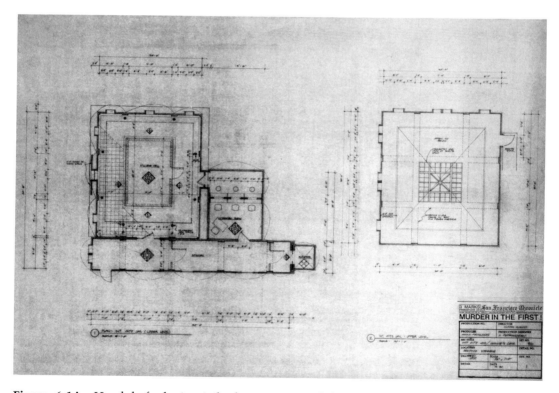

Figure 6-1A Hand-drafted city jail plan—upper and lower levels—by Maya Shimoguchi. MURDER IN THE FIRST © 1994 Warner Bros., a division of Time Warner Entertainment Company, L.P. and Le Studio Canal + (U.S.). All Rights Reserved.

corridor, running along its bottom length and connecting to an elevator at its far right end. The reflected ceiling plan, Fig. 6-1A of the main holding cell room is shown to the right of the floor plan. Fig. 6-2 shows the same ceiling, containing a skylight that loomed almost twenty feet above. The center of the skylight, where all structural ribs met at a central circular hub, was also expanded as a full-size detail, calling out molding and mitered angles.

The pieces of the cage—four walls and ceiling—sitting at the center of the main holding set, were as real as any built for a zoo or maximum-security prison with $3/4"$ steel rods woven through a $1/2" \times 1\,1/2"$ steel bar sitting on a heavily reinforced 6" platform scenically painted as concrete. All sections were wild as per the director's request. Fred Murphy, cinematographer (*Secret Window, Auto Focus, October Sky*), figured a way to seamlessly pull out of a side of the cage and begin a circling motion around it, by not drawing attention to the fact that one of the heavy metal walls had swung open, allowing a Steadicam to continuously shoot without cuts or edits. The execution was astonishing when you think about the heft of all that metal and the sound that it might make during the choreography of the shot.

Two drafting styles are tolerated in Hollywood art departments: the architecturally derived style (Maya: Fig. 6-1A, Fig. 6-1B, Fig. 6-2, Fig. 6-5) and a theatrical style used for theater and opera (Mine: Fig. 6-4, Fig. 6-6).

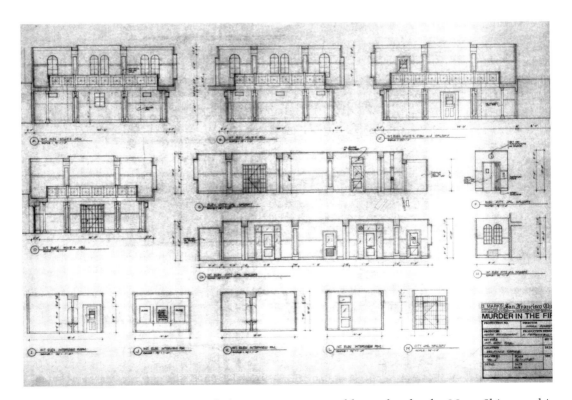

Figure 6-1B　Hand-drafted city jail elevations—upper and lower levels—by Maya Shimoguchi. MURDER IN THE FIRST © 1994 Warner Bros., a division of Time Warner Entertainment Company, L.P. and Le Studio Canal + (U.S.). All Rights Reserved.

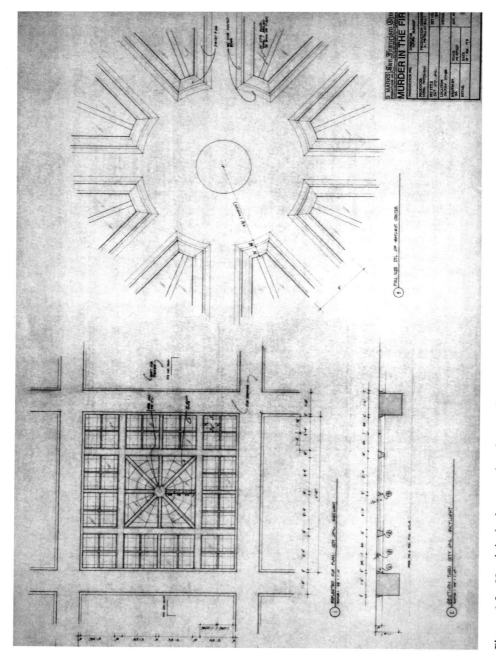

Figure 6-2 Hand-drafted city jail ceiling: reflected ceiling plan, section through ceiling skylight, and **FSD** of skylight center by Maya Shimoguchi. MURDER IN THE FIRST © 1994 Warner Bros., a division of Time Warner Entertainment Company, L.P. and Le Studio Canal + (U.S.). All Rights Reserved.

Figure 6-3   Foam sculpted courtroom angels pictured, with art department crew. MURDER IN THE FIRST © 1994 Warner Bros., a division of Time Warner Entertainment Company, L.P. and Le Studio Canal + (U.S.). All Rights Reserved.

Both are valid and useful, just so long as information on the page is clear and readable, although the former is a preferred convention. The drawings for the interior courtroom set, *Body of Evidence* (1993), were originally drawn by me in theatrical style and later revised as the courtroom set for *Murder in the First* two years later. It was decided that the original *Body of Evidence* set would be purchased as is, and added to or subtracted from in order to satisfy set budget limitations at the time. **Retrofitting** significant architectural detail on the original set with redesigned windows, judge's bench, and column capitals was an oddly familiar exercise. The twin angels wielding swords, Fig. 6-3, were newly designed additions to the original set. This kind of serendipity was atypical of the movie business and provided an unusual continuity of business as usual.

The courtroom and judge's chamber sets were constructed and assembled in Stage 12 at Culver Studios in Culver City, shown in Fig. 6-4 as a spotting plan for the sets. A prominent hero set scheduled for several weeks of continuous shooting, the courtroom set's placement and location onstage were important considerations. It was home for the shooting crew during that section of the shooting schedule, making everyone's experience more effective and enjoyable. Everything around the judge's bench wall changed between films, as each designer interpreted the contents of their respective

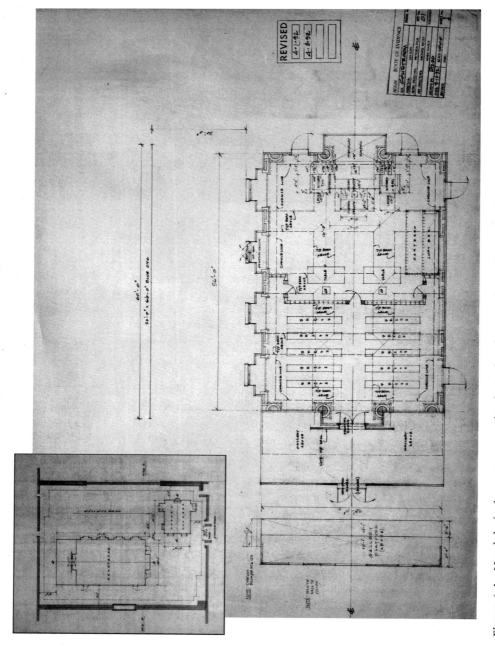

Figure 6-4 Hand-drafted courtroom and judge's chamber sets drawn by Michael Rizzo. Inset: Spotting plan, indicating placement on Stage 12, Culver Studios.

Figure 2-3 The revised art department. Courtesy of Alex McDowell © 2002.

Figure 3-1 Typical locations folder: Left: Bradford Building, L.A., Top panorama: Ford Theatre, D.C
Middle panorama: Farmhouse, Luxembourg, Bottom panorama: Moab, UT.

A

B

Figure 3-8   Concept sketch drawn by James Clyne for **A)** *Tron 2*. **B)** *Instinct*.

A

B

Figure 3-9 **A)** CG model of interior newsstand set for *The Terminal.* **B)** Set shot of the interior set for *The Terminal* showing elliptical backing and reflective ceiling. Courtesy of Alex McDowell. Photograph by Merrick Morton for the motion picture *The Terminal*™ © 2004 DreamWorks L.L.C., reprinted with permission by DreamWorks L.L.C.

A

B

Figure 3-10 **A)** CG model of the exterior of the terminal set for *The Terminal.* **B)** Aerial view of JFK airport showing CG addition (circled) for *The Terminal.* Courtesy of Alex McDowell. Photograph by Merrick Morton for the motion picture *The Terminal*™ © 2004 DreamWorks L.L.C., reprinted with permission by DreamWorks L.L.C.

A

B

Figure 3-11 **A)** White model of *The Terminal* set. **B)** Finished CG model of the exterior detail of *The Terminal* set. Courtesy of Alex McDowell. Photograph by Merrick Morton for the motion picture *The Terminal*™ © 2004 DreamWorks L.L.C., reprinted with permission by DreamWorks L.L.C.

Figure 4-6 Set shot of Clavius lunar site in *2001: A Space Odyssey*. Courtesy of Metro-Goldwyn-Mayer/THE KOBAL COLLECTION.

Figure 6-12 Concept illustration by James Clyne for the Hall of Containment. Courtesy of Alex McDowell. MINORITY REPORT © 2002 Twentieth Century Fox—All Rights Reserved.

Figure 6-7 Form Z model of interior house set for *The Cat in the Hat* by Victor Martinez. Courtesy of Universal Studios Licensing LLLP.

Figure 6-9 CG model of exterior neighborhood for *The Cat in the Hat* by J. Andre Chaintreuil. Courtesy of Universal Studios Licensing LLLP.

Figure 6-10 Pre-Cog chamber showing concept model of the set. Courtesy of Alex McDowell. MINORITY REPORT © 2002 Twentieth Century Fox. All Rights Reserved.

Figure 6-11 Set shot of Pre-Cog chamber. Courtesy of Alex McDowell. MINORITY REPORT © 2002 Twentieth Century Fox. All Rights Reserved.

A

Figure 6-20   A) Dan Sweetman's storyboards showing White House Rose Garden speech.

B

Figure 6-20 B) Laminated photo showing construction progress of the White House Rose Garden. MY FELLOW AMERICANS © 1996 Warner Bros., a division of Time Warner Entertainment Company, L.P. All Rights Reserved.

Figure 6-13 The Biltmore Estate, Asheville, North Carolina.

Figure 6-17 In-process construction photo of the back of the West Wing scenery. MY FELLOW AMERICANS © 1996 Warner Bros., a division of Time Warner Entertainment Company, L.P. All Rights Reserved.

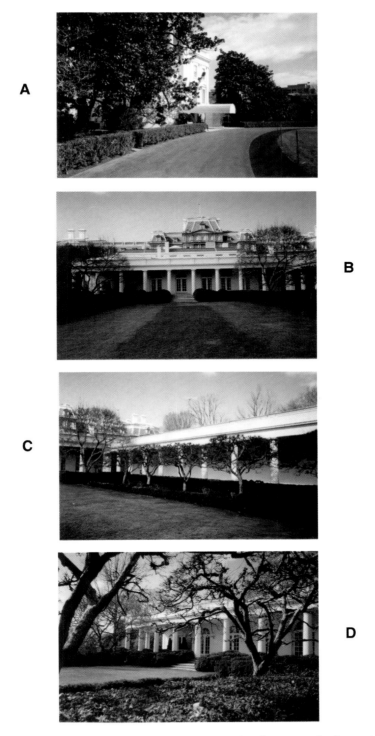

Figure 6-21 White House research photos: A) The driveway flanking the South Portico steps in Washington, D.C., B) White House East Wing colonnade seen from the center of the Rose Garden, C) White House Rose Garden side colonnade, D) White House Rose Garden looking toward the East Wing. MY FELLOW AMERICANS © 1996 Warner Bros., a division of Time Warner Entertainment Company, L.P. All Rights Reserved.

Figure 6-24 Finishing up: Set photos of: **A)** White House southwest lawn and West Wing, **B)** South Portico and **C)** Rose Garden Pergola, **D)** East Wing facade, **E)** White House East Wing and Rose Garden. MY FELLOW AMERICANS © 1996 Warner Bros., a division of Time Warner Entertainment Company, L.P. All Rights Reserved.

scripts into visual terms. For instance, the retrofitted columns were repainted as dark malachite with gilded detailing throughout the set as well as the witness stand, designed as a movable set piece on casters for the *Murder in the First* set. These changes are obvious in the drafting compared in the plates provided, Fig. 6-5 and Fig. 6-6.

We have briefly explored some traditional aspects of scenery drafting and design, as well as creative decision-making based on collaboration and script requirements. The advent of CGI has incorporated technology into the mix and spawned digital drawing and drafting. Many questions arise as a result of this evolutionary step into the twenty-first century. Perhaps it's best to analyze the perceptions of digital set designers regarding traditional vs. digital filmmaking. From a recent interview, **Victor Martinez** (*The Terminal, The Cat in the Hat, Minority Report*) had this to say:

> Digital film environments are becoming more accepted as normal, although it will probably be difficult to find art departments that are just digital; the same goes for films that will be solely hand-drawn. In any art departments I've worked in, there are sets that lend themselves more to being drawn by hand and others being drawn on computer (see Fig. 6-8 and Fig. 6-9). On *The Cat in the Hat*, I worked on a very complex interior set, the inside of the house that is transformed (Fig. 6-7), and it wasn't your typical process of designing a set. There were days when I was just modeling in clay in order to whip out sketch model ideas for the more resolved digital model. I'm not one who's going to close the door on any process. A good digital designer must have training in handcraft as a way to problem solve, otherwise the process of working is robotic and straight out of a manual. My physical art background is very important to this. The people I work with and respect have worked by hand or at least understand that mode of working.[1] Also see Fig. 6-7 in the color insert between pages 142 and 143.

CG modelers and CAD draftspersons in digitized art departments work in tandem with each other and their traditional counterparts. A digital modeler might clearly see a structural problem in a set that an analog draftsperson might otherwise overlook. In this way, all bases are covered. The beauty of CAD is the speed of making changes, regardless of whatever caprice is tossed at the draftsman. To use an example from the *Minority Report* (2002), the rendered Rhino model and resulting AutoCAD drafting for the building of the interior Pre-Cog chamber evolved through many permutations. From digital set designer, **J. Andre Chaintreuil**'s perspective:

> A few of us worked together on a piece of the Egg interior set, or chamber, where the Pre-Cogs were kept: Victor Martinez played with the exterior, and David Chow and I worked on the interior. In the end, it became my job to do all the construction documents for the Egg interior. On that Egg, every single angle was unique so I worked with the 3D model in Rhino and then drafted everything in AutoCAD. I would often section or slice the model by extruding or projecting curves through it at any angle that was appropriate. In the

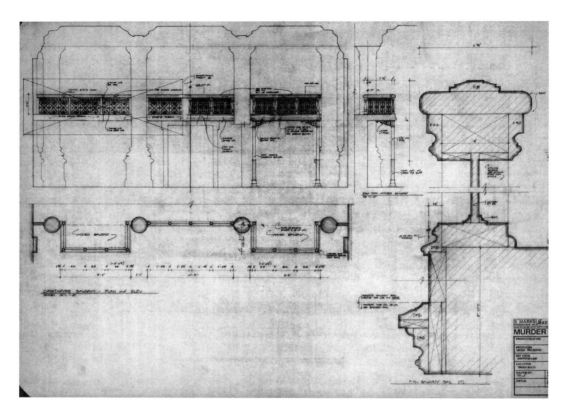

Figure 6-5 Hand-drafted courtroom gallery wall elevations and FSD of gallery rail drawn by Maya Shimoguchi. MURDER IN THE FIRST © 1994 Warner Bros., a division of Time Warner Entertainment Company, L.P. and Le Studio Canal + (U.S.). All Rights Reserved.

same way, I could take any plane and fold it flat or develop any surface I wanted. The pages you see (flipping through a wad of CAD drafting) are just a small percentage of a ream's worth of paper for one set of working drawings. (Laughs) It was massive, but it was the best way to communicate with construction about how to cut every angle on every unique piece. The construction crew made the frame of the Egg set, which we called "the cookie cutter." While the frame pieces were individually being cut and assembled, we sent the computer files out to a company in San Francisco called Kreysler & Associates, who used their **CNC**, or computer-numerically-controlled, milling machine to carve the interior sculptural surface of the Egg. These CNC pieces were then fitted into the cookie cutter frame as the finished interior surface was crafted. It was composed of two overlapping waves moving in opposite directions creating a beautiful, woven texture from Styrofoam blocks.[2]

As you can see, the options for visualizing are limited to the imagination and subsequent needs of the designer. The Egg was derived specifically from the aesthetics of working in the computer (Fig. 6-10 and Fig. 6-11). Alex McDowell, the designer, specifically hired digital designers because he

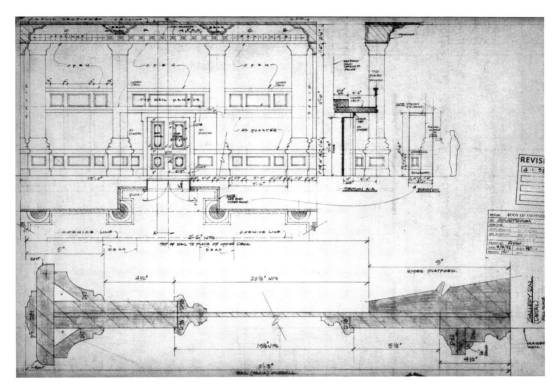

Figure 6-6 Hand-drafted courtroom gallery elevation, plan and section and FSD of gallery rail drawn by M. Rizzo for *Body of Evidence*.

wanted a digital aesthetic for the movie. The same process of concept designing applied to other aspects of this film. See also color insert between pages 142 and 143. **J. Andre** explains,

> My main set for *Minority Report* was called the *Hall of Containment* where the prisoners were confined to vertical sleds that rose out of the ground as a telescoping, horizontal arm swung around to access them. The visual image was like blades of grass in the wind or much like a device called "Pin Art" you've probably seen where you can press your hand onto a frame of blunted pins that mimic the shape of your hand. I collaborated with illustrator James Clyne on this set (Fig. 6-12 and also color insert). In 3D it's so easy for me to create a shape quickly and accurately, then share renderings with an illustrator like James. A benefit of sharing files like this is that it saves the illustrator the time to properly set up a perspective view so more time can be spent adding textures, creating mood, and furthering the set design. We already know from the 3D model how much of the set will be built for the camera. The other beautiful thing about these modeling environments is that everything is life size—my one-quarter, my three-quarter, and my full-size are all the same image, just printed out at different scales.
>
> I really was thrilled in the end and very happy with the world we had created. Alex McDowell, production designer, composed some books we

Figure 6-7 Form Z model of interior house set for *The Cat in the Hat* by Victor Martinez. Courtesy of Universal Studios Licensing LLLP.

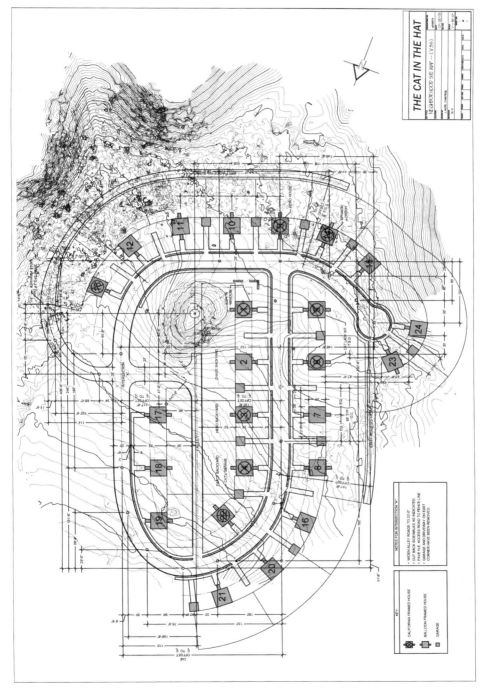

Figure 6-8 LIDAR exterior neighborhood plan for *The Cat in the Hat* by J. Andre Chaintreuil. Courtesy of Universal Studios Licensing LLLP.

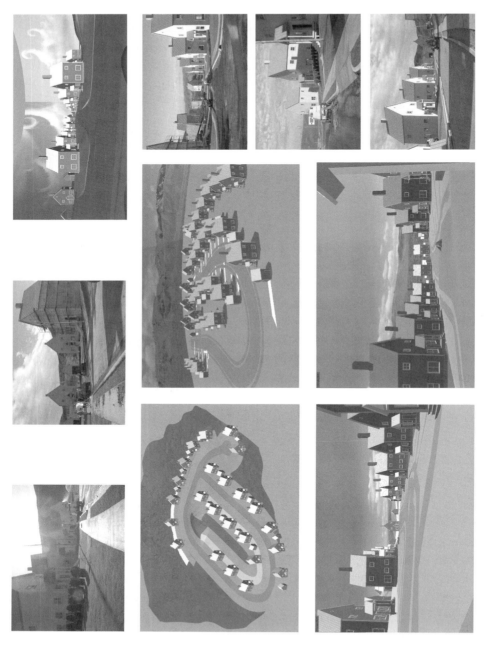

Figure 6-9 CG model of exterior neighborhood for *The Cat in the Hat* by J. Andre Chaintreuil. Courtesy of Universal Studios Licensing LLLP.

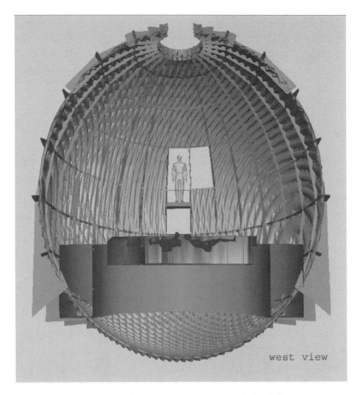

west view

Figure 6-10   Pre-Cog chamber showing concept model of the set. Courtesy of Alex McDowell. MINORITY REPORT © 2002—Twentieth Century Fox—All rights reserved.

Figure 6-11   Set shot of Pre-Cog chamber, courtesy of Alex McDowell. MINORITY REPORT © 2002—Twentieth Century Fox—All rights reserved. (Also see Figs. 6-10 and 6-11 in the color insert between pages 142 and 143.)

eventually called The Bibles for *Minority Report*. They explained the theory of the city so if you ever got stuck and couldn't find an art director, you could pick up one of these reference books and find your answer. It was brilliant. I've never seen it on another show. Also, the research material was over-whelming, and it was everywhere.[3]

EXTERIOR SETS

My Fellow Americans (1996) required the design and construction of the South façade, South Portico, and Rose Garden of the White House on the sycamore grove of the Biltmore Estate, Asheville, North Carolina (see Fig. 6-13). Another architecturally trained, senior set designer, Harry Otto (*The Terminal, 8 Mile, Minority Report*) wrestled with the $\frac{1}{8}$" scale eleva-tions provided by the White House PR department and reliable photo book research to achieve a realistic and architectural believability in his larger scale details. Our phone relationship with our contacts at the Oval Office was less encumbered before 9-11 than it is now. One fact hasn't changed—location shooting in and around the White House is not an option. It com-pelled us to design believable and accurate scenery. We amassed a ton of applicable research and designed an identical, digital-quality copy of the original in Washington, D.C. Harry's drafting shown in Fig. 6-14 and Fig. 6-15 shows the level of meticulousness to architectural detail necessary for the brief glimpses of believability we see onscreen, even for a high-concept comedy. (Also see Fig. 6-13 in the color insert between pages 142 and 143.) **Harry Otto** reminisces:

> A contact through the *Dave* (1993) art department was kind enough to send us some of the blueprints of the South Porch with the stairs that radius around and down to the driveway. The problem with these drawings is that the plans were drawn at a reduced scale for two reasons: 1) That part of the White House was shot at a distance and 2) They wanted to cut costs. Although our timeframe was compressed, those drawings just couldn't be traced off, retitled, and blueprinted for building, especially when you consider the staircase treads were 8" and the risers were 3", making them unusable unless reconfigured to full scale. I remember searching through some terrific reference material from the Wilson period—1913 through 1921—that included aerial shots of the White House and close-ups of him in the Rose Garden. I remember going over those with a magnifying glass to discern what the profile of the moldings looked like, and what the scale relationships were. Several days later, other well-photographed, contemporary coffee table books showing other excellent detail were brought into the office to complete the picture, so to speak. With all of those pieces quickly snapping together, I was able to blast out the drawings for our set. All in all, it was a real challenge and a good learning experience to do it fast and get it right.[4]

Figure 6-12 Concept illustration by James Clyne for the Hall of Containment. Courtesy of Alex McDowell.

Figure 6-13 The Biltmore Estate, Asheville, North Carolina.

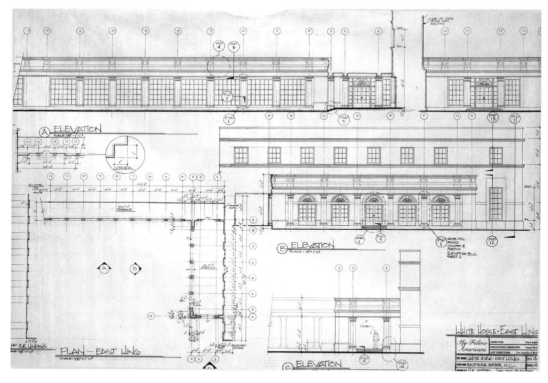

Figure 6-14 Hand-drafted White House East Wing plan and elevations A, B, and C by Harry Otto. MY FELLOW AMERICANS © 1996 Warner Bros., a division of Time Warner Entertainment Company, L.P. All Rights Reserved.

The plates of drafting shown here are a small sample of the larger bulk of work Harry turned out in several weeks' time. All of the plates were drawn in architectural style and most of them held full-scale details of the miles of finishing molding eventually air-stapled onto the completed building façades.

As Harry was working out the building details, I had arranged a topographic survey of the sycamore grove where the sections of White House would stand. The survey, Fig. 6-16, indicated existing trees, underground water pipes, and most importantly, which areas of the grove were prone to flooding. If you look closely at the back of the West Wing section under construction (Fig. 6-17 in the color insert), you will see that the walls are supported by telephone poles securely set into the ground. Knowing exactly where the water main and other vulnerable buried utilities were located allowed us to complete the set pieces without worry. Finally, with all of the details of the survey in place, we could determine how the White House building sections should stand relative to the sun's position and the quality of daylight in early spring.[5] This is a consideration of all cinematographers shooting exterior scenery and acting sequences in a motion picture—ours was not a special case.

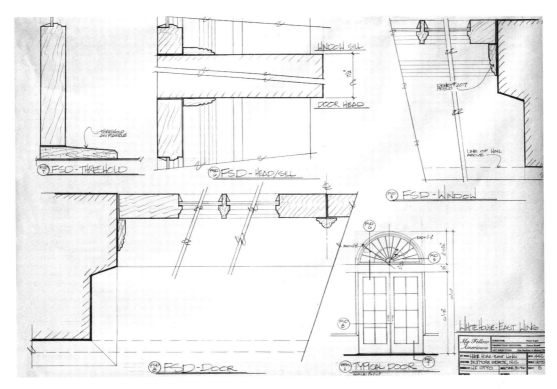

Figure 6-15 Hand-drafted White House East Wing FSD 5-8 and typical door elevation by Harry Otto. MY FELLOW AMERICANS © 1996 Warner Bros., a division of Time Warner Entertainment Company, L.P. All Rights Reserved.

During the first stage of White House construction, production designer Jim Bissell was with the main shooting crew in L.A. There, the art department crewmembers had built a replica of the White House in $\frac{1}{8}$" scale, Fig. 6-18. It was used to plan the shooting sequences of two former Presidents galloping on horseback around the building from the North Porch to the East Wing Rose Garden on the North Carolina set. The result of these shot planning meetings was a series of sketches and other visual material developed by the designer. He began with a rough sketch (Fig. 6-19A) as a quick visual outline for several key exterior day shots, scenes 227, 228 pt., 235, 237, 240, and 242A, and later completed a more developed Director's plan (Fig. 6-19B). As I was emailing progress shots of our daily work to him, Jim was composing a revised storyboard sequence of shots against what we were building in North Carolina by sketching on top of my photos (Figs. 6-20A and B, see color insert as well). Jim's enhanced storyboard sequence provided a clear indication of how he saw the shots in terms of how they would finally play on the exterior set at the Biltmore Estate. As these pages provided more fodder for our discussions, the crew continued their work.

Imitating the greenscape of the existing White House exterior was the daunting project of head greensman, Henry Dando (*Wrestling Ernest*

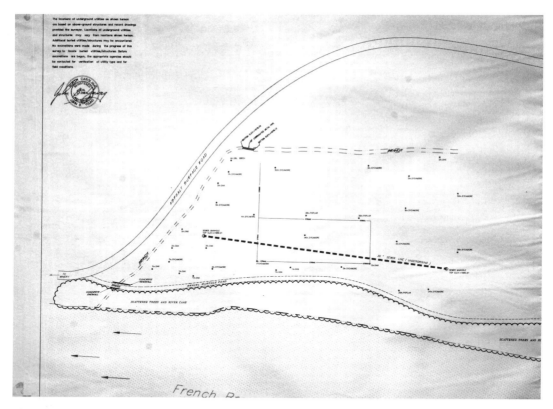

Figure 6-16 Site survey of the typography of a section of field and French Broad River at the Biltmore Estate by Webb A. Morgan and Associates, P.A., Asheville, NC.

Figure 6-17 In-process construction photo of the back of the West Wing scenery. MY FELLOW AMERICANS © 1996 Warner Bros., a division of Time Warner Entertainment Company, L.P. All Rights Reserved.

Figure 6-18 Replica of the White House constructed by L.A. art department model makers. MY FELLOW AMERICANS © 1996 Warner Bros., a division of Time Warner Entertainment Company, L.P. All Rights Reserved.

Hemingway, Striptease, Sunshine State), with the help of Stephanie Girard, landscape architect and set designer. Their collaborative effort required just as much zeal for detail as Harry's, but in the texture and dynamic terms of this large, green exterior set. Thousands of square feet of sod and rows of manicured box hedges and small trees helped anchor the overall look of the landscape. Our greatest challenge was creating the 200-year-old magnolias flanking both sides of the South Porch steps. Henry's solution was to build two armatures into which huge magnolia boughs could easily be inserted. Early spring in the western hills of North Carolina could not provide us with usable boughs, so we were forced to investigate sources in the warmer regions of Georgia and then transport truckloads of refrigerated magnolia limbs to our Biltmore location. This specific set was an expensive one (see Fig. 6-22). The eight-day shooting timeline on the finished set happened without a schedule change, which would have jeopardized the freshness of the Jeffersonian magnolias and greenscape, requiring continual irrigation and maintenance.

The overall design of this vast exterior set was the brainchild of Stephanie Girard (*Any Given Sunday, Holy Man*). It developed from her patient skill with a magnifying glass and photographic landscape details of the Rose Garden taken at the existing White House grounds (see Figs. 6-21A–D and also color plate section). Keep in mind the fact that the existing

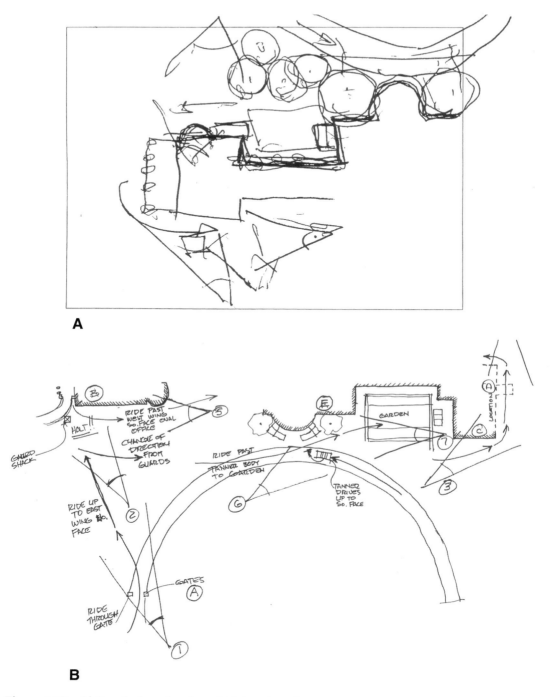

A

B

Figure 6-19 **A)** Rough shot sketch and **B)** Developed Director's plan drawn by Jim Bissell of the White House South Lawn exterior set. MY FELLOW AMERICANS © 1996 Warner Bros., a division of Time Warner Entertainment Company, L.P. All Rights Reserved.

sycamores dotting the Biltmore field had to be located, plotted, and worked into the larger design; the site survey also helped her develop her design. Stephanie's experience as a landscape architect imbued her drawings seen in Fig. 6-23 with the authenticity and credibility the set demanded as the greenscape neared its completion (see Fig. 6-24). It's interesting to see how precise our efforts were by comparing the research shots of the existing Rose Garden and laminated, finishing-up shots of our completed scenery.

The timeline, including my arrival to Asheville, meeting with the locations manager and Biltmore representatives, enrolling the surveyors into the project, completing the survey, orienting the set to the site, overseeing the building, painting, and dressing of the set sections, as well as the design of the landscaping and finishing the set for shooting, took eight weeks. In retrospect, big thanks to Harry, Henry, and Stephanie for their vision, experience, and collaboration—all visible in the set photos—and for Jim's unerring guidance.

The rhythm from page to scenery outlines an art director's daily pre-production routine. Awake at 5 AM and in the shop by 6 AM to begin the day with the folks in the construction shop to answer any related questions, then back to the art department by 8 AM for check-in with the PD and the art department folks, and participate in various interdepartmental meetings including mechanical effects, set decorating, and production office considerations, fills the early morning hours. The late morning is spent running to locations to view building progress or double-checking details or solving problems, digitally photographing the progress, and helping solve PR problems that might have arisen between the location point-person and the activity of our construction crew. The early afternoon might require a return to the shop periodically throughout the remainder of the workday to check on progress or solve additional problems, then back to the office to check email, Photoshop progress images and email them to the designer or other department heads, and talk through changes in scenery design and modification. Any free time in the office demands the completion of current paperwork, the double and triple checking of schedules relating to the construction timeline, inserting revised script pages, updating the PDA with shooting schedule changes, quickly drafting $\frac{1}{4}$" scale plans or elevations on a sheet for the designer's emergency meeting at day's end, and reviewing the next day's agenda. Final check-in with the art department folks happens by early evening. Design changes are noted, approved, or modified, and, if time allows, prints are made in multiple for construction and other departments, and setting out whatever is physically necessary to take along to the shop for the 6 AM visit, including drafting, printed material, color photocopies of research, paperwork, or materials samples. The day ends by around 8 PM This briefly outlines a typical day and workload in general terms. At various points in the day, mobile phone calls from the art department coordinator, the production office, designer, set decorator, and locations department interrupt the process. Most often, meals are gulped on the fly or missed altogether as the pre-production schedule quickly moves toward our first day of shooting.

Figure 6-20 A) Dan Sweetman's storyboards showing White House Rose Garden speech.

B

Figure 6-20 B) Laminated photo showing construction progress of the White House Rose Garden. MY FELLOW AMERICANS © 1996 Warner Bros., a division of Time Warner Entertainment Company, L.P. All Rights Reserved.

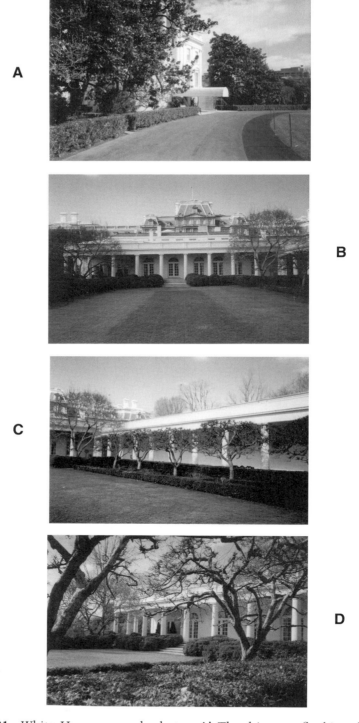

Figure 6-21 White House research photos: **A)** The driveway flanking the South Portico steps in Washington, D.C., **B)** White House East Wing colonnade seen from the center of the Rose Garden, **C)** White House Rose Garden side colonnade, **D)** White House Rose Garden looking toward the East Wing. MY FELLOW AMERICANS © 1996 Warner Bros., a division of Time Warner Entertainment Company, L.P. All Rights Reserved.

"My Fellow Americans" Construction Estimate				Last modified	3/16/96	

Script Date: March 8, 1996 **Director:** Peter Segal **Production Designer:** Jim Bissell

Producer: Warner bros. Michael Ewing Jean Higgins

Production number:

Page number: 7

Set #:	Loc:	Type:	Set Description:	Const. Estimate	Sign Estimate	Greens Estimate
445	Ashevill	Ext	White House gate/N. Lawn	$50,000.00	$0.00	$5,000.00
445	Ashevill	Ext	White House Front entrance	$100,000.00	$1,000.00	$10,000.00
445	Ashevill	Ext	White House Kennedy Garden	$100,000.00	$500.00	$10,000.00
445	Ashevill	Ext	White House Southwest Lawn	$100,000.00	$500.00	$10,000.00
446	Ashevill	Int	Factory Lunchroom-Cleveland	$5,000.00	$2,000.00	$0.00
447	Ashevill	Int/Ext	Hollis Kitch/Ext Barn	$15,000.00	$0.00	$0.00
701	2nd Unit	Ext	Sky/Airforce 2	$0.00	$0.00	$0.00
702	2nd Unit	Ext	Moutainous area	$0.00	$0.00	$0.00
704	2nd Unit	Ext	Train barrels through N.C. Countryside	$0.00	$0.00	$1,000.00
705	2nd Unit	Ext	"Scoggin's" truck barrels down hwy	$0.00	$0.00	$0.00
706	2nd Unit	Ext	Maison Blanc restaurant	$0.00	$0.00	$0.00
			Totals:	$XXX,XXX.XX	$XXX,XXX.XX	$XXX,XXX.XX

Figure 6-22 A Construction Estimate page showing the item cost of the White House South lawn green set budget.

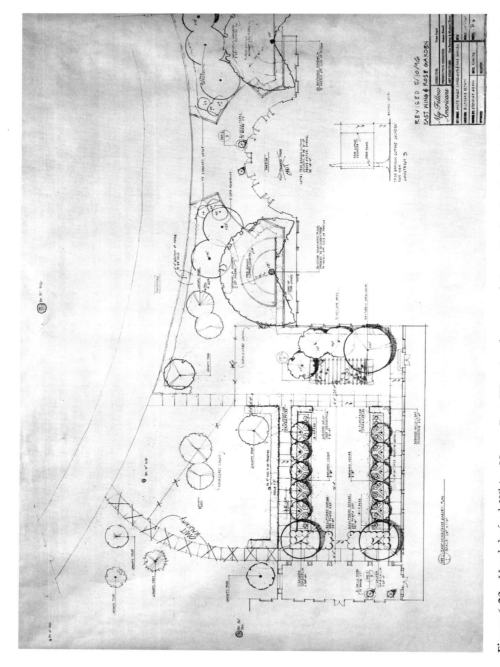

Figure 6-23 Hand-drafted White House East Wing Landscape and Rose Garden by Stephanie Girard. MY FELLOW AMERICANS © 1996 Warner Bros., a division of Time Warner Entertainment Company, L.P. All Rights Reserved.

Figure 6-24 Finishing up: Set photos of: **A)** White House southwest lawn and West Wing, **B)** South Portico and **C)** Rose Garden Pergola, **D)** East Wing-façade, **E)** White House East Wing and Rose Garden. MY FELLOW AMERICANS © 1996 Warner Bros., a division of Time Warner Entertainment Company, L.P. All Rights Reserved.

VENDORS

An enormous industry of support businesses was established both within and outside of the studio system in Hollywood. At this time it exists to service all Indie and studio filmmaking projects. Everything an art director can imagine or need can be found in the greater Los Angeles area. The remainder of this chapter will focus on the highlights offered by studio facilities, rental backing companies, and industry support vendors.

Studio Facilities

The major studios in Los Angeles in 2004 are 20th Century Fox, Disney Studios, DreamWorks SKG, Paramount Pictures, Sony Pictures, Warner Bros., and Universal Pictures-MCA. (See Section III. Appendix A: Reference and Source lists.) A comprehensive list of the major studios helps to determine which offer the following production services: mill and molding shop, painting and sign shop, hardware shop, **staff shop**, metal shop, and scenic backings. Detail items like latches, pulls, knobs, escutcheon plates, special wood or plaster molding for period windows, doors and walls, or painted and photographic backings used for interior, onstage sets are easily found in any of the studio shops. For the most part, the studio prices for these services and items are as competitive as those of any other vendor. The advantage of using major studio facilities is experience; they have decades of know-how and a vast stockpile of options that work for all production needs.

Warner Bros. staff shop has an 80-year archive and the largest selection of architectural, plaster model detail available as fiberglass capitals, corbels, brackets, rosettes, ropes, and friezes, as well as a large assortment of brick, stone, and rock options, including Bumstead and Murder Your Wife brick, for all production construction needs. A CD version of the catalogue is available to anyone who calls to request one—guild membership affiliation is not a prerequisite. Unfortunately for digital draftsmen, there is not an AutoCAD compatible CD catalogue at this time. According to the WB production marketing office, continuous requests are made by architects and landscape designers eager for this data, as well as designers and draftspersons in the movie industry. Apparently, it will be awhile before the studio shops can fulfill the demands of our digital requirements.

Sony, Disney, Paramount, and Fox studios have vacuum form and fiberglass staff shops providing light, paintable, durable capitals, rosettes, and brick skins. To a greater or lesser degree, all studio facilities offer full services for carpet and drapery, state-of-the-art graphics capability for signage, and limited greens. Their products are time-tested and competitively priced.

Paramount Studio's set hardware shop is as extensive in metalware as WB is in carved plaster molds. Its set hardware inventory periods span 28 various styles from Louis XIV–XVI, to English styles, to Moorish and Greek, German Gothic, Art Deco and Contemporary/Moderne. Every kind of door hardware including peepholes, knockers, and kick and mop plates; every elevator detail such as operator panels, floor indicators, and operator seats;

specific hardware for bathrooms, windows, refrigerators, light switches, and electrical outlets and bells, including boxing, cable car, fire, train, and mission; and of course, mailboxes are available for rental. This studio's hardware shop is the definitive place to rent hardware.

20th Century Fox Studios is unique among the majors because of its library service, offering historic and archival materials: An extensive Library of Period Architectural Drawings (ships, planes, trains, and motor vehicles), Production Drawings (from 1940 to present), and Collection of Set Stills (from 1935 to 1965)[6] are available for use. The collection is split into two separate sections. The book and periodical library located in the basement of the current art department building is a fully staffed and comfortable facility, available to the research needs of any film project. Ed Hutson, the original art department's one surviving member, is the keeper of period and archival materials stored in 50 file cabinets organized in chronological order in the basement under Stage 15.

Lower budget film and Indie projects might still find prices for rental space at the major studios unaffordable. The Appendix A, L.A. Soundstage listing includes a plethora of other, smaller spaces at reasonable prices. These mini-soundstages and warehouse spaces do not offer the same level of facilities as the big guys, but do offer any low budget production the luxury of control of image, sound, and scheduling. A Web link to Entertainment Industry Development Corporation, http://www.eidc.com/Location_ Information/Soundstages/eidc/owa/dis_ByStage/alphastages.htm displays the same list of soundstage names, locations, and Web addresses for further, detailed information. Any of these lists organized in the Appendix exists to assist a young art director in determining the best sound stage for upcoming scenery.

A quick solution to a limited construction budget would be to visit the Molding Center in North Hollywood, inventorying a solid selection of standard moldings, stairway items, and pre-mitered door sets. They do not have a Web site. Another source for pre-built scenery items such as walls, doors, windows, kitchens, and architectural details like arches, columns, bookcases, cabinets, staircases, and fireplaces can be found at IDF Studio Scenery at www.idfstudioscenery.com and its land-based store in North Hollywood.

Rental Backings

This category explains the significant differences between source options for a range of rental or custom **colortrans** and **translite** photographic backdrops, painted backings, digital imaging sources, and rental or custom fabric backings available in Los Angeles.

To date, Sony Picture Studios is home to JC Backings, owner of over 4,000 rental backings, including historic stock from MGM, Fox, Universal, and Disney. Its Web site at www.jcbackings.com/home.html showcases its land-based warehouse containing five **paint frames** and a state-of-the-art photo lab with digital print machine. Its quality and prices are competitive with those listed in this section.

Pacific Studios, with no Web site, does provide catalogues containing over 1,200 chromatran photographic backdrops for rental, or custom fabrication, shot on location for film production. As a prime quality, large-format photo company, it is well known in the industry and has serviced film production companies since 1928.

According to its Web site, Rosco has been servicing the entertainment business since 1909. It is competitive with JC Backings and Pacific Studios not in its inventory of stock, but in its ability to custom photograph quality translites, trademarked as Roscolite™ backdrops. It also offers RoscoJet™, super large format photo for graphics, and lenticular 3D prints available in billboard sizes. Its extensive portfolio showcasing both TV and film projects is impressive and should be considered as a viable alternative.

Both Grosh Scenic Studios and Schmidli Backdrops are painted backdrop companies, differing only in placement on an historic timeline. Grosh rents older, extremely well preserved, thematically painted backdrops where Schmidli, a newcomer, provides exquisitely painted, abstract products for rental. Both are capable of custom work. Specifically tagging them in this sourcing section signifies the high level of the quality of their work.

Fore-Peak, Rose Brand, and ShowBiz Enterprises rent and custom sew black velour and duvetyne **drops**, **borders and legs**, blue/green screens, a range of **sharktooth scrims**, **bobbinettes**, fabric **cycloramas**, fiber-optic curtains in extra-wide, flame retardant, theatrical fabrics. They are the mainstays of standard backing products offered at reasonable rental prices.

Three companies, owned and operated by the same partners, offering diverse support and service to the entertainment industry are: Sky Drops® for rental and custom painted backdrops and photographic translites; Really Big Skies, an onsite mural painting company; and Really Fake Digital, state-of-the-art digital production services. The owners complement one another as jacks-of-all-trades, including art directing and designing sets and graphics. They are another viable option for budgetary or subcontracting consideration.

Industry Service Listings

As you might well imagine, the phonebook roster of movie industry service listings is as gigantic as the sprawling landscape of Los Angeles. A practical solution to compiling the definitive source listing for this overwhelming task began over a decade ago, as the search for resources became a continuous activity. The resulting entries, FILM-POCKET LISTINGS, are compiled in Appendix A in the most comprehensive list my successive art departments and I could collectively manage for the first edition of this book. I have included only the sections from a larger list that are applicable to art direction. What has been overlooked is included in one of a handful of print directories available, listed below:

LA411® and *Debbie's Book*® continue to vie as "the" premier print and online resource for the industry. As vast databases in either category, each resource has its strengths.

LA411® (as well as NY411®) has been a print directory for 24 years. The seminal source for crew-related or production resources, *LA411®* is an indispensable directory in book form, or click on http://www.la411.com. It includes listings for production companies and ad agencies, financial services, crew listings, sets and stages, location services and equipment, support services, camera and sound equipment, grip and lighting equipment, props and wardrobe, post-production services, and hotel and related services. It is comprehensive and provides an online service for a fee for adding and updating personal and business listings in *Crew411®*. It is a tremendous resource for newcomers.

Debbie's Book®, originally known as *The Prop & Set Yellow Pages*, has been a print directory for 22 years. Where *LA411®* is more crew or production service oriented, *Debbie's Book®* is more of a vendor source. Organized primarily by category, you can find most film things and services in this comprehensive, spiral-bound resource. Debbie's Book Online at http://www.debbiesbook.com is a fast and convenient Web site directory of companies and individuals that supply merchandise and services to the entertainment industry and planners of events, theatrical productions, themed environments, and parties. It is organized into almost 1,000 categories to help you quickly find the exact item you need, and it is constantly updated to provide accurate contact data and new sources.[7]

The following two source books are excellent supplemental directories in their own right. *Creative Industry Handbook®* is one of six print products for various LA markets including: the *Interior Design Resource Book*, the *Los Angeles Resource Book*, *Advertising and Print Services Resource*, *Medical and Health Industry Handbook*, and *Universal City: North Hollywood and Toluca Lake*, printed by GMM, a marketing company. Its Web site at www.creativehandbook.com is simple, direct, interactive, and less cumbersome than those at LA411.com and Debbie's Book.com online counterparts, easily straddling both land and Web-based distribution options.

aCMe LiTe Resource® has the potential for becoming the most prolific of the four print and online entertainment related sources, highlighted in this chapter. In addition to its comprehensive, spiral-bound print directory, The Acme Web site, click www.theacme.com contains links for architecture, art, books, building materials, design centers, design research, design furniture and accessories, libraries and museums, motion picture and television, online reference tools, and world news. It is in the process of compiling a highly interactive resource featuring regular, online radio interviews at www.theacme.com with movers and shakers in the movie business, ranging from young artists just beginning careers to lifers writing memoirs. The implications for this are as far-reaching as becoming a cutting edge forum for information and issues facing creative film industry participants and newcomers. In addition, it plans to host a gallery of changing designer work: hand sketches or CGI modeling, reflecting upcoming film productions or as a supplement to whatever interview happens to be appearing on the site. Organized by fellow art director, Libby Woolems, The Acme is on its way to becoming a fully connected and more deeply integrated resource on a level that the dynamic changes in the movie industry currently demands.

The following chapter continues the scenery construction process in terms of how mechanical effects are preconceived, executed, and designed into the scenery.

ENDNOTES

1. Victor Martinez Interview, 4/21/04, N. Hollywood, CA.

2. J. Andre Chaintreuil Interview, 4/28/04, N. Hollywood, CA.

3. Ibid., Andre Chaintreuil.

4. Harry & Suzanne Otto Interview, 4/25/04, Silverlake, CA.

5. Sunlight should not be confused with daylight. Sunlight is the light of the sun only. Daylight is a combination of sunlight and skylight. For consistency, 5500°K is considered to be Nominal Photographic Daylight.

    Rob Hummel, Ed. *American Cinematographer Manual*, 8th Edition, 2001. Hollywood: The ASC Press, page 130.

6. Retrieved from the World Wide Web at http://www.foxstudios.com/los_angeles/supportservices/support.htm

7. Hamela, Deborah A. *Debbie's Book: The Source Book for Props, Set Dressing and Wardrobe*. Pasadena, CA: Deborah A. Hamela, 2004.

CHAPTER 7

Mechanical Effects: A Practical Guide

CLARIFICATION

In Chapter 1, a distinction was drawn between the production designer and the art director in terms of definition, function, and areas of overlap. Within the world of effects, distinctions must also be made. As you might already imagine, visual effects are vastly different from special effects. The former is created on a computer screen, the latter happens in the physical world. Still, these terms are used interchangeably in error. Like the term art director, "special effects" has been a term used throughout the twentieth century as a catchall phrase to explain that "Hollywood trick photography," defining the elusive magic of the movies. There is nothing tricky or facile about it; special effects have developed as a craft around and for the film industry. Generations of stuntmen and women, a parallel guild, continue to act as stand-ins or body doubles in the danger zone of Hollywood. The symbiotic relationship of the effects crew and the stunt persons mirrors the designer/art director relationship in terms of concept or strategy vs. tactical application in cinematic problem solving. In simple terms: the stunt people do what the effects supervisors dream up—and, they do it perfectly, take after take.

Before the advent of digital moviemaking, mechanical effects, formerly called *special effects*, defined Hollywood worldwide. These technical tricks-of-the-trade continue to be an integral part of the physical filmmaking process: bathroom shower stall sets continue to need running water, exterior street scenes still require controllable rain, fog, or snow supply, and stunt people rely on the expertise of mechanical effects' fire monitoring, as they run from burning buildings. The purpose of this chapter, then, is to familiarize the reader with some of the fundamental techniques used in mechanical effects production today. Understanding that these techniques are based on common sense and safety provides a good foundation for the untrained visionaries in the art department. Details on how the physical world works and of the science/physics that support mechanical effects solutions should be left to the adept professionals who perform "the effects."

169

Mechanical effects are designed and built into physical scenery. Squibs or bullet hits, fire, smoke, steam, breakaway and crumbling scenery walls, all types of explosions, water, rigging for tanks or pools for underwater work, rain, snow, wind, electronics, mold making for retractable weaponry and breakaways, moving set pieces, i.e., centrifuges and gimbals, use of air cannons, rigging for accidents, crashes, near misses, flying rigs, and vehicles are basic items on a mechanical effects to-do-list. The coordination of draftsmen, construction foremen, and effects foremen is where an art director's participation can be an asset. More complicated sets requiring involved mechanical effects attention should always be at the top of an art director's scenery-to-design-and-build lists, next to other more involved, challenging scenery demanding a longer timeline for completion.

During the mid-nineties on *Rocketman*, I met one of my most enduring mentors, mechanical effects supervisor, **Jeff Jarvis** (*Cast Away, The Replacements, Firestarter, Poltergeist*). By experience and example, he taught me how to focus and be more logical, how to stay well ahead of the shooting schedule, what "No" really means, and that the simplest solution is oftentimes the most elegant. He challenged me and taught me how to make decisions I would've never considered, but in doing so, tripled my learning curve. What he didn't do was to convince me to become an effects supervisor, but his effect on me must be shared here. As usual, an interview will continue to act as the most accessible way to deliver the goods:

☐ *In the movie* Poltergeist, *there is a superb mechanical effects scene: the swirling cyclone of wind in the young boy's room carrying a spinning bed; the flurry of books; the cowboy riding the rearing horse; the lampshade twisting itself onto the top of a self-lighting lamp and the 45-rpm record played by a drafting compass were extraordinary considering the level of technology then. Were there any big challenges there for the art department?*
For the record, the cowboy and phonograph were optical effects, but the rest was mechanical. Those spinning objects were easy to figure out and pull off—if you think about each one long enough, you can come up with a simple way to make it work. There were other things in there that you probably didn't notice—that was filler—like the thousand superballs we tossed into the set from above. They moved so fast and sustained their velocity for such a long time that even if you couldn't focus on them you were still aware of a whoosh that went by every other second. On top of the other stuff listed in our scripts we *had* to give the director, the extra stuff was what made working on that scene a lot of fun.[1]

Our conversation didn't go into set construction detail beyond this section of interview. I would assume that the set would have to be "effects proof" by fastening wall dressing including anything else in the room needing to be stationary, the bed would have to be reinforced or just built by the effects team from scratch, and the ceiling and walls designed in removable sections for easy access. Substantial mechanical effects performed in this or any other interior set will most likely require custom design and art direction.

Always (1989), a noteworthy fire effects film, provides an example of utmost collaboration between art and mechanical effects departments in creating the best non-digital, realistic, exterior fire set. By continuing this interview, some of the more memorable highlights were recounted by this forest fire master:

☐ *Jeff, the forest fire in* Always *was not a controlled burn on a Hollywood back lot or computer-generated as a blue screen filler. What location allowed you and your crew to burn dozens of 40–100-foot high trees?*
I actually started on *Always* on second unit. At around the same time there was a huge forest fire up in Montana so we took a helicopter with key crew people and a director to the site and shot some footage that could be added to the main picture. Mike Woods, who had coordinated the show, asked me to supervise all the exterior fire footage up in Montana. So I set up rigs for fire in the scenes where characters were supposedly trapped.

☐ *How many rigged trees were there?*
We built 25–30 propane trees. We plumbed the bottom with propane hoses and mixed liquid and vapor propane to fully develop them for film takes. Once that was done, we had each tree re-dressed by the art department with multiple takes of branches that burned away so quickly under the intensity of the heat. Our burning set was all mounted in the same area where a recent fire was, just outside of Libby, Montana. This location was secured by the locations manager and production designer as a believable, burned-out area as a background for our forest fire. We also got permission to crawl up the backside of the real burned-out trees to lace them with propane pipes so that we could create the appearance of a much larger fire. Of course, we had split-second control of the fire for the shooting crew and just had miles and miles and miles and miles of propane hose. To show you how huge this was, the first day we went through 12,000 gallons of propane because the first day, they were shooting a lot of master shots. Then we slowed down, but the semis were still lined up off camera waiting to be used—that was still 750–1,000 gallons of propane a day.

☐ *The bottom line for you is safety. Would you talk about your perspective on safety and control?*
Fire is one of my specialties. Whether we're using fire pipe, propane hose, truck, or propane bottle with manifolds, it's all carefully laid out. I stand out in front of whatever we're going to burn with a schematic showing a number corresponding to a name of a technician who is operating a specific propane valve. *Firestarter* is where I learned to develop this system, and it works very well for me. Another fire film was a Jean-Claude Van Damme picture, *Nowhere to Run* (1993), where there was a big barn fire and a water tank that fell over and a large propane tank that exploded. In the barn set, of course, there were horses that are normally afraid of fire and a lot of actors. In a set like that any of the wood near the fire pipes has to be made out of a fire retardant material like wallboard and painted like wood, or if it is real wood, it has to be soaked in fire retardant. During burn scenes, the whole

place needs to be cleared of loose hay and bales and anything flammable. I don't leave anything to chance. If you don't think about a precise schematic for the burn and explosions, someone could get seriously hurt. Afterwards, Jean-Claude came up to me, looked me in the face and said, "You're really good with fire." It's not about better or best—you just can't throw a fire pipe in a corner and call it an effect—you have to plan it out very carefully.

☐ *Your work on* Always *was an exceptional showcasing of your mastery with fire effects. Can you recall a project with other challenges for your mechanical effects crew?*
Earlier on, when I did that Michael Cimino picture, *Year of the Dragon* (1985), we were asked to create a tremendous amount of shoot 'em up in this Chinese restaurant set they built in North Carolina. I had over 25,000 bullet hits prerigged into the set walls. In a case like this, collaboration with the art director and the art department was crucial. Design and color of the place, then, became secondary and the material of the walls became the most important focus—and rightly so. We needed all the time we had for prep alone. That's because the squibs need to be set properly into the wall structure. I rely on a good art director to understand what physically happens when a squib goes off and how it affects the scenery material. Someone with a good head on his shoulders can make my job a lot easier by getting the practical stuff right and then working on the art. We're there to make the gags in the script work and to serve the director.

☐ *There are two other examples of collaboration of specially designed rooms that immediately come to mind that specifically used a gimbal: the Mom's room in* Poltergeist *and the spaceship vestibule in* Rocketman. *Would you care to elaborate?"*
There are many types of gimbals for different rotation and use (see Fig. 7-1). The *Rocketman* scene where the characters danced on the curved walls of the spaceship was really about the placement of the camera. The rotation speed of the room and the fixed camera position had to be equal or it

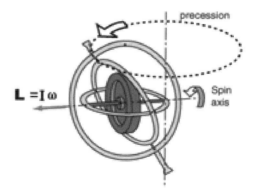

Figure 7-1 Schematic of a typical gyroscope/gimbal mechanism. Two opposing rotational directions, one on a horizontal plane and another on a vertical plane, "maintain its angular orientation with respect to inertial coordinates." In other words, both directions of rotation keep it balanced and in motion.

wouldn't have worked. The gimbal for that particular room versus the one we built for *Poltergeist* had a different function and approach. Mike Wood and I called in our foreman, Sam Price, to help us make sure we were thinking right. As our foreman, he was the guy who built that room. In that case, the first thing you do is build the room and balance it. That takes some patience. When you're done, a man could walk the walls of the room and by the sheer force of his weight, cause the room to easily rotate, even before we attached any hydraulics. That particular room was on an A-frame with a center pick at dead center of the set, similar to a Ferris wheel, without a metal exoskeleton. On the other hand, the *Rocketman* room was built with two-channel iron frames in a wheel shape. Instead of using hydraulics, we used two air-winch motors that were cable driven. One was used as an airbrake and the other made it rotate. Even though the effect is similar, each one solves a different, specific problem for each project.

If you remember the *Poltergeist* scene in the Mom's bedroom, there was very little dialogue but a lot of screaming and sliding around on the walls. [Laughs.] Usually when we get into heavy mechanical stuff, it gets pretty noisy; it didn't matter for *Poltergeist*, but it did for *Rocketman*. The spaceship had no props that could move or fall away because if anything moved, it would give away the illusion of this room rotating in space. Also, when you're building anything mechanical, the simplest way is usually the best way. Many times you can get into out-tricking yourself by not keeping it simple.

I didn't invent these tricks. We've all learned from the guys before us by improving on their mistakes and their successes. Eventually, every improvement makes it better and easier, so nobody gets hurt and nothing unfortunate happens.[2]

Rocketman was a heavier mechanical effects show than most. The script called for a full-scale, working centrifuge. Early in the design process we contacted NASA to begin our research through the Ames Research Center in California. They were compliant with our requests and generously provided more data than we could use. Some of it is presented here (Fig. 7-2A and Fig. 7-2B) to give the reader a more comprehensive idea of how involved research on a scientifically based film can be. Both NASA documentation and non-government image research allowed us to cover all bases in order to design the best centrifuge for this Disney comedy.

Recalling the plan and section for the centrifuge set reminds me of the list of requirements we had to consider: 1) Both director and cinematographer specifically requested the viewing booth be at a comfortable height so that the window would not be more than five feet above the centrifuge bucket, allowing the actor's face to be clearly visible for a tilt down-shot. Fig. 7-3A shows that specific relationship, 2) In addition to the viewing booth, a camera window was cut in the compound-curved wall to catch sight of the bucket as it whizzed past at maximum speed, 3) To address budget constraints, we only designed and built the viewing booth with wild back wall and ceiling pieces, access stairs, and two-thirds of the centrifuge's circular perimeter wall. Aside from saving a few dollars, this was done for easy crew access for operation of the centrifuge or for emergencies that might arise. 4) The viewing booth glass had to be gimbaled, or angled, to avoid reflection and be easily removable, 5) Jeff Jarvis and crew only requested the plan and section you see here and not a fully developed set of drawings for the centrifuge base and arm (Fig. 7-3A). The rationale was that the mechanism was delicate in terms of weight balance and movement physics; rather than be a design piece, it was to be used as a functional, engineered piece. As a rotating truss system, it would have its own mechanical aesthetic. 6) Finally, in our overall design, we had to be mindful of four shots that would complete the shooting of this scene: the medium tilt-down from the inside of the booth [1], the medium close-up shot from the camera window [2], a medium-long shot from the removed section of perimeter wall [3], and close-up shot from a remote camera mounted directly in front of our screaming hero in the bucket [4]. The final set piece (Fig. 7-3B) shows the rig during dress rehearsal.

The mechanical effects crew did an outstanding job designing the centrifuge arm and base. Not only was it beautiful, but also it worked without a problem at various speeds. Once the unit was assembled in place at our shooting stages in Houston, the director, cinematographer, and key shooting crew personnel arrived for a brief show-and-tell session. The arm was rotated with and without a passenger as lenses and focal distances were double-checked by respective shooting crewmembers. Grips and 1st assistant director asked technical questions about the operation of the rig, even though the centrifuge would be solely operated by the mechanical effects foreman who built it on the actual day of shooting. Once the formality was over, several of us took turns in the bucket, celebrating a job well done in our mini-amusement park.

☐ *Are the* Matrix-*inspired rigging effects more intricate than mechanical effects rigs?*

Not really. It seems that way only because they hyped it. We were doing that stuff years ago. There was a lot of fancy ninja fighting on *Robocop 3*. After Glen Randall, English effects supervisor, came off *Raiders of the Lost Ark*, he visited Mike and me and showed us pictures taken at a British air force base of "free-fall simulators," used to teach paratroopers how to properly jump out of planes. For us, this technology revolutionized high falls off the tops of buildings. They're now called **descenders**. Basically, a person's weight determines how large an air paddle is used on the device. Originally, we used $3/_{32}$-inch airplane cable, but now with advanced opticals we can get away with $1/_4$-inch cable. For a long time Glen, Mike, and I were the only people in the United States who had them. A lot of people will tell you that they were the first to use them, but they're lying. British paratroopers were the first, and *we* borrowed from them.[3]

National Aeronautics and
Space Administration

Ames Research Center
Mountain View, CA 94035-1000

For Release: Immediately

Photo No. AC89-0097-15

20-g Centrifuge

     One cab of the Ames Research Center's 20-G centrifuge is shown in this photo. With its 50-foot diameter arm and its two cabs, one at each end, the centrifuge is structurally capable of operating at levels up to 20-Gs, or 20 times normal Earth gravity. It is rated for human-occupied operations at levels up to 12.5 Gs. The 20-G centrifuge is available to conduct equipment checkouts under simulated space launch conditions and for studies of human physiological and behavioral functioning under various simulated gravity loads.

SL Hyper-G Facilities

Facility	Use	Capacity	G-Level	Species	Status
12-Foot Radius	Chronic Weeks Months (Two 1/2-hr stops per week)	20 Cages (~320 rats)	0 - 4.15 G (various radii)	Rodents Sq. Monkey Rhesus*	Operational (In use)
52-Foot Diameter	Chronic Weeks Months	Flexible Enclosed rotating room (~50 rats)	0 - 3 G (continuous radius)	Humans Rodents Sq. Monkey Rhesus	Operational *This is being rebuilt*
4-Foot Radius	Chronic Days Weeks (Two 1/2-hr stops per week)	10 Cages (~20 rats)	0 - 10 G 4-ft. radius	Rodents Sq. Monkey*	Operational

*Restrained, only

Figure 7-2A   Centrifuge research documentation.

Figure 7-2B Some centrifuge research image choices.

Figure 7-2B *Continued*

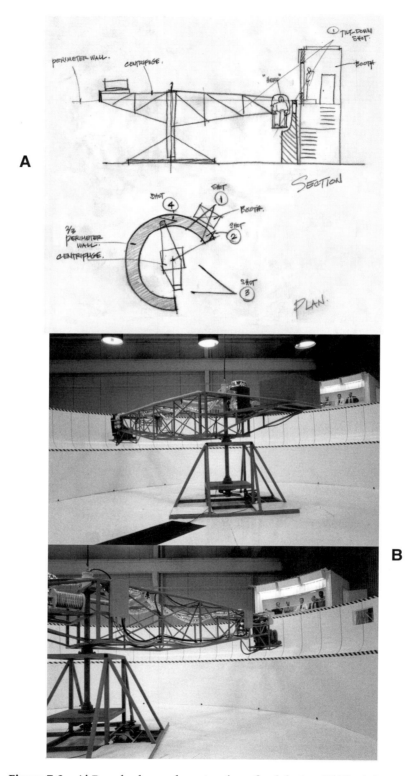

Figure 7-3 A) Rough plan and section for a final design. **B)** Final design.

SPECIALTY PROPS AND ANIMATRONICS

Filmmakers will always draw on solutions from proven options because nothing succeeds like success, especially in Hollywood. A state-of-the-art effects solution might not necessarily be the optimal solution in some cases—using a traditional technique, or better yet, improving upon a tried and true technique might provide the ultimate solution. This point of view is typical of a mechanical effects approach to problem solving. Animatronics is different. Although not scenery, animatronic objects like the half cockroach, half manual typewriters created for a movie like *Naked Lunch* fall into a specialty props category, likely to be initially designed by a concept illustrator or digital modeler in the art department. It is a specialized subdivision that thrives on innovation and unbounded creativity. **Jamie Hyneman** and his electronic effects production company, M5 Industries, fit that description. He is a specialty prop supervisor working in the Bay area for 20 years, who talked at length about his attempts to reconcile the demands between his training in traditional mechanical effects and visual effects components now demanded for TV and film projects. He also appears regularly on the HBO show, *Mythbusters*.

☐ *Jamie, were you the shop supervisor of the 21-man animatronics team for* Naked Lunch *(1991)?*
  No, I was not, though I was one of the lead mechanics responsible for a number of the major mechanical effects on that show. I cut my teeth on the animatronics for *Arachnophobia* (1990). I interviewed at Chris Walas Inc., who did *Naked Lunch*. At that time I was told about a film they would be doing about spiders that would be starting up in a couple of months. I went home and overnight made a spider out of wire with steel tips on the ends of its eight legs, and ran it across the bottom of a broiler pan lined with two rows of magnets. The effect made a very creepy, spider crawl as each leg moved across the path of each magnet. I went back the next day and showed them my spider. They were actually impressed and when they crewed up, I got my job. That gag never was used because it was too inflexible, and it would have to run on a track. But I did learn two things: 1) that ingenuity and passion will get you a job and 2) I also learned patience.[4]

It was obvious that M5 Industries warehouse/office space is a place of serious creative business as Jamie gave me a well-rehearsed tour. Neatness prevailed despite the company's relentless activity and the palpable sense of creativity and chaos all around. Larger specialty props were sturdily hung from the truss system above, imposing floor items were pushed carefully aside to allow easy flow around machinery and worktables, and hand-sized objects were carefully strewn across many rows of wall shelving (see Fig. 7-4). **Jamie** diligently continued his monologue:

  My skill designing more flexible, lifelike spiders improved through using super magnets. We made simple, rubber spiders and embedded very tiny

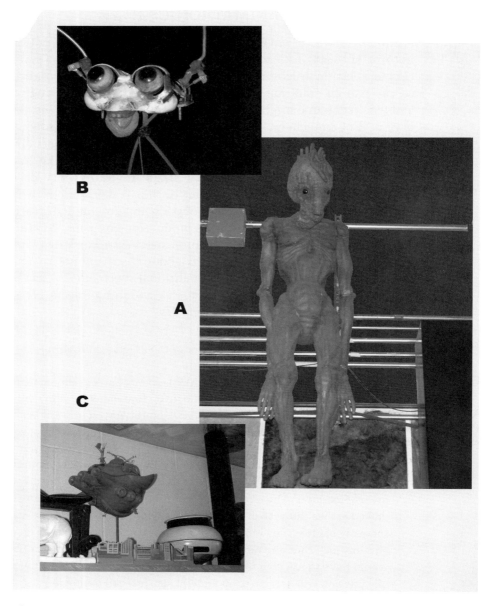

Figure 7-4 M5 Industries ANIMATRONICS: **A)** Latex creature prototype, **B)** Mechanical Mogwai head, **C)** A shelf of recognizable specialty film props.

D

E

F

Figure 7-4 D) Animatronics for an overscale spider puppet, **E)** Latex tarantula prototype, **F)** Radio-controlled puppet developed for a TV commercial—a considerably advanced puppet incorporating miniature radio, servo, and battery technologies not available before 1990. Courtesy of M5 Industries.

super magnets into the tips of each leg. The idea was to toss them at a metal wall surface and as they neared the metal surface they actually looked like they're reaching forward and grabbing to latch on. It was a wonderful, simple effect they used all the time. Later on, my particular contribution to the show was the leg joint design for the more articulated spider in close-up scenes. I simplified the process by perfecting the mechanics of one-cable-in-one-leg by pulling at the base of it and curling up the whole leg. It worked on the principle of the parallelogramming arms of an architect's lamp. As I refined it, I found a way to have one cable do the work of the equivalent of three cables with a solid linkage not being as sloppy or as jerky as it can when this type of mechanism gets more complicated. My solution made the process more elegant and more bulletproof.

☐ *Much of the work you've done is object-oriented. Have you done any work within scenery like in the movie* Delicatessen *(1991), for example, in which the physical effects and scenery were combined?*

Since we've been doing *Mythbusters*, people have been asking us to do that a lot more. Anyone can do the traditional effects—pyro, rain, fog, and wind— but I'm the guy you come to when things get problematic. I'm a generalist and a problem solver. A production company would approach me if there were something that required a solution that went outside of the normal range of physical effects. An upcoming movie called *The Darwin Awards* will require the supervision of traditional wind, rain, fire, and explosions, a welcomed change to our show, *Mythbusters,* in which we actually do the real stuff and don't fake anything. By working outside of L.A., we have the advantage and disadvantage of being a premier boutique shop for animatronics here in the Bay Area.

☐ *Jamie, is this machine used for 3D sculpting? (Pointing to a smaller CNC rig in the upstairs prototyping room.)*

Yes, and that's why it intrigued us enough to buy it for the work we do. The fine sculpting ability of this machine rivals what any gifted modeler can do with clay by going beyond human capability. For example, the $\frac{1}{2}$" × $\frac{1}{2}$" relief figure of this tiny prototype you see is at 200 percent. Its normal size was eventually put on the side of a pen as part of a packet for kids. To sculpt this detail in reality with traditional sculpture methods is impossible. But in this medium, I can fill the monitor with the detail of this animation character's finger.

☐ *What is its non-commercial name?*

It's a CNC, computer-numeric-control, digital milling machine (see Fig. 7-5A–D). Once it is programmed with a digital design including the scale of the desired object, the machine will run all night and produce the high quality detail you see on the surface of this object, or just carve the object itself. FreeForm Plus software works with the Phantom sculpting tool; otherwise, we typically use Rhino software to model polygonal surfaces. It outputs a file that generates a tool path, or series of locations, for the cutting bit to remove material and create the image. The CNC is a versatile machine tool to carve a shape out of plastic or wood in the case of a sculpture, or metal in the case of a mechanical part. We chose this because of the dual purpose and economy of the machine. You can set it so it will take a pass and then move over a thousandth of an inch and take another pass—so you can get an extremely fine resolution to carve things that it would be practically impossible for a human to actually sculpt in clay. For sculpting alone, a printer is easier to use, although not capable of as fine a resolution. Scale and design changes can tip the balance in choosing between CG vs. traditional options; if it is anticipated that many, minor changes may be needed in the production of a piece, then the computer is the best choice because it can make the changes more often with ease, and be much more cost effective.

☐ *So, this is a prototyping machine.*
Exactly. The larger machine, the 3D printer, downstairs is the same kind of machine. The difference is that the CNC subtracts surface and the 3D printer adds or builds surface to create a sculptural form.

☐ *Explain how a 3D printer works.*
Digital information is fed to the printer, and it reads it and sculpts the object in wax, cornstarch, UV curing resin, or even metal powder that gets centered by impregnating it with another metal that wicks into it and solidifies it. We've limited our CG adventure to designing models for prototypes when 1) the work is too small for a clay sculptor, or 2) multiples of the same metal parts need to be replicated quickly and efficiently. (Pointing to a desktop PC.) This SenseAble Forced-Feedback™ system works optimally for projects with scale issues; otherwise, a traditional human sculptor can handle it.
    (His assistant, Cris Rocha pulled up a 3D model of the profile of one of the *Mythbusters* crew on a nearby computer screen.)

☐ *So your approach to CG is very practical—you're not making art for art's sake.*
Yes, by being practical we're not biased. We use whatever method, traditional or digital, that gets the job done. Our practicality is about speed and efficiency. An interesting little detail about this SenseAble™ tool is the 3D mouse. The operator simply moves this 3D wand in space and that's where the digital model goes. For speed in determining the screen model, there's nothing like it. The only flaw in doing a prototype as opposed to a purely CG model is actually being able to tell what you've got. The image on the monitor is an educated guess or estimate of what you would really have in actual vs. virtual space. This is one of the biggest flaws we found as a reality check for this type of technology in terms of the crossover between the digital and physical models. We find that it's a worthwhile tool to have, although our first inclination is to put a sculptor on the project first.[5]

Cris, the 3D modeler, suggested I grasp the wand and "feel" the solidness of the onscreen sculpture (Fig. 7-6). Holding the stylus and running it over the surface of the sculpted profile on the PC screen was a remarkable feeling. My fingers actually sensed the tactical sensation of sculpting in 3D, especially when I ran it around the tip of the nose or to the edge of the cheek and behind to the backside. This unexpected virtual lesson with a 3D mouse

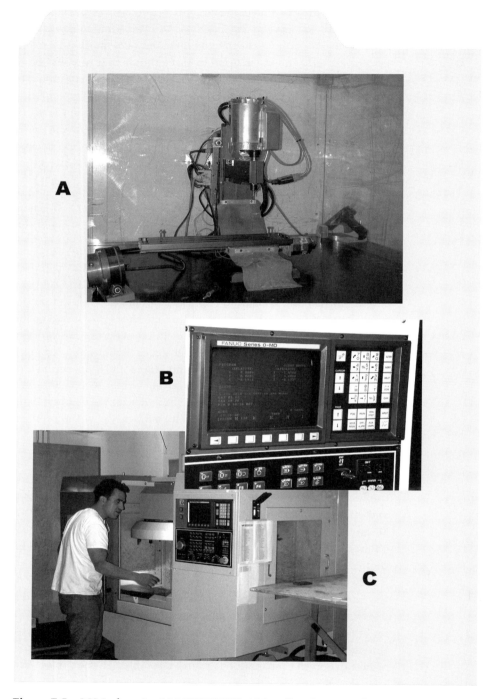

Figure 7-5 M5 Industries MACHINERY: **A)** Smaller CNC machine, **B)** Larger CNC machine, **C)** Insert: CNC readout screen.

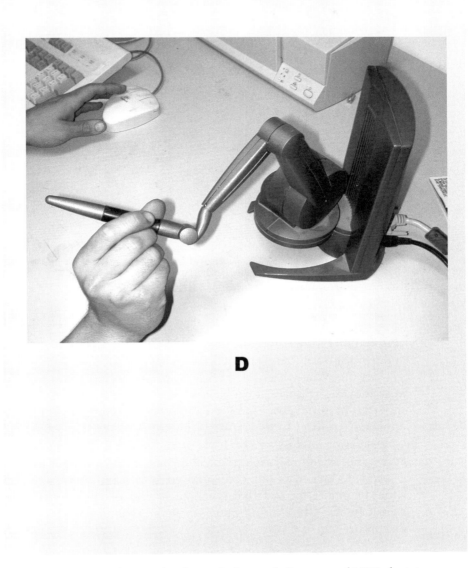

D

Figure 7-5   **D)** 3D stylus for sculpting tool. Courtesy of M5 Industries.

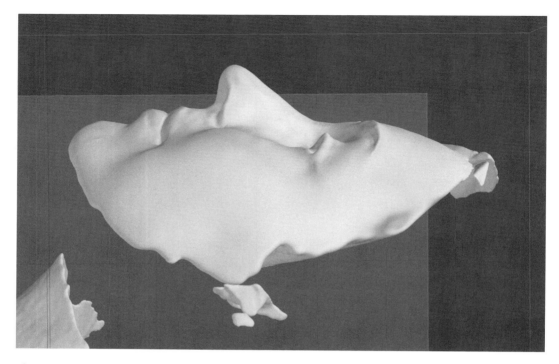

Figure 7-6   Screen capture: Side view of a human profile transferred from a 3D scanner into a FreeForm™ software document. Courtesy of M5 Industries.

clarified just how powerful this technology really is. It also drove home the concept that experience is the best teacher.

Art directors who have a working knowledge of mechanical effects and how they're integrated into built scenery are at an advantage. Understanding what materials should be used in scenery for multiple retakes of a series of physical effects shots, not only supports the success of the gag, but it prevents compromising of the look of the scenery. To review an important concept in Chapter 7: Achieving believability through our highly developed craft of deception is our continual goal. What we have encountered here should support the fact that mechanical effects continue to be an intrinsic aspect of the filmmaking process. Physical effects and stunts will never disappear.

ENDNOTES

1, 2, and 3. Jeff Jarvis interview, 9/05/02, Saugus, CA.
4 and 5. Jaime Hyneman interview, 6/26/04, San Francisco, CA.

Production and Post-Production Processes

CHAPTER 8

Paperwork and Production Tasks

Film production companies generate stacks of paper during the activity of delivering a film product to the studio. Script revisions run the gamut of white, blue, pink, yellow, green, goldenrod, buff, salmon, cherry, tan, gray, and ivory. The remainder takes the shape of contracts, forms, lists, and memos. The good news is most production companies provide large recycling bins for the waste; the sobering news is an art director will fill at least two three-hole, four-inch binders per show. Super microchip technology has, for some unexplained reason, increased the volume of paper, not lessened it. I've recently managed to keep the number of binders I keep in my car to one; I rely on the laptop and PDA to hold the bulk of the data for easy retrieval, with a fraction of the weight. If you are serious about doing this work, you might want to consider this or develop a similar system of data entry and rapid retrieval. It will save time—and ultimately, forests.

THE ONSET OF PRINCIPAL PHOTOGRAPHY

Production Meetings

The final production meeting is a formal, well-structured event held at the end of the pre-production phase. The first assistant director presides over the meeting. It is well publicized and requires the mandatory presence of all department heads and their assistants. The meeting opens with brief, round table introductions, then proceeds directly to an item-by-item review of the **one-liner schedule** and **shooting schedule**, highlighted in Figs. 8-5 and 8-6 and Appendix D: Production Lists, respectively. The bulk of this 3–4 hour meeting is focused on giving general clarification and commentary on the shooting schedule, providing detailed answers to the items specified on the shooting schedule, updates from various departments, and production office news and information pertaining to 1st Day of Principal Photography. Additional in-depth conversations are inevitable and become sidebar, or post-meeting discussions, extending the time away from the daily routine well into the afternoon. As a result, everyone is asked to make his or her questions, comments, and information as brief as possible. The tone and efficiency of the final production meeting is a good indication of the swift and efficient working style of the 1st AD. During this meeting, the 1st assistant director assumes responsibility for the organization of the shooting schedule, the shooting crew, and commits to the timeline of delivering the film on time.

THE SCHEDULES AND LISTS

The following schedules and lists seem repetitive but have different purposes and will be discussed in more detail in the following pages. They are created by the assistant directing staff, e.g., the 1st AD, 2nd AD, and 2nd 2nd AD, reviewed by the 1st AD and UPM, and distributed by the production office into manila pouches, push-pinned onto a designated production office wall. In more technically updated film production offices, this same information is digitally distributed over the company intranet (server), or simply emailed to everyone on the production crew by the production office staff.

Script Breakdown

The text and evocative imagery of the script are transformed into a list of tangible sets for shooting. As you might recall in Chapter 6, the sequential process of text to sets looks like Fig. 8-1.

The pivotal item in this sequence is the Script or Design Breakdown (Fig. 8-2), providing essential data for each set, derived from every scene in the script. From this small, encapsulated version of vital information, the set list and corresponding construction budgets are generated. Of course, the format for any of these lists is dependent upon which text-generating software is used; this is not as important as what information is included. Every art director has his/her own organizing quirks. In addition to the Set Breakdown page shown here, take a look at the Set Breakdown Item Page in Appendix D. The information for each set is included on one page. I prefer to use both the list and per/page items in order to comprehensively cross-reference and double-check the data. These lists are only effective if they are updated on a daily basis. The Set Breakdown Item Page was designed in Microsoft Word. In preparing my set list for construction estimate or budget breakdown (Fig. 8-3), I've found Microsoft Excel to be indispensable because each page of a typical document is set up as a table by default, allowing automatic subtotals to be generated as item costs are entered. Fig. 8-4, shown as Set List, was created in FileMaker Pro. Rule of thumb: Choose a software format that is universally compatible but supports your comfort level.

Text > Script Breakdown > Set List > Budget > Sets

Figure 8-1   Progress from text to sets.

"My Fellow Americans" Design breakdown				last modified: 3/20/96

Script Date: March 8, 1996		Director: Peter Segal		Production Designer: Jim Bissell
Producer: Warner Bros.		Michael Ewing Jean Higgins		Production number:
				Page number: 5

Set #:	Loc:	Type:	Set Description:	To be Designed:
434	Asheville	Ext	Hollis Farmhouse	
A.D.: Michael Rizzo		Shoot Date: 6/8/96		
Set Des:		Design Completion Date:		
435	Asheville	Int	Hollis Horsebarn-night	
A.D.: Michael Rizzo		Shoot Date: 6/8/96		
Set Des:		Design Completion Date:		
436	Asheville	Ext	Maryland Road-Day	
A.D.: Gae Buckley		Shoot Date:		
Set Des:		Design Completion Date:		
438	Asheville	Ext	White House Kennedy Garden	Design and build
A.D.: Michael Rizzo		Shoot Date: 5/15/96		
Set Des:		Design Completion Date: 4/1/96		
441	Asheville	Int	Witnaur's bedroom	
A.D.: Michael Rizzo		Shoot Date: 6/2/96		
Set Des:		Design Completion Date:		
444	Asheville	Int	Wayne & Genny's Trailer-night	Int. Trailer Set
A.D.: Michael Rizzo		Shoot Date: 5/22/96		
Set Des:		Design Completion Date: 4/5/96		
445	Asheville	Ext	White House S.W. lawn	White House Facade
A.D.:		Shoot Date: 5/17/96		
Set Des:		Design Completion Date: 4/1/96		
445	Asheville	Ext	White House Southwest Lawn	
A.D.:		Shoot Date: 5/15/96		
Set Des:		Design Completion Date: 4/1/96		

Figure 8-2 Typical Set Breakdown page organized by Jim Bissell, production designer, for *My Fellow Americans*.

"My Fellow Americans" Construction Estimate				Last modified	3/16/96		

Script Date: March 8, 1996		Director: Peter Segal		Production Designer: Jim Bissell			

Producer: Warner bros.		Michael Ewing Jean Higgins	Production number:				
			Page number: 4				

Set #:	Loc:	Type:	Set Description:	Const. Estimate	Sign Estimate	Greens Estimate
309	Wash	Ext	**Street-Wal and Talk**	$0.00	$0.00	$0.00
310	Wash	Int	**Reynolds' Outer Office**	$0.00	$0.00	$0.00
311	Wash	Int	**Reynolds' Office**	$0.00	$1,500.00	$2,000.00
312	Wash	Int	**Office building corridor/Elevator bank**	$0.00	$0.00	$0.00
313	Wash	Ext	**The Mall-Washington -Morning**	$0.00	$1,000.00	$1,000.00
314	Wash	Ext	**Street bordering White House**	$0.00	$1,500.00	$5,000.00
317	Wash	Ext	**White House West Wing**	$5,000.00	$0.00	$0.00
401	Ashevill	Ext	**Private Runway**	$0.00	$0.00	$0.00
402	Ashevill	Ext	**Funeral/Cemetery-D**	$3,000.00	$2,000.00	$3,000.00
403	Ashevill	Ext	**Baseball Field**	$0.00	$0.00	$5,000.00
404	Ashevill	Ext	**Another wooded clearing-explosion**	$3,000.00	$0.00	$2,000.00
405	Ashevill	Int	**Train Station Restroom**	$18,000.00	$2,000.00	$0.00
406	Ashevill	Int	**Train Car**	$3,000.00	$3,000.00	$0.00
407	Ashevill	Int/Ext	**Small town train station-night**	$15,000.00	$1,500.00	$1,000.00
408	Ashevill	Ext	**Another Train station platform**	$30,000.00	$2,000.00	$1,000.00

Figure 8-3 Typical Design Breakdown page organized by Jim Bissell, production designer for *My Fellow Americans.*

192

"My Fellow Americans" Set List					last modified: 3/17/96
Script Date: February 19, 1996			Director: Peter Segal		Production Designer: Jim Bissell
Producer: Warner Brothers			Michael Ewing Jean Higgins		Production number:
					Page number: 4

Set #:	Loc:	Type:	Set Description:	Scene Numbers:
301	Wash	Int	Kramer's Limo-day	39,41
302	White House	Ext	White House-establishing shots	21,47,200
303	Wash.	Ext	Wasington Street	39
305	Wash	Ext	Union Station	56
306	Wash	Ext	Street/Union Station	57,58,59,60,61,62
308	Wash	Ext	White House roof	229,330,238,242
309	Wash	Ext	Street-Wal and Talk	46
310	Wash	Int	Reynolds' Outer Office	42
311	Wash	Int	Reynolds' Office	43,45,49
312	Wash	Int	Office building corridor/Elevator bank	44
313	Wash	Ext	The Mall-Washington -Morning	147,148
314	Wash	Ext	Street bordering White House	234
317	Wash	Ext	White House West Wing	234a

Figure 8-4 Typical Construction Estimate page organized by Jim Bissell, production designer and John Samson, construction coordinator for *My Fellow Americans*.

One-Liner Schedule

As you can see, the One-liner Schedule (see Fig. 8-5) is very straightforward and self-explanatory, as a shorthand version of the longer, more detailed Shooting Schedule (see Appendix D), by distilling the information down to: shoot day number, date, scene number, single-line scene description, scene time of day (Day, Night, etc.), scene location type (INT, EXT), location place (Stage description or Location description), and number of pages to be shot (noted by eighth of a page increments, e.g., $2^5/_8$ page).

Shooting Schedule

This is the master list for the shooting process (see Appendix D), compiled by the unit production manager and 1st assistant director, but ultimately the responsibility of the 1st AD. It is generated from the script breakdown of scenes into information items like day, night, interior, exterior, scene name, scene description, and shoot location. It further distills the script down into workable, daily units of shooting: number of scenes and corresponding scene numbers, and total number of pages of script to be covered. For example, each day of the shooting schedule has a number (shoot day #15) and on that particular day specific scenes are scheduled to be shot based on script requirements, logical sequencing, and actor availability. Cast required for that day are listed as principles, stand-ins, and atmosphere (atmos) or background/crowd people. Additional data is provided to each department, where necessary, indicating special equipment, special effects, specific hero props, costuming, set dressing, scenery pieces or even special painting notes, i.e., "light aging on hero car." The Shooting Schedule is updated when significant changes occur because it acts as everyone's "shooting bible" for the duration of the production phase of filmmaking.

Fig. 8-6 shows an additional version of the Shooting Schedule plotted on a calendar page. This example tracks art director, shooting crew, and actor movement to and from distant locations, as well as set prep and how many days a specific set is scheduled to play. The calendar page version of the Shooting Schedule can also be found on the walls of the art department. There, large-scale calendar pages are similarly color-coded to easily track the same items mentioned above. (Sadly, the color coding is not shown here but is presented in black/white.) Again, this data is also repeated on PDA screen readouts and laptops.

Day Out of Days

This chart called a *Day Out of Days* (see Appendix D) almost always pertains to actor working schedules. It is significant for an art director to use as a guide for special equipment, such as boats, vehicles, planes, or other craft, on pictures that specify their continuous use. This is a particularly good tool for refining "hero detailing" in conjunction with the Shooting Schedule so that no item is forgotten.

End Day #36 -- Total Pages: 2 4/8

Shoot Day #37 -- Wed, May 15, 1996

Scs. 6	INT	Century Plaza - Backstage Haney prepares to go on stage for his victory speech ID 3, 4, 5, 81	NIGHT	4/8 pgs.
Biltmore Hotel		Pete's Sequence Name: Cold Opening		
Scs. 20,22pt	EXT	Arlington Cemetery Matt and Kramer continue their discussions; Matthews gives his eulogy ID 1, 2, 5, 18, 19, 35, 36	DAY	5/8 pgs.
Biltmore House, Asheville,North Carolina		Pete's Sequence Name: Cemetery		

End Day #37 -- Total Pages: 1 1/8

Shoot Day #38 -- Thu, May 16, 1996

Scs. 214pt	EXT	White House South Lawn Haney at reception; Tanner gets call ID 3, 7	DAY	2/8 pgs.
Biltmore Estate, North Carolir		Pete's Sequence Name: Guest Quarters		
Scs. 235	EXT	White House South Lawn Haney speaking at ceremony ID 3, 26, 27	DAY	1/8 pgs.
Biltmore Estate, North Carolir		Pete's Sequence Name: Horse Race		
Scs. 243	EXT	White House South Lawn Matt and Kramer arrive at ceremony; Ask to speak to Haney ID 1, 2, 3, 26, 27, 100, 101, 102	DAY	3/8 pgs.
Biltmore Estate, North Carolir		Pete's Sequence Name: Horse Race		
Scs. 227	EXT	White House Gate House Tanner spots the boys riding away; They give chase ID 1, 2, 7, 8, 100, 101, 102, 111	DAY	3/8 pgs.
Biltmore Estate, North Carolir		Pete's Sequence Name: White House Gate		
Scs. 228pt	EXT	White House Northeast Lawn Presidents riding across lawn ID 100, 101, 102	DAY	1/8 pgs.
Biltmore Estate, North Carolir		Pete's Sequence Name: Horse Race		

End Day #38 -- Total Pages: 1 2/8

Shoot Day #39 -- Fri, May 17, 1996

Scs. 248	EXT	White House Matt tells Kramer that he taped the conversation ID 1, 2, 18, 19, 23, 35	DAY	2 1/8 pgs
Biltmore Estate, North Carolir		Pete's Sequence Name: White House Drive		

Figure 8-5 Typical One-Liner page authored by the assistant director's team for *My Fellow Americans*.

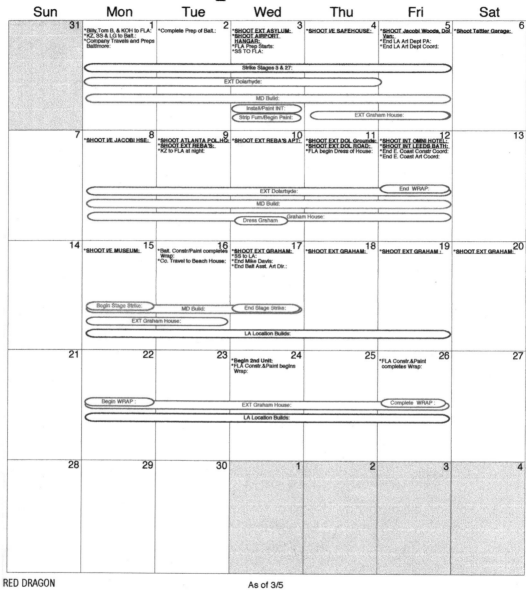

Figure 8-6 Typical Shooting Schedule calendar page 3 of 5 from *Red Dragon*. Courtesy of Steve Sablad, art director.

Call Sheet

The Call Sheet is a daily reminder of expectations and activities, planned for the shooting crew and remains the responsibility of the 2ⁿᵈ AD (see Appendix D). It includes scenes to be shot that day, the weather forecast, and shooting location, and also lists by department all crew and actors either needed on set or expected to be on stand-by during various times of the day. It is the final, printed, daily version of the more general Shooting Schedule previously distributed, and it demands drop-dead, faithful commitment from all crewmembers. The actual signature of the 1ˢᵗ AD on this sheet confirms the data, and it signals to the accounting department and the studio the budget expenditure for that particular day of shooting. Now, the process has become serious business.

Cell Phone and Pager List

All company and crewmembers' names, addresses, mobile phone numbers, pager numbers, and email addresses are compiled on this extensive list by department. The list is arranged hierarchically beginning with department heads and ending with assistant crewmembers; it is the precursor of the final crew list distributed by the production office at wrap.

DIRECTOR'S PLANS

The art department PA reduces, photocopies, collates, and delivers every set scheduled to be shot from its original 24' × 36' blueprinted format (typical) onto an $8\frac{1}{2}'$ × 11', three-hole paper format. A small booklet of plans is distributed to all key people in the production office, shooting crew, and art department who need access to the footprint of every location and onstage studio set. Final distribution of the director's plans packet happens at the final production meeting. For those who prefer digital files, a production office PA provides the same data electronically via the server from laptop to laptop.

Figs. 8-7 and 8-8 display how various aspects of a typical director's plans are drawn for use. As shown, several generations of the same location sets are combined in the overall packet to provide more specific information. You can never provide too much detail or too much seemingly insignificant information. The minutiae will always fill in the gaps somewhere for someone.

ART DEPARTMENT PRODUCTION TASKS

The first day of principal photography marks the first day of the production or shooting process, normally ranging from 60–70 days, but at times extending to a year. It is a time when the camera stops only at scheduled intervals like national holidays and for few emergencies. Otherwise, the course of the film is driven by the shooting schedule.

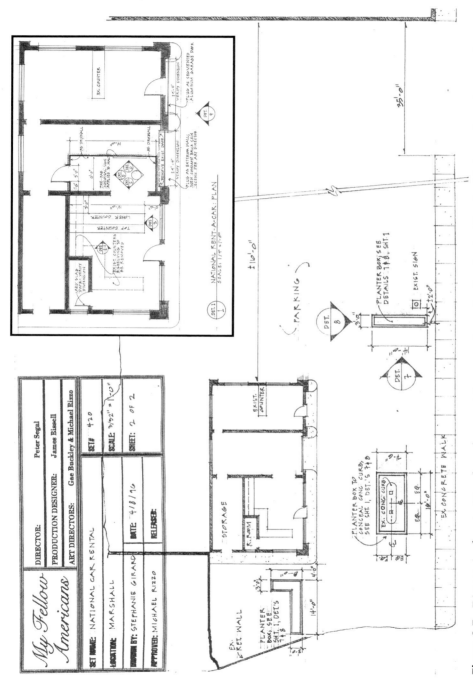

Figure 8-7 Director's plan-A: Site plan of car rental agency drawn by Stephanie Girard with inset: Location set plan. MY FELLOW AMERICANS © 1996 Warner Bros., a division of Time Warner Entertainment Company, L.P. All Rights Reserved.

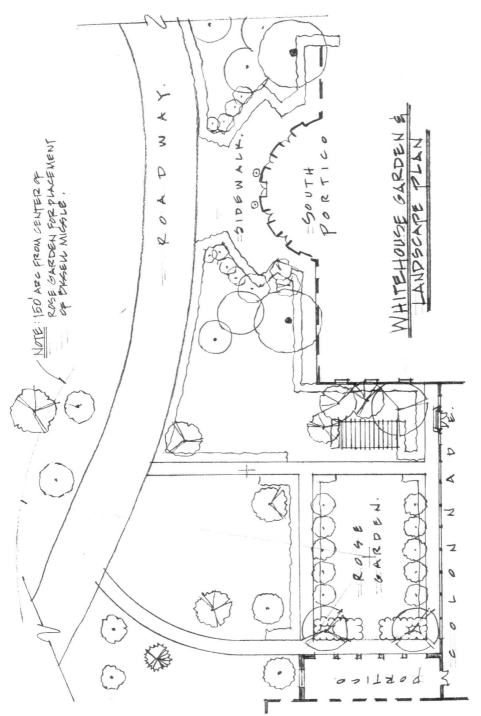

Figure 8-8 Director's plan-B: Set plan of White House Rose Garden and Landscape drawn by Michael Rizzo. MY FELLOW AMERICANS © 1996 Warner Bros., a division of Time Warner Entertainment Company, L.P. All Rights Reserved.

Clearances and Product Placement

A product placement and clearance coordinator employed in the production office, the parent film studio, or from an independent company must clear any likeness, individual name, business name, telephone number, license plate number, street addresses, actual product depiction, signage, or item of set dressing or clothing placed in front of the camera displaying a logo, graphic, or icon for use on a particular film project. If this clearance is not sought or if the process is not effective, lawsuits are not unlikely.

Although placing a can of Coke as set dressing in a kitchen set is actually free advertising, the Coca Cola company reserves the right to know how the product is displayed. It also needs to be assured that its product is not used in a way that will defame it or show it in a negative way. The art director should be actively involved with a product placement/clearance person by supervising important hero items mentioned above, in order to carefully control details in a timely manner before any special content is shot. Wrong information can create a damage control situation that can easily turn into a nightmare if not properly handled.

Keeping Ahead of the Camera

Once the camera begins to roll, it remains faithful to its relentless shooting schedule. During the shoot, focus is on the set. It is the job of the art director to remain far ahead of the shooting timeline while supplying the daily needs of the shooting crew in terms of scenery or special props and effects listed on the daily call sheet. The goal is to make the shoot as smooth as possible despite unexpected changes or events that will occur. This goal can only be attained if a solid, pre-production strategy is in place and is continuously monitored and adjusted as needed. Communication is the key to resolving any issue. Here are some helpful suggestions for exercising that skill.

On-Set Presence

During the shoot, an art director's task list becomes longer as the length of the day remains the same. The shorthand communication already established within your working relationships during the pre-production phase becomes an asset in getting the expanding job done. Wireless phones as prime communicating devices enhance the speed of receiving and exchanging of information. While art directing on *Vanilla Sky*, we were first introduced to the newest line of Nextel™ cell phone/walkie talkies—now they are ubiquitous. In the midst of a transmission with two other people on the lot, I was able to put them on hold, dial a vendor, ask questions and check supplies, finish that call, then resume the original conversation with the new information. Speed like that is expected during the shoot; it counterbalances the weight of the growing list.

An art director is in many places throughout the day. During production, the rhythm of "the daily routine" adjusts to accommodate the needs of the shooting crew. Before anything else can be accomplished during the day, the set needs attention. Awake at 5 AM and on set by 6 AM, the art director begins the day with the art department running crew to discuss any last minute questions for scenic requirements for either later that day or short-range considerations for the rest of that week. Details are constantly in flux and in need of modification and fine-tuning. As on-set art department crew are constantly with the shooting crew with no time to leave the set. Supplying the physical and emotional needs of your on-set people, especially on location, is important. Spending time with the on-set art crew also allows time to get a sense of how they are relating to the rest of the shooting crew and vice versa. Often, misunderstandings between departments result from vague commitments as to who will actually deliver what to the camera on smaller productions with less experienced crew. Guidance from an art director can help resolve the issue at hand. The intensity of the work requires special attention to conflicts and productive relationships by resolving issues and encouraging onset harmony.

Opening a new set with the production designer and director is a welcomed ritual. It signifies the culmination of another job well done by the entire art department. This event happens well before call time the day the new set is scheduled for shooting. Those involved do a **walk through** to point out pertinent details and scripted features in the set. The director or 1st AD delivers last minute notes with the on-set crew in earshot; the art director gives further instruction to hasten the process. The trick is to be the first group to receive notes so that tasks can be completed while other departments are receiving their marching orders. The experience and skill of your on-set crew rallies to make moments like this effortless. Once notes are completed, the art director is free to visit the catering truck for a quick breakfast. It is time to take a moment to relax and wait for the shooting crew to get the first shot off. Again, "first time" sets need much attention until the first scene is in the can to assure a smooth, continued process for that day.

Walking over to a standing set and physically checking it over is a good idea. Actively looking for discrepancies with working parts of the set, i.e., doors, windows, and built-in special effects sections, might avert potential problems. Scenery suffering the effects of extended use might need minor repair or touch-up paint overlooked during a demanding shooting schedule. Expensive or irreplaceable set dressing should also be examined or noted as missing in action, as well as other conditions around the set like dangling lighting instruments, poorly hung backings, and other accidents waiting to happen. Nothing is too obvious to be overlooked or triple-checked.

After watching the completion of the first scene during setup for the next shot, quick informational exchanges with other onset departments forwards communication. There are often details or changes gathered from on-set crewmembers that happen before there is a formal notice on a call sheet. A conversation-in-passing with a director's personal assistant, for example, might provide a significant heads-up and require further investigation. No one's participation is too obvious to be overlooked or used to get a jump on new changes—everyone on the set is a wealth of information.

Talk directly to the directorial staff to get advance reports on any formal, upcoming changes and double-check any on-set rumors. The production office, location's department, and the directorial staff monitor weather forecasts throughout the day. Need for cover sets is directly dependent on that incoming data. Surprises, or finding oneself out of the loop, belies sloppy communication and on-set networking skills. Daily check-in with the 2nd AD over hot coffee and a breakfast burrito is a habit worth developing. Being a great communicator ensures good PR both on the set and with production.

If there are no pressing issues for an art director in the woodshop, in the art department, or on a location being prepped, remaining on the set throughout the day ensures art department presence and staying fully within the loop. Participation in various interdepartmental meetings including set decorating, mechanical effects, visual effects, and production office considerations can be done on a conference call or on set in a standing set or the **feeding tent**, if necessary. Otherwise, the late morning is spent running to location(s) to view building progress or double-checking details or solving problems, digitally photographing the progress, and helping solve PR problems that might have arisen between the location point-person and the activity of the construction crew. WiFi service, where available, allows easy email access for sending scenery progress images from a laptop or cell phone. If this service isn't available, Internet hook-up is surely available in either the production trailer or directorial staff trailer. In addition to emailing set photos, Web connectivity enables the completion of current paperwork, the double- and triple-checking of schedules relating to the construction building schedule, reviewing the next day's agenda, and keeping up with vendors and subcontractors' delivery timelines.

Leaving the set in early afternoon might require a return to the woodshop to check on set construction progress or to solve additional problems in person by talking through changes in scenery design and modification. A quick call to a set designer relays those changes or alerts that draftsman to emergency adjustments to be made to $\frac{1}{4}$" scale plans or elevations for the designer's new meeting time in the next twenty minutes. If distances aren't too great, then returning to the set is an option. Otherwise, final check-in with the art department folks happens in person by early evening. Additional design changes are noted, approved, or modified, and, if time allows, prints are made in multiple for construction crew and other departments. Before leaving the office, setting out whatever is physically necessary to take to the set for call time includes drafting, printed material such as revised director's plans, color photocopies of new research, paperwork for on-set crew, or materials/construction samples, which all goes into the backpack. The day typically ends by around 8 PM at the set to gather last minute bits of information or to just hang as the crew gets the **martini shot**. An important point to remember: an art director is always on call when the crew is shooting.

Cover Sets

Weather conditions can be one of the few things altering or stopping the shooting schedule altogether, and must be avoided at all costs. The art department is directly responsible for keeping the shoot on schedule by providing cover sets. An art director does not accomplish this alone. Assistance from locations, production, and the directorial staff help forecast and communicate changes in weather and scheduling tactics. Ideally, cover sets are established early during pre-production and are fully dressed and ready to be utilized. The location of the film and time of year will determine the number of cover sets. For instance, if you are shooting the bulk of a film in Ireland, chances are that every interior set will be considered a cover set. During the shoot for *White Sands* in New Mexico, summer weather delivered an expected, late afternoon thunderstorm—it was factored into the weekly shooting schedule plan. The ability to be fast and flexible arms a vigilant art director.

Communication with the Trinity

Diligent service to the director, cinematographer, and UPM are expected (see Chapter 2: "Hierarchy of Responsibilities"). Both direct and indirect communication with these key players supports the efficiency of the production. Showing digitally-enhanced idea changes to upcoming locations or scenery progress images to the director, especially, encourages excitement for upcoming sets and inspires continued creativity. Presenting new research or new data not previously considered enhances the continuation of the collaborative creative process. Making self-inspired changes to scenery, dressing, or visual and mechanical effects, for instance, are also reasonable suggestions to entertain. But, sometimes it's also important to say "No."

The creative filmmaking process is an organic one. Most changes a director or cinematographer makes mid-stream are acceptable. How do you determine which are unacceptable? Additions or changes that affect the scenery budget in a big way demand immediate attention and analysis. Having a strategy already in place regarding the inevitability of these requests helps the speed of decision-making. Experience helps determine early on which sets will most likely receive additional work: hero sets will probably require this kind of attention, some sets are important for storytelling but not critical, and other sets are dispensable. As a result, the original set list is continuously modified throughout production, as well as corresponding budget items. Your job as budget watchdog requires your active participation. Input from the construction coordinator or mechanical effects supervisor is helpful, but the final decision is in the hands of the designer or UPM once your financial caveat is delivered. This is not to suggest stubbornness or unreasonableness on the part of the art director. Rolling with the changes is a big part of the job description. But it is important to remain firm in your judgment of what changes will be acceptable or not. Shooting from the hip is necessary, but not at the expense of your budget, your crew, or yourself.

Telling the Truth

Stress is a given while principal photography progresses: demands are great, tension is high, time is metered, and personalities are volatile. Having knowledge of up-to-the-minute changes, ability to quote budget numbers on the spot, and having critical data at hand are several ways to offset the stress an art director experiences. A practical art director is well prepared to negotiate every situation that arises. Understanding the facts and telling the truth matter the most. On-set disputes look for the level-headed, logical, and factual input of an art director. Although sometimes difficult to hear, the truth will dispel fear and resolve a conflict. Combining diplomacy with the truth makes all the difference.

ART DEPARTMENT TACTICAL STRATEGY

Handling Changes

Moviemaking is a changeable process. Developing an operational plan flexible enough to withstand small and large scale shifts is practical. Most of the changes are likely to occur within the building and finishing stages of scenery production, once the designing process on the page is done. For instance, repainting an interior set is an inconvenient task that disrupts the timeline. Because the construction crewmembers have already been assigned to a given number of sets, additional crew would have to be hired as well as additional materials to complete the job. Annoying at best, it is achievable mainly because each budgetary item on the set list is figured with a 10–15% contingency cushion, allowing for these kinds of budget and time disruptions. While this same, small emergency crew of painters is still on payroll, they might also be utilized on other sets where crew is getting into a jam—this is another justification for hiring additional crew in the first place. A major addition to the timeline schedule, such as building a duplicate of a set, demands special attention. Most likely, it will require an emergency meeting with the producer or UPM, construction coordinator, mechanical and visual effects supervisors, the head accountant, and art director to decide on the best tactical solution. (Details will be discussed later in this section.)

The art department coordinator handles the bulk of paperwork generated in the art department for production and studio files. This includes the filling out of art department crew time cards, keeping track of check request forms, organizing petty cash disbursement and receipt envelopes for the production designer and art director, pagers and cell phones' distribution lists, accident coverage and worker's compensation forms, designing and distribution of car cards and similar ID tags for admittance to a hot set, securing certificate of insurance forms required by certain vendors, and tracking of most clearance materials and information for product and name usage. Free from these smaller, vital operational tasks, the art director can more fully concentrate on onstage scenery production and finishing touches, set dressing, hero props, completion of location sets, and cover sets. From time to time personality or stress-induced conflicts in the art department will erupt but end quickly, simply because there is little time to sustain an argument. Any lingering discord needs to be immediately resolved by an intruding art director to keep morale high and productivity on schedule.

Vendors

Vendors are a vital part of the support structure of the film industry; as subcontractors, they provide relief to a demanding workload. Graphics and signage, billboards, or site surveys for location sets are examples of many jobs outsourced to other companies. The progress of those projects requires daily management scrutiny. Dealing with vendors in Los Angeles is simpler, in many ways, because they understand how urgent the time factor is in the overall process. In some cases, you will receive outsourced work before a deadline, and this is good. When working out of town, most art directors are subcontracting to vendors who are highly motivated to participate but lack the ability to move quickly. If the options are narrow, then an art director must impress on the vendor the fact that their participation requires them to make sure the needs of the film take precedence over anything else. This is an arrogant request, but it must be made up front and verbally agreed to, otherwise not having established that basic understanding will surely cause setbacks in production schedules. Be clear, firm, and thorough to prevent any misunderstandings. An excellent idea worth noting is to set a precedent by being highly organized and providing exactly what the vendor will need to fulfill the demand—a sloppy art director can't expect much more. Another point to consider is properly reading your audience. Depending on where you are located, cultural rules are better followed than not. If you are in an area where politeness and a certain amount of small talk precede business, it might be worthwhile to follow suit. Enrolling other people's help and enthusiasm by respecting their cultural expectations will most likely satisfy your time constraints and produce a better product.

Minding the Budget

Adjustment reflects the dynamic nature of a set budget. Set overages will occur as a result of directorial request, acts of God, or actor availability, but usually happen as a result of a director modifying a creative decision. Consider the following scenario: The original decision to digitally film sections of a hero house in flames changes ten days before shooting. Having watched several films as reference during late pre-production phase, the director and cinematographer decide that technology hasn't perfected digital flame and smoke well enough to satisfy the visual and emotional aspects of the storytelling. Instead, the director opts to have a duplicate of the house built as an exterior shell on location for the burning sequence. It is felt that real flames will inspire more compelling performances and dispel any reservations that the director might have about digital flame and smoke.

The emergency meeting that ensues between the producer, or UPM, location manager, construction coordinator, mechanical and visual effects supervisors, the head accountant, and art director might produce the following tactical decisions: 1) The original, two-story house set budgeted at $187,000 primarily as an onstage cover set, per the director's request, will now cost twice as much. For starters, the art director might suggest building a 3" = 1" exterior miniature of the house constructed in high detail, shooting it digitally and compositing in smaller scale, real flame and smoke. 2) In addition, sections of the interior could be duplicated as greenscreen floors, walls, and ceilings, incorporating fire pipe and figuring multiple-burn takes onstage. Shot digitally, the real flames could be used in full size or in miniature for both interior and exterior scenes to be shot. 3) The foreground action could also be composited with the mid-ground flames and background interior shots of the house. 4) With some quick figuring by the three supervisors present, the additions by combining construction, visual, and mechanical effects' budgets arrive at an additional cost of $85K or $282K total cost. Your producer will most likely be satisfied with a $94K savings over the $374K total cost of building a duplicate set on location. If agreed upon, this solution would minimally compromise all budgets involved, would give the director what she wants, and aesthetically enhance the final product. It is questionable whether this scenario might ever happen or resolve itself in this way. Quick thinking and collaboration are key points to consider in this kind of emergency situation. In order to more fully convince the director, photographic and film examples of proven successes with miniatures, fire, and digital compositing work of all participants will help sell the idea.

Although the idea works for those at the tactical meeting, the director might remain unconvinced. Variations of the solution should exist as options. One of the options will prevail, at which point, all department heads will speed the respective changes along within the scope of the new budget item and the blessing of the producers. Scenarios like this are creative shell games an art director and other department heads manipulate to adequately shift the weight of impromptu decisions to balance the budget. It happens on every show. Experience is the determining factor in making the right solutions happen.

Keeping a Chronicle

Entering daily agenda data into a PDA is a foolproof way to chronicle art department events. A Palm Pilot® is an indispensable organizing tool but backup detail is also important. Even if blessed with a photographic memory, a written documentation of a phone conversation with a vendor or crewmember will help jog a memory working on overtime, recalling data items like budget figures and shooting schedule details. You can't remember everything so put it down on paper or save it electronically as an Adobe Acrobat file.

I've found that keeping a personal diary and a separate production notebook are helpful. Packets of five spiral-bound, letter-size notebook pads are inexpensive, and the end of a show fills all five. The notebook pages are dated and provide an informational base for organizers, vendor forms, check requests, etc. Idea sketches, design development, and graphic explanations accompanying conversations link the note taking between the pages. At the end of each week, it's a good idea to have the entries photocopied and kept by the art coordinator as a backup when the notebook is sitting at home or lost.

A database of vendors, contacts, and networking information can also be created from the notebook or its copy. Your art coordinator can create this data file in Microsoft Access. If you find yourself on location with WiFi access, then the information is easily uploaded or downloaded from laptop to laptop. By the end of the show, this database list and other printed material collected in a 4" binder becomes the art department production binder. This tome of visual and written data becomes your bible in post-production phase or for re-shoots of various sections of the movie.

Protecting the Crew

In general terms, the well-being of the art department crew, including the production designer, must be ensured. Optimal physical and psychological conditions enhance optimal performance. Obstacles need to be constantly removed, even to the point of providing comic relief to cut the level of stress and promote a positive working vibe. "Quote of the day," shared emails, and contests keep the laughs coming and the atmosphere relaxed. Creatives seem to work best in this type of minimal stress, maximal inspiration environment. On more reasonably scheduled shows, I insist on the art crew leaving the premises for lunch and organizing regular group lunches or dinners whenever possible. Also, enforcing regular morning and afternoon breaks are refreshing segues to all the intense work and stress it generates. Personally, getting regular exercise and eating well have proven beneficial to manage continuing physical, mental, and emotional health. Bottom line is: consistent communication and cheerleading make a difference.

POST-PRODUCTION

Finishing Up

A typical show will have an art director and art department operating at top speed through the last day of principal photography—slow, steady easing off of workload is rare and should be enjoyed. Take advantage of being in production mode during the last week of shooting by reconnecting with your network and announcing your imminent availability for a new project. In the meantime, there is still much work to do.

Archiving

An art director's principal activity after the last formal day of shooting is archiving, as it provides the basis for the other categories included in this section. This process should have been an ongoing one since your first weeks in the art department, and it concludes with the organizing of final documents and images into both the art department production manual and its digital counterpart in database format. With the continued help of the art coordinator and archivist, this final task can be swift and comprehensive.

Wrapping the Art Department

Unless the art department is located in a furnished office suite found in any of the L.A. Studio complexes, the physical activities of returning rental furniture, Xerox and fax machines, $\frac{1}{2}$" tape players, DVD players and monitors, and the boxing physical models, prototype props, document and drafting duplicates all fall within the jurisdiction of the art coordinator and PA staff. For anyone in the department who has generated creative documents, files, or prints, it is a time to collect copies for portfolio use in the ensuing job hunt. Legally, all artwork created for the show is the property of the studio or producing entity, and it must be packaged for storage.

Wrapping Hero Sets

The art director is more involved in the process of dismantling sets. Hero sets are of special importance, but all built sets are "folded" and held in a designated storage facility until the show has officially wrapped. Once the director has determined exactly what scenes need to be re-shot, the art director and construction coordinator can discuss which sets will be discarded or refurbished for additional photography. It is rare for any hero scenery to be inventoried at a studio's storage facility unless there are plans for a sequel.

Re-shoots

The shooting schedule for a film is prescribed at 60–70 days. When a UPM figures the length of the shooting schedule, a fairly accurate, educated guess determines that decision. So many factors are considered that any one of them has the potential to shift and consequently affect the others. "Making the schedule" is the positive attitude everyone adopts throughout the shooting process, and it is rarely compromised. In cases of mechanical failure, accident, or natural disaster, days are lost and must be retrieved.

Re-shoots typically happen at the end of principal photography and might also include problematic scenes needing to be re-worked for physical, timing, or aesthetic reasons. Depending on how extensive the list of scenes, one can figure on an additional two to three weeks of work. This process should not interfere with post-production editing and must happen as quickly as possible. It requires a greatly reduced number of crew and equipment. The most logical head of the re-shoot crew is the 2nd Unit director accompanied by key shooting crew personnel and key department representatives required by the new shooting schedule. Re-shoots are mini-productions and should not be confused with "pick-ups" or close-up shots never gotten during the production schedule.

With new shooting schedule and one-liners in hand, a short production meeting is held to discuss the scope of the next few weeks. Interior sets marked for re-shooting are spotted onto the ground plan of a warehouse or available stage floor; sets are then erected, rigged, retouched with paint, and redressed. Exterior locations are prepped according to the specs of the new shooting schedule, and the process continues with daily call sheets until final day of wrap. After a month of down time, the director returns to begin the post-production process, editing in the additional material with the rest of the footage already in the can.

Sequels

Having worked on the first film of several headed for sequel status doesn't guarantee steady employment. Interviewing for the next job and getting it is the only sure guarantee of employment. One might expect the original production designer to be hired back to design a sequel in order to maintain an outstanding visual look for the next film in the series, but this also is not guaranteed. The phrase, "You're only as good as your last job," certainly comes to play in this situation. In general terms, the only thing that *will* guarantee that you work at all is a steady track record with your designer, director, and producers. An art director is in an enviable position to be all things to all people. Attend to your position, perform outstandingly, and leave without any regrets—it's all you can do.

Tossing your name in the hat and being called back to art direct a sequel is a turn of great luck and an advantage to you. Your last efforts on the previous film have left you with the art department production book, a larger database, and a research-rich digital image file. Even if the production designer or a new director will not be following the same visual path, this is certainly a good place to begin. Main hero sets in storage will certainly be considered for use—and that includes the built props and dressing that furnishes them. No doubt some of your past images and ideas might also be considered, and your experience will be respected. At this point in time, you can pat yourself on the back for a job well done.

Landing the Next Job or Taking a Vacation

The instability of keeping actively employed in the movie industry compels most lifers to accept whatever projects are offered in order to remain solvent. The mixture of a slight bit of workaholic ethic and superstition prevents the enjoyment of our time off between jobs—there are few people who actually know how to relax and catch a breath. For some, working on location is vacation enough; for others, the buzz of just doing what they love day in and out, precludes the thought of some time off. Phil Dagort has this to say:

☐   *At the end of your process, when do you begin your search for the next job?* I'm not especially good at that kind of multi-tasking. I've always been a one-job-at-a-time kind of person. Maybe by the time the job is winding down, I just want time off. Plus, a lot of my daily phone time is devoted to multi-tasking on the current work. I usually don't have time to make calls about another job. If I did, I wouldn't be doing the current job very well.

     Lately, on smaller to medium projects we are working like crazy up to our last day. A week or two after the project has wrapped is when I begin my phone calling, after enough down time to just change gears. If I plan anything first it's a vacation after a job ends, and that's the first week after wrap. The next job usually waits until after that. But once I've returned, there's going to be at least a month of job-hunting for the next project, sometimes more.[1]

Playtime is just as critical as making a living. Taking time to recharge by doing nothing, catching up on reading, taking a short class, or jumping into a favorite hobby needs some serious consideration. This has to be said because there are people who overlook the opportunity. The truth is that there will always be a new show to jump onto, most often when you least want it or expect it.

ENDNOTE

1. Phil Dagort interview, 6/06/04, Toluca Lake, CA.

CHAPTER 9

Networking and Self-Promotion

This category is a purely selfish one. Networking is how we create careers. It incorporates every aspect of our managing skills and our personalities into what an interviewer sees and how this person is convinced to hire us. Self-promotion is a place where *you* get to be the product or service. If you were going to market yourself, how would you begin? Probably the best way is to define your target audience. The production designer is your obvious target market, but you will also be interviewing with the UPM to negotiate your deal memo. Each prospect in your target market will be receptive to different metaphors and some will overlap.

INTERVIEWING

Production designers expect loyalty, amenability, creative thinking, leadership, follow-through, and attention to detail. Unit production managers expect attention to detail, follow-through, leadership, budget focus, frugality, and flexibility. Notice the overlaps and the outliers. Tweaking the *outlier* attributes addresses the niche market you happen to be playing to at the moment; the middle range or overlapping attributes cover the normal range. These guidelines are worth thinking about before interviewing with the designer or the UPM. Lack of experience is a blatant non-attribute. Projecting the qualities you do have is sometimes more convincing than a range of experience. Think about your personal qualities and prepare your "pitch" that will indicate who you are, what your accomplishments are, skills you have, where your passions lie, and what job you are seeking. The point is, be honest and sincere. Although you are playing to a particular audience during an interview, your focus isn't artifice—the greatest actors come from a place of sincerity and honesty in order to create believability. Reading your audience at the time of an interview, or understanding who you are playing to at the moment is the key: you are a mirror for the PD or UPM as you sell yourself, playing back to that person an eager romantic who once sat where you are sitting. Project a positive, likeable memory, and you most likely will be hired. The fascinating thing is that we tend to surround ourselves with likenesses of ourselves as it provides a good comfort zone. Using these parameters for an interview and landing the job are the payoff of a good networking strategy.

THE NETWORKING PROCESS

The networking process that unfolds before getting a job interview provides the foundation for a solid career. Networking style varies among people. Those strategies used by highly successful people in any given industry are worth analyzing for obvious reasons. Catherine Hardwicke, director (*Lords of Dogtown, Thirteen*) and production designer (*Laurel Canyon, Vanilla Sky, Three Kings, Two Days in the Valley, Tank Girl*), recalls her early years working on films like *Thrashin'* (1986), *Mr. Destiny* (1990), *and Tombstone* (1993), and provides insight as a designer, screenwriter, and director.

☐ *As I remember you telling the story, you were too creative for architecture and encouraged not to be an architect. How did you react to that news—was it difficult to hear?*
(Soft laugh.) Exactly (Overlapping.) Yes, it was because I had worked for five years in college, and I had busted my butt and I loved it. Then at the end of it, my instructors said that my creativity would be so stifled doing just architecture that I'd probably be disappointed. They predicted I would be put in a box and just be asked to do the graphics for the firm. Needless to say, it didn't sound too good, but I did immediately go and make my own project as an architect: a 20-acre subdivision containing 120 townhouses. That was really fun, but people wanted me to re-create the same look again and again. Since I had created this successful design, new clients only wanted that, but I didn't want to repeat myself—at that point I had already thought that design was kind of boring. I wanted to do something wilder. That's why I *thought* film would give me the opportunity to do more creative stuff. It's just not always the case. (Big laugh.) On most projects you're asked to re-create reality. Unfortunately, there aren't that many *Cat in the Hat* projects around.

☐ *Having had some solid architectural training, did you also take courses on directing?*
I fulfilled a five-year professional degree in architecture, then I worked as an architect and contractor for three years, then I went to UCLA grad school for film for one year and studied animation and live-action. I made a small animation/live-action film that won a Focus Award. An agent at the awards festival for the film noticed me and signed me because I had also written a screenplay with Michael Werb (*Lara Croft: Tomb Raider*), while we were at UCLA. After the film was greenlit and budgeted, the head of the studio changed, and it never happened. Not soon after, I met a producer dancing in a club here in L.A., who was working on a skateboard movie. Knowing I was an architect, he suggested I production design his movie called *Thrashin'* (1986). I didn't know or understand the names of the categories of PD or Art

Director at the time but it was a non-union film, so I did everything on a creative level. I also hired three people on my staff who stayed at my house or lived in the art department truck. It was a $1M movie, but I learned a lot and met all these famous skateboarders who I'm working with again on my current movie, *Lords of Dogtown*, which I have directed. (Giggle.) Full circle. It's all come full circle. So, I accidentally, randomly wandered into art direction and loved it. After that I got offered many other movies.

When I first moved here I didn't know anybody in L.A. or the film business. After I got that first job by dancing like a crazy person, I continued going to the clubs. People would meet me, dance with me, and hire me. (Raucous laugh).

☐ *So, for anyone who is coming up in the ranks, is studying architecture essential for designing?*
It's really fantastic. I've had mostly architecturally trained people work for me. By the way, Carnegie Mellon has a theater design program that's just as hard-core and radical as UCLA. I think anything can work, but the architecture is clearly helpful. If I were advising somebody, I would suggest that and also photography. AFI has a great production design program, as well as UCLA. Any well-known film school program will do. And . . . of course, there's no substitute for just working in the business.

☐ *In your early career, then, did you do any art directing?*
After designing several movies in the $3–4M range, I decided to do bigger movies at the higher end of the independent film range. I found an agent who suggested I art direct for a designer one time for a studio feature. That's why I took *Mr. Destiny* (1990) as an art director. The experience taught me what I needed to know about the studio system. It's the only art direction job I had.

☐ *Would you give us your thoughts on three aspects of designing low budget films by addressing these questions: 1) What is a good deal vs. a bad deal? 2) Is screen credit enough or should you ask for more, and 3) How do you resolve creative vision vs. budget?*
As a director, I just made *Thirteen* (2003), a $1.5M film. Carol Strober, my production designer, had to work under the same constraints I did about thirteen years ago. In retrospect, it was fascinating to see how you pull it off with no money and lots of passion and inspiration. To answer all of your questions, my best advice is: If you think the director is prepared and talented, and the script has integrity, then commit yourself. With those two things in place, it's a good indication that the project could get released and might see the light of day, and then it doesn't matter if you get paid. The goal is to work on a good movie. Always try to work with the best people you can. This could jump-start a career faster than anything else. Then if you have an opportunity to contribute to a project headed by a talented director, writer, and producer—well—anything could happen. Once you're in, you need to put your heart and soul into it every minute of every day and do whatever it takes to be the best you can possibly be.

Last year at Sundance, there were 900 entries. That means 900 art directors and production designers worked on 900 movies probably for free or little money on Indie movies. Twelve made it above the competition to finally be screened at the festival. Our little movie was one of those. The people who worked with me were paid a box of dirt, almost nothing, but they busted their butts, and the movie was not only good but also recognized. For them, having *Thirteen* on a resume as an Oscar nominated movie has to help a helluva lot more than getting paid a decent wage.

So, you've got to find a way to get to the good people. Join IFP West,[1] volunteer at the film schools in L.A., find out who has something special that's going to make a good Indy film. Then do anything to work on it. On *Thirteen*, even though I was the director, the set decorating five-ton truck backed up to my house and took half of my stuff to the set. My current movie, *Lords of Dogtown*, is a $30M for Sony, but still we took stuff out of my house. Having an attitude of entitlement isn't going to do anybody any good. You're only going to succeed if you work real hard and your work is great.

☐ *Thank you. You nailed it. What did you enjoy or not enjoy about art directing?*
I like the whole process: coming up with an idea and seeing it built five minutes later [Laugh], and making it look good, and having to solve unseen problems. I like all those challenges. I like to have to come in on a budget. In some ways I think it makes your job better. You have to be more creative.

I don't like the politics: figuring out which producer to go to in order to get on your side to release more money for a set or pay people to stay on an extra day. There's always the psychological game playing. If the director doesn't have as much vision as you have, then it's your challenge to convince them that your idea is their idea. The trick with that is to get him or her excited or inspired but not overwhelmed by you. As an art director, your biggest challenge is how you manage your crew. Most of those people are artists and that can make it more stressful for an art director to make the experience a creative one for everyone in the art department. It's hard to have your crew understand that they are significant and are making a substantial contribution. It's just hard to do your job and to keep all those artistic temperaments happy—that's the biggest challenge for an art director. Most of us never went to business school; most of us were never trained in management styles. I'm sure that hundreds of decisions I have had to make in my career could have been solved more easily if I had had a couple of management courses under my belt. When I finally started catching on, I realized that when I was talking to the line producer/production manager they only care about one thing—that I'm doing something smart for them. I'd come up with an idea that saves money. I'd recycle this set into that set or reconfigure scenery in other ways. I'd have to tell them about my ideas in terms that they'd understand. When I go to interviews, I not only take drawings and photographs, but I take budgets, just in case a line producer is sitting in on the interview.

☐ *What qualities do you expect and prefer in an art director?*
Super-organized. Someone who is so organized that even if they're out on a job site, I can go to their desk and look at a copy of their notebook or a PC file

to get the information I need. Now more than ever, I need someone who is multi-talented and can jump on the computer and do great stuff. Also, I always consider someone who's creative and provides good ideas and contributes to the process. You know, I just want the best person on the planet—someone that blows *me* away.

☐ *Describe your designing process. How do you previsualize?*
Different projects require different processes. Some projects are historical and require research. What does Iraq look like now? On *Three Kings* (1999) that was all just research for me at first, and then I started getting excited about it through the process. We called the Kuwaiti Embassy, found lots more research, and investigated newspaper footage. And then sometimes it's more imagination where you do just, "Ahhhh—I'm going to design the coolest set." And, I then just start sketching out something crazy. So, it really depends on the project.

☐ *Have new technologies made your relationships with the director easier or more challenging?*
Easier. It helps you to see how things might look a lot faster. It's a plus.

☐ *Generally, how do you create a healthy relationship with your visual effects coordinator?*
The projects I've done have not been as visual effects intensive as Alex McDowell's have. On my former projects somehow, instantly, because visual effects people are all great artists, we just end up sharing fun ideas and inspiring one another. It's more inclusive and about being a fun, creative process. I've really just had super-positive experiences. In my post-work for *Dogtown*, I'm having a great relationship with Gray Marshall, of Gray Matter, who is doing our visual effects. I stop at his office on the way to do post at Sony to work out ideas and do sketches. It's fun, and I love it. I worked at a visual effects company when I first got here while at UCLA so I have some understanding of what's currently being done.

☐ *How can the art department operate more smoothly?*
Every member of the staff is vital. From the art coordinator to the PA, everyone can potentially make a vital contribution. On *Tombstone* (1993), a non-union film, my art department PA became an art director by the end of the movie. Chris Gorak is now a big production designer. On the same movie, there were seven people with master's degrees in architecture on my staff, so everybody was brilliant. Everybody was able to leap to the challenge with more or less experience in film. It made the project a success.

☐ *So, do you think the visual effects and art departments are beginning to merge with all the sharing and overlapping that's going on at this time?*
Yes and no. Finishing my current movie, the art department production people are going to be gone when a lot of the heavy visual effects start. That's an interesting question that needs to get figured out over time. How much does a production designer stay actively involved in post? When do the overlaps occur and how can they be positive, especially with new advancements coming into play? On past movies when I was off payroll,

I was involved with the visual effects people because I wanted to be. There's always more to know.[2]

Other art directors' job finding experiences are worth considering. Excerpts from longer interviews with Gae Buckley, Phil Dagort, Steve Saklad, Christa Munro, and Linda Berger provide equally valuable examples of networking strategy.

Gae Buckley

(The Sisterhood of the Traveling Pants, Coyote Ugly, What Women Want)

As a child I studied painting and drawing with my mother, an artist. I also worked as an architect in NYC and wondered about continuing when I got an offer to work on a music video. The next year I worked in music videos in many different aspects of production, but still decided to try architecture again. Another friend called to lure me into scenic painting and art directing music videos, commercials, and small TV shows. Beyond that, my goal was to be in Los Angeles working on features. I moved there from New York in 1988.

When I arrived in L.A., I knew no one. I was first hired in a set building shop as a sculptor on a commercial. The next commercial they hired me as a scenic painter, and the next as a set designer. Soon after, Penny Hadfield, the queen of MOWs and mini-series, called to ask me to be a set designer. A few weeks later, Cynthia Charette, the art director, left to design a Wes Craven movie so I moved into her position. Penny and I worked together for a couple of years and when I left her I began my career as a feature art director.

☐ *The process is different for everyone. And, if we dig a little deeper, the network lines will emerge.*
Well, the reason I got the job with Penny was because Cynthia Charette had just come off a show in Boston, and I had worked with some Boston crew in New York. She had heard my name so when I arrived in L.A. she recognized it, and I was hired. So, yes, it was that direct and that simple.[3]

Phil Dagort

(Six Feet Under, X-Files, The Hunted, Hard Target)

☐ *After graduating architecture school, how did you begin your film career?*
The irony is that soon after I graduated with an architectural degree in the late seventies there was a recession. There were not as many jobs as before I started and with a shrunken architectural market, the film business was the perfect place to look for a job. Of course, I had planned to do this all along. My parents just wanted me to have a degree to "fall back on." Little did I know I was way ahead of my time. After I got into the industry, people I went to school with were calling looking for work.

When I first started in the business, like most people, I knew no one. I began by getting designers' names and setting up interviews, and I suppose I did this by six degrees of separation: somebody knows somebody who knows somebody. I asked everyone I knew and finally had a list. Only one designer I met actually had an opening for an assistant, but during my interview he was dwelling on my lack of experience and familiarity in knowing where to shop for set dressing. At another interview the same day, I met Debbie Hemela. She was selling this guide for set dressing that she had just completed. So I bought one and turned around and went back to the interview I had just left, placed the book on his desk, and said, "Now I know where to find stuff." The designer then hired me on the spot. So, I guess landing a first job is about a bit of chutzpah and a bit of luck. (That book has now blossomed into *Debbie's Book*.) I went right to work and learned on the job, mistakes and all. In the beginning, I came up into the business as an assistant in videotape where we all crossed over job positions. We drafted the set first, supervised set going into the shop for building and finishes, and then went out and shopped the set dressing. Videotape at the time wasn't governed by the film agreements, so the benefit was that it was excellent overall training ground to learn all the pieces of the puzzle.

Now my process for finding work or hiring people is based on whom I like to work with because of their taste and how well we get on. I look at the *Hollywood Reporter* to get a sense of what's going on and that might springboard me into a possible job contact, but I tend to refer to my list of every person I met and have worked with which I started at the very beginning of my career. The list just builds on itself. It might take 20 years, but an original contact might eventually land me a new work situation.[4]

Steve Saklad

(*Spiderman 2, Red Dragon, The Mambo Kings*)

☐ *Explain your networking process going from Yale Drama School to film.*
Out of Yale, I first assisted Broadway set designers David Mitchell and later Tony Walton on a series of Broadway plays and musicals. During the eighties in New York City, I was typically involved in segueing between assistant art directing/drafting on movies and working as assistant designer on Broadway shows. I first met art director, W. Steven Graham, when he hired me to draft on *Radio Days* in 1985, and later hired me to work as a set designer for Stuart Wurtzel on *Old Gringo* in 1988. Stuart and I hit it off, and eventually it was Stuart who gave me my first shot at art directing for him when we made *Mermaids* in 1989. I attribute the rest of my film career to Steve and Stuart, as these two connected me with a solid networking base in film. In the early nineties, there was a lockout by the West coast studios against the New York unions' demands for better pay scales. Most movie work dried up, signaling a large exodus for many of us to the West coast. Knowing no one in L.A. at first and waiting for East coast designers coming west with projects-in-hand, I began designing commercials for TV. For the last ten years, my career has

bounced back and forth between designing commercials and art directing on features.

I never seem to know what my next project will be while I'm still working on the current one. That's where designing commercials for the same director/producer team since 1994 has been a godsend for me. By 2000, I'd chosen an agent at ICM to represent me for commercial design on the proviso that he would make his percentage from all projects other than this particular commercial company I had already secured. One great dividend from my connection with ICM has been a growing relationship with their team of agents devoted to feature films. It was one of those who secured my first feature film design job, *Shadowboxer*. Now the question presents itself: Do I want to art direct a $50M movie or wait around for the next low budget script I can design? Even the small Indie project to design can be more satisfying in a way that the biggest summer blockbuster to art direct may not. Ultimately, as a creative person, I get to try it all as a production designer in a way that you don't as an art director.

☐ *Any advice for working on Indies?*
You only get to be a virgin once. The idea of throwing away that status on a Santa Claus-gore-fest-horror-thriller shot in Canada is something to think hard about, considering you might become known as the designer of gore movies. The important things to consider are the script, a credible director, and notable actors. Then you have something; you have credibility, a calling card.[5]

Christa Munro

(*Erin Brockovich, Forces of Nature, Hope Floats*)

☐ *Did the beginnings of your networking experience grow out of the theater, art school, or something else?*
While working in a local art store connected with the Art Center here in L.A., I was aware of this guy who graduated from Art Center who I would bug for freelance work. One afternoon he came into the store and offered me a job. He needed drawings for large-scale models he was working on at his studio for the ancient library of Alexandria, Egypt for Carl Sagan's show, *The Cosmos*. We went over to Paramount Studios to check in on how the shooting crew was getting on with the models and *Wham!* That was the beginning of it. It was like giant doors had been thrown open by a cool gust of wind on a hot day. I continued on that project until it wrapped. Through the contacts I made there, I was introduced to some L.A. companies that did commercials, a couple of the feature contacts, and it just took off from there. Eventually, the networking lines crisscrossed back to my college acquaintances at Art Center who had continued into filmmaking. We reconnected, started working together doing *Playboy* projects, and having a ball. Needless to say, this was a classic networking experience. Combined with your technical skills, it's the people skills that make a career—and for that matter, what moves the whole industry.

☐ *How do you handle the stress?*

As you know, the 14-hour days, five days a week, in addition to any weekend work make it overwhelming. Playing polo is really the only activity I do that totally overrides the effects of the work schedule because you have to be extremely focused on the game at hand. I guess the intensity of one has to equally balance the other.[6]

Linda Berger

(Angelmaker, Forrest Gump, Death Becomes Her)

☐ *Linda, what's your networking story?*

It's pretty brilliant—not my brilliance—but I essentially did it twice: once in 1985 in videotape and then in 1990 with film.

Let me quickly backtrack. From the age of 11, I knew I wanted to design films after seeing a double billing re-release of *The Man Who Shot Liberty Valance* and *Forbidden Planet*. Watching two films of totally diverse genres told me that the sky was the limit. Creatively, it was possible to design a black-and-white historical Western, or a Technicolor, cinemascope sci-fi drama based on Shakespeare's *Tempest*. Another film that deeply impressed me even earlier was *Helen of Troy* (1956)—it was one of the first films I ever saw. I was very young and my Dad took me—he loved historical epics and he wanted me to see this one. I still remember how I felt when I first saw the giant horse onscreen. When I met Ken Adam—to be able to ask him about working on that film as an assistant AD was a high point in my life.

Determined to creatively be in both worlds, I went to the Goodman Theater and Art Institute of Chicago as a theatrical designer and fine artist in a magnificent reciprocity program that no longer exists. Soon after graduating, I lost track of a fellow lighting designer classmate, Edgar Swift, who was one of my very best friends all through school. The CBS affiliate television studio in Seattle hired me as an art director. I did everything from news graphics, *TV Guide* ads, PSAs (public service announcements), sets for Special Programs, and a Sunday 60 Minutes-style news show called *KIRO Newsline*. I also did hundreds of commercials for a related in-house commercial production company. I did J.C. Penney's regional/national commercials there. This all tested my creativity and earned me several Emmy nominations and an Emmy Award. Photographs of some of my work were published in a book put out by the Broadcast Designers Association. The head of the art department of ABC in Los Angeles at the time saw my work, and we got in touch. He extended the invitation to see him at ABC when I came down next. Once there during my interview, he gave me my first networking list of television contacts, including the Head of Operations and Supervising Head of the Art Department at NBC, Ed Swift. I did not make the connection. I was escorted into his office, and there was Edgar, my art school friend. He took my portfolio, put it in a corner, and took me out to lunch. I couldn't believe my eyes. We were both flabbergasted. It was outrageous. But it was wonderful. That was the beginning of my five years at NBC.

It's never been easy, but it's always astonishing. I feel like I'm riding on a train watching the ever-changing scenery and stepping off along the way to explore—then stepping back on to enjoy the ride—not having a clue about where I'm headed, but I know it's somewhere wonderful.

In 1990 came a second serendipitous and lucky opportunity via a connection at Paramount Studios. I was aware that Hermann Zimmerman (*Star Trek: Nemesis, First Contact, and Generations*), whose work I admired, was on the Paramount lot so I took a chance and knocked on the door of his office. I thought that perhaps he might give me an appointment for an interview later, but instead he invited me in right then to speak with him. What a wonderful thing! (Little did I know then that literally one brave chance would change everything for me and send me off into a new direction—one I had actually been striving toward since I was a young girl of about eleven—to design motion pictures.) Anyway, I always had my portfolio with me so Hermann Zimmerman looked through every page. I asked lots of questions, and he gave me really helpful direction and advice and real encouragement about my potential and design skills. I described working at NBC among many other assignments, as an assistant to the late John Shrum, creator of the *Johnny Carson Show* settings and many of the now classic television shows. John had spoken with great pride about one of his earlier assistants, Hermann Zimmerman, and I related John's story and my pleasure at having had the opportunity to work with this great early television designer, for he had been so wonderful to me. Toward the end of our talk, Zimmerman graciously offered to call J. Michael Riva (*Charlie's Angels, Congo, The Color Purple*) on my behalf, and as a result I was able to get an appointment to see him the following week. I went to the Columbia Pictures lot, now Sony Pictures, and J. Michael Riva and I sat and talked for at least an hour. He gave me excellent advice, a lot of encouragement, and thought enough of my work to give me a list of the names and phone numbers of 15 people to see, including Patrizia von Brandenstein, Albert Brenner, Dick Sylbert, and Rick Carter. The final person on this list I saw was Rick Carter (*Polar Express, Forrest Gump, Jurassic Park*), who was working in a trailer at Universal Studios filled with drawings and concept models as he prepared the initial ideas for the future *Jurassic Park*. There were the most amazing drawings and illustrations on every wall—models of the future buildings of the island—and dinosaurs everywhere. Like the others, he was so very generous with his time and willingness to offer great advice and direction. Several weeks later I invited him to lunch to talk again. I asked lots of questions, and his advice and insights were of great value to me. To my great surprise and excitement, several months later he called and invited *me* to lunch with him and his Art Director, Jim Teegarden; it was then that they offered me the chance to work with them as an assistant art director on *Death Becomes Her*.

Earlier in the process of enjoying the gift of this wonderful list Michael Riva had given me, I had the great opportunity to interview with Richard Sylbert (*The Bonfire of the Vanities, Dick Tracy, Splendor in the Grass*). Talking with Dick Sylbert was really a lesson in designing film scenery when the conversation moved to the film *A Face in the Crowd* (1957) he designed with his twin brother, Paul, for Elia Kazan, and starring Andy Griffith. I asked him about designing this film because I felt the settings were so powerfully evocative of the story, and I wanted to understand why. One of the last images in the film had stayed with me since I first saw the film: Griffith's character's penthouse apartment with the bridge-like path in front of huge windows leading from a tall winding staircase. He explained how the scenery clearly defined how the main character keeps going up in life, but really goes nowhere after all. Through my discussion with Dick, I learned how images could be symbolic for storytelling and character analysis; this clearly showed how he designed character development into his films. I was later thrilled to be asked to join his art department on *The Witching Hour*, a project that had a couple false starts and then never happened. Sylbert was a mentor to Rick Carter so I was doubly fortunate.

When I was hired by Rick Carter on *Death Becomes Her* as assistant art director, Rick went to Gene Allen, the head of the Art Directors Guild, on my behalf to plead my case because I had only worked in "tape" in L.A. After a long process of filling out forms, petitioning the Guild with my record of working hours at NBC, and submitting the full body of my work, I was given the status I needed. I owe it all to Rick Carter—and of course, Hermann Zimmerman.

We had to shoot several endings for *Death Becomes Her*, and I was asked to art direct the re-shoots while Rick and Jim Teegarden, art director, were in Hawaii beginning pre-production for *Jurassic Park*. I ran everything I needed to do by Rick and then shepherded the last part of the movie for him. I later joined them on *Jurassic Park* and later again on *Forrest Gump*.

Rick had such tremendous trust and respect for those of us who worked closely with him. What I learned most from Rick was that the art department must be a place of pleasure and respect where it was our job to simply create the movie. Rick ran political interference for us so we could do just that. That was a particularly wonderful experience for me.[7]

PAYING DUES

Your film relationships are your most vital resource. The maxim, "You're only as good as your last job" must have originated in Hollywood. From what I've seen, people are hired primarily for attitude, especially newcomers whose skill level is questionable. So, be prepared to do whatever it takes, even if it means erasing your personal life for the duration of a project. Eve Light Honthaner, author of *The Complete Film Production Handbook*, reinforces this point: "The trick is to be the very best production assistant, runner, apprentice, or secretary that ever existed. Short of being totally abused and terribly exploited, don't whine or groan when asked to do something you don't want to do. Accept tasks willingly. No one is asking you to do anything just to make your life miserable. If it has to be done and falls within your sphere of responsibility, you don't have much choice. Do not complain. Everyone is busy, and no one wants to hear it. Be a pleasure to have around; be a team player and if you have any extra time, volunteer to help others with their work. Everyone will agree that you are wonderful, and they will all want you to work on their next picture and the next one after that."[8]

As harsh as it sounds, the people who hire you want to see total commitment. The harsher fact is the line around the building is long, and we are all replaceable. The positive side is that the rewards of going the distance are reaped by eager recommendations at the end of a film project. Sublimating your will and life to the project proves that you "are one of us" and that you have the stamina for the process. When the baptism of fire is over, calls will begin to fill up your voice mailbox and email.

FAQs

I am constantly asked a handful of questions that might be of help here:

☐ *Do I need a degree to work in the art department?*
No, a degree for art department work is not necessary. Solid training in a reputable film school or university or college film program or art school is preferred—the degree is secondary to the school attended and academic training experience.

☐ *Which are the best education choices?*
With film design in mind, a school choice should complement your personality and needs. A film school per se will stress technique, theory, and hands-on experience, university or college education might be more general in scope but might offer excellent computer graphics courses, art schools will focus on hand skills and computer skills that directly refer to art department creative work. In addition to these suggestions, you must do a good deal of research here in order to tailor your training to your temperament.

☐ *What should I study?*
With film design in mind, you should study architectural drafting, art history, cinematography, and CADD or computer-assisted drawing and drafting software.

☐ *Which computer programs are most important to know?*
You must have a solid working skill level with Adobe Photoshop & Illustrator, Macromedia Director, AutoCAD, and Vector Works. A good, basic understanding of Maya or 3D Studio Max will help navigate the modeling environments. Microsoft Office Suite, especially Word, Excel, and Access, is an important software package to know extremely well because it will help you correctly interface with other film departments and keep yourself organized.

☐ *What other skills are necessary?*
Communicating ideas through drawing and sketching are paramount skills. Well-developed interpersonal and social skills are the basis of the collaborative nature of the film business. The rest is found in Section Two of this book.

☐ *Should I work as a production assistant first?*
If it is the only job available in the art department, it is an excellent place to begin hands-on education. Experience on one non-union film from the first days of pre-production to the last days of art department wrap provides a good basis for all you will need to know for the rest of your career as an art director or designer.

☐ *Are there sources for lists of art department jobs?*
Trade papers including *The Hollywood Reporter*, *Daily Variety*, and *Below the Line* magazine should be checked regularly for shows in development or various stages of prep with pertinent information on resume submission. Also industry related Web sites such as LA411.com, Crew411.com, and TheAcme.com are all indispensable for posting a resume through modest membership fees. Spiral, printed versions of these sites are also available, as well as other helpful industry site links found on these Web sites. Appendix A of this book contains FILM-POCKET LISTINGS, covering movie industry categories and accompanying Web addresses, as well as other resources for additional information.

☐ *Do I have to live in Los Angeles?*
The film industry is now global. Presently, international hot spots are located in Canada, Mexico, Australia, New Zealand, Czech Republic, England, France, and Germany. In the U.S. filmmaking centers are currently located in New York, Florida, and North Carolina. What's been outlined above are major centers of film activity; in addition to being global, moviemaking is done locally at every level.

Doing your research homework for filmmaking in the area you are going to school or living is practical and most often overlooked. For example, you will not only get your feet wet working on an Indie in Buffalo, New York, you also will have invaluable experience and a final crew list of references for your next gig. Using the information outlined above will transport you directly to where you are headed, and might present some unimagined possibility. Organizing the unplanned situations that might randomly appear into opportunities you *can* choose to be helpful stepping stones on your career path is a vital skill that deserves deliberate, creative thought. Call it sorting the chaos or learning to roll with the punches, but developing the ability to make any situation work to your benefit is priceless. Don't dismiss anything or reject an offer because it doesn't perfectly fit the parameters of your goal set. Regardless of how you might have planned your career path, the most unlikely surprises along the way might prove to be the most beneficial in the long run. Taking that temporary job as an assistant editor for two weeks might open another door to designing you hadn't considered or ultimately introduce you to your real niche, revealing that you have been misguiding yourself with thoughts of production designing. If anything, a career in movie work can provide a template for life lessons as well as nourish creativity and career success.

ENDNOTES

1. "The Los Angeles Film Festival, held annually for ten days in June, showcases the best of American and International Independent cinema. With an attendance of over 40,000, the festival screens over 200 narrative features, documentaries, shorts, and music videos. Now in its tenth year, the festival has grown into a world-class event, uniting new filmmakers with critics, scholars, film masters, and the movie-loving public." http://www.lafilmfest.com/faq.htm

2. Catherine Hardwicke interview, 6/22/04, Venice Beach, CA.

3. Gae Buckley interview, 9/04/11, Studio City, CA.

4. Phil Dagort interview, 6/06/04, Toluca Lake, CA.

5. Steve Saklad interview, 8/17/04, Silverlake, CA.

6. Christa Munro interview, 9/11/04, Flintridge, CA.

7. Linda Berger interview, 8/16/04, Studio City, CA.

8. Honthaner, Eve L. *The Complete Film Production Handbook*. Boston: Focal Press, 2001, page 345.

CHAPTER 10

Non-Union vs. Union Status

MAKING THE GRADE OR NOT

A majority of the readers of this book will begin working in the industry with a non-union status. There is great freedom at this level of filmmaking. Not bound by union restrictions, crewmembers are free to double-up on job responsibilities—an especially good thing if you are learning the ropes and need to experience all aspects of your chosen job description. A young art director will work in the art department with an assistant or two, and will most likely be doing research and graphics, designing and drafting scenery, shopping for dressing and hero props, acting as art department coordinator, construction foreman, and lead scenic artist. In the process, an enterprising art director will see to it that both assistants are quickly trained to act as art department coordinators and help with the graphic design, drafting, and dressing search, respectively. Salary and fringe benefits, hovering between 15–20% are lower than union wages and fringe set at 33 percent, but the potential for training in a chosen department and gaining experience, not to mention screen credit, is invaluable.

Many non-union films are shot in **right-to-work** states because film companies are not required to hire crew with union status if they choose not to. Seeking out films on these locations have their drawbacks: neither housing nor per diem will be provided and, as is the case with all non-union films, overtime and penalties associated with union film work will rarely happen. Payment of proper wages is negotiable but not guaranteed. At times these conditions are harsh, but it's important to remember that *everyone* working with you, including the producers, are experiencing the same learning curve. To compensate for the range of advantage and disadvantage, the morale is generally high and the quality of the overall experience reflects the freedom from the non-union situation.

DESIGNING INDIE FILMS

In some ways Indie movie production is a smaller scale version of its commercial Hollywood counterpart; otherwise, it operates as its own animal. Financial constraints force low budget production to be infinitely more creative in format and style, compelling those involved to adopt a more realistic attitude. A smaller, leaner, optimal crew inspires greater creative intimacy and multi-tasking. Creative restrictions force all participants to make decisions out of practicality. Overall, it is an excellent training ground for economy and pragmatism not found elsewhere.

Before we begin, here is a big word of advice: If the financing for the prospective film of your interest has *not been completed*, then walk away. Courteously ask that the director and producer keep you in mind when financing is complete. But, don't stay on a promise; whether they do phone you back or not, they will respect you for your decision. It is terribly disappointing to work passionately on something that may or may not happen. What I'm also suggesting here is to do as much homework before your interview as you possibly can. Use www.imdb.com to properly investigate prior work of Indie producers and directors—the subcategory of "Independent Film" on the title bar of the Web site will link you to pages of very helpful data. Remember that you are interviewing them as much as they are interviewing you.

PRODUCTION VALUE = BUDGETING + SCHEDULING

A designer is hired to develop the visual aesthetic of a film. S/he also gets to be art director, set designer/draftsperson, prop person, mechanical effects supervisor, set decorator, and shopper. Multi-tasking creates long lists, but it affords the eager designer near total visual control. Insist on as many bodies to inhabit the art department as possible and be organized enough to use everyone.

In the commercial film arena, an art director is required to think like a director; in the realm of the Indie, an art director is required to think like a producer. More than aesthetics, budget is the most important obsession. On any given day, a coin toss will resolve this argument, as learning to blend both considerations into an effective solution provides a win-win for all involved. How? The following discussion on budget types based on film size and scheduling based on budget type will answer this question.

Budget

Gone With the Wind (1939) was considered a blockbuster in its time. *Cleopatra* (1963), adjusted for current inflation rates, was the most expensive movie ever made at the end of the twentieth century—its budget of $44 million is equivalent to $270 million in 1999 dollars. Current blockbuster budgets range from $180 to $280 million. Typical Hollywood studios consider making 18–30 films per year for budgets ranging from $40 to $80 million. Inflated actor salaries and the high cost of marketing are reasons for these figures in the upper and middle range movies. Up-and-coming actors and directors, as well as creative teams, make a mark on smaller budget films made by subdivisions of the studios, comprising the lower end of the Hollywood studio range from $20 to $40 million. In general terms, anything falling below $10 to $20 million is considered an Independent film—this

Production Costs for a Less-than-a-Million-Dollar Film		
Accounting code	**Description**	**Amount**
Above-the-Line Costs:		
100	Script	5,570
200	Producer	13,000
300	Director	13,000
400	Talent	36,750
500	Fringes	3,675
Total: Above-the-Line		**71,995**
Pre-Production & Production Costs:		
600	Production staff	18,615
700	Camera staff	11,510
800	Art department staff	17,270
900	Visual effects staff	4,800
1,000	Locations department staff	5,015
1,100	Electrical department staff	6,315
1,200	Grip department staff	3,620
1,300	Sound department/equipment	3,100
1,400	Stunts/SFX	12,470
1,500	Camera rental	11,140
1,600	VFX equipment costs	16,900
1,700	Raw stock/developing	46,365
1,800	Sets/prop rental	20,980
1,900	Locations fees	19,200
2,000	Grip-electrical package	28,485
2,100	Wardrobe/Makeup	16,000
2,200	Transportation	14,760
2,300	Picture vehicles	835
2,400	General office	18,350
2,500	Craft service/catering	17,150
2,600	Police/Fire/Safety	465
2,700	Accommodation	5,570
2,800	Insurance	13,925
2,900	Legal	13,200
Sub-total: Below-the-line		**326,040**

Table 10-1   Sample budget for a Less-than-a-Million-Dollar Film.

Production Costs for a Less-than-a-Million-Dollar Film		
Accounting code	**Description**	**Amount**
Post-Production Costs:		
3,000	Editing	20,000
3,100	Music	3,175
3,200	Post-production Sound	35,235
3,300	**Answer print**	9,140
3,400	Titles and Opticals	10,575
Sub-total: Below-the-line		**78,125**
3,500	Miscellaneous	41,700
3,600	Total: Above-the-line	71,995
3,700	Total: Below-the-line	404,165
3,800	3,600 + 3,700	476,160
3,900	Applicable taxes	39,283
4,000	Contingency	47,616
TOTAL [US Dollars]		**604,759**

Table 10-1   *Continued*

	< < < < O N E W E E K > > > >						L O N G W E E K E N D			
Friday	Saturday	Sunday	Monday	Tuesday	Wednesday	Thursday	Friday	Saturday	Sunday	Monday
Pickup rentals end of day.	< < < < T H E S H O O T I N G S C H E D U L E > > > >									Return rentals early morning.

Table 10-2   Sample rental schedule for a one-week film shoot.

fact will be argued by anyone you might encounter. Regardless, an excellent script supported by passionate, talented artists can attract the attention of or even change the cultural Zeitgeist.

This table features reasonable costs on a film budgeted at less than a million dollars. It was composed to demonstrate how all aspects of a basic film budget are allotted and where the art department monies stand in contrast to the remaining budgeted items. Efficient scheduling of rental items keep limited budget lines in balance. Most low budget shooting schedules are three weeks long, but consider the advantage of a one-week shooting schedule regarding rentals and apply it to three-week schedules.

A three-week shoot is common, but a one-week shoot is smart. You might find yourself shooting 10 pages a day (double the normal 5–6 pages a day), but cast members, especially, will be more eager to commit to it than for three weeks, which translates into a month when all is said and done. With some persuasive coercion, an extended one-week rental can work to the benefit of your limited budget. Your ability to convince a vendor demands that you keep your end of the bargain by returning goods on time with no excuses. Vendors renting props and set dressing to small film companies have heard every story imagined about why a rental item cannot be returned on time. Either return items on time or be prepared to pay another week's rental fee. In the big picture, you are cultivating a customer base here; respect the rules and the intelligence of your vendors, and you will have their loyalty for the duration of your career.

Schedule

Timing is of the absolute essence. Get your hands on the most current copy of the script revisions and the **strips** as soon as you can to get an idea of how the shooting schedule will be organized. On a three-week shooting schedule, the strips (Table 10-3) will indicate that the antique domino set might play intermittently throughout the first few weeks of shooting. A location can also triple its production value if it is located on an intersection with usable front, side, and back view both painted and dressed differently to suggest different locales. Don't wait for the UPM or 1st AD to tell you the schedule, but work out the logistics of when a specific piece of set dressing, or a hero prop should play based on its availability, and present it to the makers of the production board. You'll be seen as a valuable team player, and you will also safeguard your budget. Remember that you have three options to always consider: 1) You can be on time, but over-budget, 2) Overtime but on budget, 3) On time and on budget. Strive for the latter.

Four and a half months into Indie film prep, the crew is hired. Four weeks later, casting will be completed, as well as locations secured, equipment, dressing and props rented, and scenery in finishing stages. Two weeks later, at six months into prep, the shooting begins.

The strips enable an art director to use tools discussed in Chapter 8, namely the script breakdown, set list, and day out of days (see Appendix C and D). Efficient use of time and money will establish your reputation with producers and directors—the people who count. Your aesthetic skills and delivering on time will ensure your being rehired.

Understanding how to talk about the budget of a film without talking dollars and cents is a valuable skill in terms of understanding how an Indie producer operates and also adding to your general knowledge of film production. For example, most 35 mm Indie films shoot 50,000 feet of film to get a 90–minute product. That translates into a 6 : 1 ratio, that is, every six minutes of film stock that is shot equals one minute of finished screen time. In other words, it takes 90 feet of exposed film to equal one minute of film time; a 90–minute film equals 8,100 feet of exposed film. But in order to get that final 8,100 feet you need to shoot 50,000 feet of film (before editing), e.g., the 6 : 1 ratio. Successful designing means doing the math and understanding

	DAY 1				DAY 2			DAY 3		
SHOOTING DAY										
DAY/NIGHT	D	D	D	D	D	D	D	D	D	D
INT/EXT	EXT	INT	INT	E/I	EXT	EXT	INT	INT	INT	EXT
LOCATION/STUDIO	S	S	S	L	L	L	S	L	L	L
PAGE COUNT	5/8	3/8	11/8	3/8	6/8	5/8	14/8	10/8	9/8	7/8
	THE TEMPLE	TEMPLE HALLWAY	TEMPLE ROYAL QUARTERS	TEMPLE COURTYARD	STREETS OF BOSTON	STREETS OF PARIS	PEASANT HUT	ROBERT'S BEDROOM	ROBERT'S STUDY	ROBERT'S GARDEN
SCENE NUMBER	12A	12C	38D	14	1	4	8	44	22	41
CAST:										
ACTOR 1 ROBERT	1		1	1	1	1	1	1	1	1
ACTOR 2 ANTOINETTE		2	2	2	2	2		2		2
ACTOR 3 CHARLOTTE		3	3	3	3	3				
PROPS:										
1 DOMINOES (DO)			DO					DO		
2 QUILL PEN & LEDGER (PL)			PL					PL		
CAMERA EQUIPMENT:										
1 DOLLY (DO)		DO	DO	DO				DO	DO	DO
2 CRANE (CR)	CR			CR	CR	CR				CR
3 GRIP (GR)	GR	GR	GR	GR	GR	GR	GR	GR	GR	GR
SPECIAL EFFECTS:										
1 FIREPLACE FIRE (FF)			FF					FF		
2 FOG (FG)				FG						FG
3 BLOOD (BL)				BL			BL			BL
ANIMALS										
1 DOGS (D)			D	D			D	D	D	D

TITLE: FLESH & BONE
DIRECTOR: NANCY WEEMS
PROD CO.: PIEBALD PROD.

Table 10-3 Typical Production Board (Courtesy of Nancy Weems, screenwriter of *Citizen Darmont*).

these formulas. This is especially true in the twenty-first century where art and science meet to create a new product.

IMAGE AND FORMAT

Most likely, the smaller films you encounter will first be shot on digital video format, then transferred to 35 mm film, *or* shot in DV and left in that format for distribution. In Indie terms, the former way is customary, and the latter seems to be the current trend. Why? It is cheaper in the long run, and the quality is excellent. A working understanding of digital video format is another important aspect of an art director's learning curve. As a sculptor chooses a particular medium to optimally express an idea in 3D volume, a cinema artist must choose the proper digital medium to translate the "tone" of the screenplay. Truth in choosing a medium is just as important as how a story is told.

Even the finest grain film stock has a texture. This subtle surface attribute adds resonance to the literary and emotional context of a script. Consequently, it will also superimpose an additional layer of visual varnish on the design of a movie. You will never be asked to choose a film stock, but knowledge about DV camera features reinforce design concept choices. The next few paragraphs will take us back to thinking like a director by literally examining the possibilities of various shooting tools or DV cameras at your disposal.

Budget will once again determine which camera pack is chosen, with the interpretation of the script highlighted as a secondary motive. The market offers cheap, medium, and expensively priced cameras; advantages and disadvantages define each. The signal recorded on a cheap model or an expensive professional model is the same; the difference lies in the quality of the lenses and the camera's format capabilities: 4:3 is conventional TV ratio and 16:9 is HDTV quality. HD, or high definition, has four times the resolution as the Standard Definition format of a medium range Digital Betacam camera. Resolution or clarity of image captured on a less expensive camera is lost when an image is enlarged to theatrical proportion from a PC (or TV) screen. Less expensive cameras work fine for medium shots and close-ups but blur out in wide shots and rapid pans, although a few lower-priced cameras can still deliver broadcast quality images. Medium range DigiBeta cameras are typically used for SDTV digital formats (at 4:3 ratio), but for eventual 35 mm blow-up, it just squeaks by as the minimum quality. The resolution of either camera's quality range is an important consideration before rental or purchase. Of course, HD cameras promise enhanced picture quality and crystal clear resolution. Although this quality camera is somewhat untouchable in purchase price, it is a money saver on the back end; the high costs of transfer to film are counterbalanced in some cases by 30 percent savings. This is a final decision made by the producer, director, and cinematographer. In the final analysis, practical hands-on experience with any of these DV tools gives an art director a huge advantage over those who remain unfamiliar with the technology.

SECURING CG TALENT

As long as you have access to hardware and software and willing talent, you can create a small but impressive, visual effects art department core. The crew should consist of at least three animators, 1) A character animator, 2) A background animator, and 3) A supervisor. This key person should be somewhat skilled in art and commerce. Creative strengths in working knowledge of previz and visual effects, plus someone who can jump in whenever necessary to carry the load, will take care of the art requirements. Control of the budget and the willingness to make judgment calls based on experience with tools and process allow you, the art director, to supervise expenditures and the work to be accomplished on the financial end.

A prime place to look for a visual effects crew is at a local digital studio. There, salaried assistant animators would be most likely to trade their time-off hours for film credit. Non-payment is a sensitive issue that must be handled correctly. An agreement to work for credit or very little salary implies several things to you as the art department employer. Trading for credit means that: 1) All necessary equipment will be there for the artists without question and is the very least that can be expected. This should be guaranteed through the producers before you sign your contract to work on a digitally driven film project, otherwise you are fighting a losing battle. 2) You and your animation supervisor will develop a carefully devised work schedule, based on whatever strips might be available from the UPM. It should include reasonable work hours and time for meals, subsidized by the production. 3) However this shakes out, you should be absolutely clear about what you expect and what you are offering. Without good organization and honesty, you will lose your support team. If they are well informed and treated reasonably, they will stay through the rough spots. You must champion their best welfare—it is not only good policy but also good management—it will come back to you one hundredfold.

Other options for talent are film schools, architectural schools, and university/college film programs. Doing thorough crew research in these areas is just as important as visual research for your design concept. Not all Indie films will require VFX support, although films shot in DV will require digital supervision by the head of the art department to insure the truth of the visual storytelling. The art director and producers will make this judgment call, where necessary.

Cinematography in the digital video medium enhances the speed of a project, and also includes the creative participation of all key players. With heightened creativity and likelihood for iconoclastic moviemaking, there also exists the possibility of the breaking of rules in the working environment. Safeguarding this and other principal aspects of the filmmaking process is the function of the unions.

THE ART DIRECTORS GUILD

There are many unions and guilds that comprise the motion picture industry. Each organization has its own set of requirements for entry. The Art Directors & Scenic, Title and Graphic Artists Local 800 at www.ialocal800.org requires proof of a specified number of hours and days worked on a particular non-union job and proof of expertise in art directing. While working in the non-union arena, document your progress as you go. Save original deal memos, paycheck stubs, crew lists, call sheets, one-liner and shooting schedules, PDA archives, photocopied petty cash envelope information, timecards, and mileage reports. Before leaving a non-union gig, ask the producer for a written statement on production letterhead of your job responsibilities and dates worked. Be sure to photograph the stages of your film work: every set designed, drawn, built, painted and dressed, shooting crew setups, and locations photos. Leave no stone unturned. The more documentation you have organized, the easier your entry into the union will be. (See "The Roster," below.)

The Art Directors Guild presents a packet of information to newly inducted Art Director members. With the permission of the Guild, I would like to share some of the basic information with anyone aspiring for membership:

The Union exists to serve and protect your economic and creative interests. The IATSE (IA) oversees hundreds of local unions, including Local 800. Part of every member's dues is remitted to the IA to fund its various activities on behalf of all the locals, including negotiating collective bargaining agreements and organizing new productions. Your dues enable the local's staff to work on your behalf and assure you at least the following benefits of membership:

- Minimum Wage Scale
- Guaranteed Working Conditions
- Access to Employment Information
- Grievance Procedure
- Guaranteed Prominent Placement of Screen Credit
- Training and Education (seminars, symposia, etc.)
- ADG Membership Directory
- Health Plan
- Credit Union
- Pension/Retirement Benefits
- The Art Directors' Film Society
- Annual Awards Banquet
- Newsletter
- Scholarship Fund

Classes of Membership

There are three principal classes of membership in the Union. Art Director, whose duties are defined in our basic collective bargaining agreement as "an employee who directs the preparation and/or prepares sketches and designs of motion picture sets and/or backgrounds and generally supervises the execution of such designs and the decorating of sets and/or backgrounds." Assistant Art Director generally "aids the production designer and art director in the performance of their respective duties including research and helping to coordinate the work of set designers and others in the art department." Visual consultant "must possesses special and unique visual skills and talents of a nature that will assist the Art Director or Production Designer in performing his or her function with ideas relative to mood, visual concepts, appearance, etc. of the motion picture sets and/or backgrounds. Such an individual shall work under the supervision of the Art Director or Production Designer."

The titles "Art Director" and "Art Direction" are often used interchangeably with "Production Designer" and "Production Design." Production designers develop the look of a motion picture or television production through the conception and creation of stage sets and the selection and alteration of practical locations. The screen credit of "Production Designer" may not automatically be given to an Art Director on a motion picture; permission to grant this credit comes from the Local.

Initiation Fee and Dues

The initiation fee for all Art Director members is three weeks' salary for the classification in which the member joins the Local. Please contact the office for further information on initiation fees and members' dues, or click on www.ialocal800.org.

The Roster

The Motion Picture Industry Experience Roster is a list of persons, e.g., Art Directors and Assistant Art Directors who, by virtue of their work experience, are entitled to "preference of employment" over persons not on the Roster. The Roster is maintained by the Contract Services Administrative Trust Fund (CSATF) and is separate and apart from the Union. To get onto the Roster, one must apply to **Contract Services** and have worked on a total of no less than 30 days for one or more **signatory** companies within the one-year period immediately preceding application for Roster placement. Or, one qualifies for placement by demonstrating 175 days' employment as a film or TV Production Designer, Art Director, or Assistant Art Director on union or non-union projects in the three years preceding application for Roster placement. There is also a Commercial Industry Experience Roster; 30 days working for a commercial signatory is required, and an additional 90 days of commercial work qualifies the person for placement on the Motion Picture Experience Industry Roster. This is a list of individuals available for employment in their respective categories. Members should call the office when available and wishing to be placed on the List; conversely, members should call when no longer available and they then will be removed from the List.

Taft-Hartley

Taft and Hartley were two U.S. Senators who, in 1947, birthed the general, anti-labor legislation bearing their names. Among the legacies of Taft–Hartley in "grandfathering": persons who work for companies which are "organized" automatically qualify for admission into the union and must become members in good standing of the union not later than a specified 30-day period. In addition to entry through organizing, the other principal way persons join Local 800 is when they meet the experience requirements of an Assistant Art Director or Art Director side letter to the basic collective bargaining agreement. (Check with the Guild for further details.)

Training

Each year for the last four years Local 800 has received grants of several hundred thousand dollars from CSATF to enable members to attend craft-specific training courses in cutting-edge and traditional technologies. Providers of such courses are Don Jordan's Digital Media Xchange, Gnomon School of Visual Effects, and Studio Arts. For the first time in several years, such funds were not forthcoming from Contract Services in calendar year 2004; the Guild is currently exploring alternative funding and training options.

Basic Collective Bargaining Agreement Selected Provisions

- All members hired by signatory employers must be and remain members in good standing of the union on and after the 30th day following their first day of employment.
- Employees are free to negotiate terms and conditions from their employers better than those provided in the Basic Agreement.
- Any disputes with employers concerning wages, hours, working conditions, or the interpretation of the Basic Agreement concerning these matters, may be grieved and arbitrated at no cost to the employee.
- The following studio minimum wage scale is effective for the period commencing August 1, 2004 to and including July 31, 2005.

Classification	Studio Rates Per Week
Art Director	$2,670.74
Assistant Art Director	$2,006.24
Visual Consultant	$2,670.74

Table 10-4 Art Department studio rates per week as of August 1, 2004—Courtesy of The Art Directors Guild & Scenic, Title and Graphic Artists Local 800.

- Art Directors are considered weekly "on call" employees: they work no prescribed number of hours in a day or week, and are paid a guaranteed weekly wage.
- Payment for Art Directors employed on features or TV begins on the earlier of the date of script delivery to the Art Director or on the first conference of the script.
- Employees are entitled to no less than five working days' notice of lay-offs (by "lay-off" we refer not only to instances of dismissal for lack of work but also dismissal because the regularly scheduled production work has concluded).
- Rules with respect to payment for 6th and 7th days on distant location:
  ○ For each 6th day worked in an employee's workweek during a full six day workweek, the employee receives one and one-half times one-fifth ($^1/_5$) of the "on call" weekly rate in effect, the addition to the "on call" salary in effect.
  ○ For each 6th day *not* worked in an employee's workweek during a full six day workweek, the employee receives an allowance of one-twelfth ($^1/_{12}$) of the scheduled minimum "on call" weekly rate, plus pension and health contributions for seven hours.
  ○ For each 7th day *not* worked in an employee's workweek, the employee receives an allowance of one-twelfth ($^1/_{12}$) of the scheduled minimum "on call" weekly rate, plus eight reportable hours for the 7th day not worked.
  ○ For each 7th day worked in an employee's workweek, if the employee actually performs work at the direction of the Producer, the employee is paid an additional amount equal to one-third ($^1/_3$) of the "on call" weekly rate in effect.
- The amount of over-scale pay employees have bargained for may *not* be applied against any other payments due under the Basic Agreement, except with respect to allowances for airplane flights.
- You may be removed from the Industry Experience Roster for failing to pay required dues and/or initiation fee.
- Employees are entitled to screen credit in a "prominent place" on and long-for TV such as **MOW**s. "Prominent place" means single card credit whether in the main or end titles, and the only "technical" credit that may be placed more prominently is that of Director of Photography, and on short-form productions the only technical credit that can be placed more prominently, again is that of CINEMATOGRAPHER.
- Producers must come to the Union and get its approval if they wish to provide the credit "Production Designer" or "Production Design by" instead of the Art Director credit.
- The following appears in Article VII, at Paragraph 95 of the Basic Agreement under "duties and division of work":
  ○ "Art Director" shall be deemed to mean an employee who directs the preparation and/or prepares sketches and designs of motion picture sets and/or backgrounds and generally supervises the execution of such designs and the decorating of sets and/or backgrounds.

○ "Assistant Art Director" shall be deemed to mean a person employed as such to assist an Art Director in the performance of his/her duties.
○ The rough laying-out of sets and making sketches shall be deemed to be part of the duties of the "Art Director," as well as making occasional working drawings.[1]

This information is a great support to a working art director. It provides clearly drawn guidelines for hiring of art department crew, resolving confusing issues, defining changes in annual wage rates so a proper deal memo can be signed with a UPM, as well as benefits, legal support, and connection to related industry organizations and events. A working AD relies on the Union to maintain the status quo as s/he attends to the business of filmmaking.

THE NEW PARADIGM IN EXPERIMENTAL FILM

Since its beginnings nearly 120 years ago, filmmaking has always been a self-evolving, experimental medium. Computer technology has modified that on many levels. Merged media encourages Post-it snippets of everyday iconography captured on cell phones to filter into shared video blogs on the Web or into art house theaters. Virtual intelligence peering back at us through the inside of our monitor screens demands a reflective and continued dialogue from us. Digital videography captures a highly personal experience as it also enlarges the promise of improvements to everyday technology. We do not live in a static age. The paradigm shift in our culture prompted by technological advances is embraced as a necessity for survival in the capturing of the moving picture, as well as in many other facets of our rapidly changing lives.

Grad students, returning alumni, and faculty at MIT's Media Lab™ work at developing cross-media user applications. Many are Web-based and designed for easy access, and interface with all workable video formats. Much of the data presented on the Web site www.media.mit.edu is inspired by how popular technology impacts our lifestyles. The Media Lab, through its blurring of the traditional boundaries between the disciplines, and by nurturing relationships between academia and industry, is at the forefront of the new technologies that will, sooner rather than later, be a part of our daily lives.[2] Cell phones, in particular, are the focus of a great deal of attention; the development of synergies between cell phone capability and other media is found in the existence of Cinemaware™, Emonic™ environment, Movits™, and Shareable Media™. An example of **Barbara Barry**'s contribution to the laboratory's Media Fabrics paradigm[3] supports the notion of the symbiosis of man and the products of his technology:

> I'm building a mindful camera for documentary videographers. The camera uses commonsense reasoning to provide feedback to the videographer during documentary construction. The mindful camera knows, for example, what might happen at typical events such as marathons, dinner parties, and elections. It can make predictions and flag unusual events, prompting the

videographer to develop multiple story threads for their documentary. This work strives to define a new method of documentary practice in which videographer and a mindful camera collaborate to explore unfolding storytelling possibilities as they observe and record the everyday world.[4]

An implacable, creative mind can find uses for these interfaces in cinematography and elsewhere. The Media Lab at MIT encourages exploration. Symposia and proposals for new media apps are provocative—shared insight stimulates re-experience of familiar media and situations—in the process, challenging ourselves keeps our institutions flexible. Living our lives creatively, through the expanse of media and technology available to us, and by fully interacting with it, fortifies us as art directors to be the true action figures we truly are.

ENDNOTES

1. Information retrieved from "The Union—What You Should Know" a document provided by the Art Directors Guild & Scenic, Title and Graphic Artists Local 800 office as well as *Schedule of Wages and Conditions of the Art Directors Guild & Scenic, Title and Graphic Artists Local 800 (Art Directors) Handbook*, pages 80–81 (published by the same).

2. Retrieved from the World Wide Web on 11/02/04 at http://www.media.mit.edu/about/retro.html

3. "Our research focuses on a new paradigm: the "media fabric"—a semi-intelligent organism where lines of communication, threads of meaning, chains of causality, and streams of consciousness converge and intertwine to form a rich tapestry of creative story potentials, meaningful real-time dialogues, social interactions, and personal or communal art- and story-making. The fabric is characterized by six critical attributes: synergistic, integral to our everyday lives mindful, improvisational, inviting self-reflection, connected." Davenport, Glorianna. "The Storied Machine" for RTE Future Tense Science Lecture on Thursday November 11, 2004. Retrieved from the World Wide Web on 11/26/04 at http://www.media.mit.edu/~barbara/research.html

4. Retrieved from the World Wide Web on 11/02/04 at http://www.media.mit.edu/~barbara/research.html

SECTION III

Appendices

Section III is divided into several subcategories, called Appendices A–F, as listed in the Table of Contents. For your convenience, they are also shown below.

The subcategories are by no means exhaustive but give the reader a solid foundation of references, Web addresses, and documentation in order to make informed decisions. It is natural that lists will cross-reference and overlap.

	SUB-CATEGORY	ITEMS
A	**REFERENCE AND SOURCE LISTS**	Anthropometry Buckland Filmography Daily Gear List Design Reference Books Film-Pocket Listings Filmmaker's Code of Conduct IATSE 2004 Membership Directory L.A. Backings L.A. Soundstages Table of Framing Heights The Cinemarati 100
B	**CONTRACTS**	Box-Equipment Rental Inventory Crew Deal Memo I-9 Form
C	**FORMS**	Check Request Form Crew Information Sheet Invoice Sheet Mileage Log Petty Cash Sheet Purchase Order Form

D	**PRODUCTION LISTS**	Breakdown Sheet Call Sheet Call Sheet Back Day Out of Days Sheet Location List One-Liner Schedule Set Breakdown Item Page Shooting Schedule
E	**FIGURE AND TABLE LIST**	[All images used in this book from Chapter 1 through the Appendix]
F	**GLOSSARY**	[All terms that are 'bolded' in the text]
G	**INDEX**	

APPENDIX A

A	REFERENCE AND SOURCE LISTS	Anthropometry Buckland Filmography Daily Gear List Design Reference Books Film-Pocket Listings Filmmaker's Code of Conduct IATSE 2004 Membership Directory L.A. Backings L.A. Soundstages Table of Framing Heights The Cinemarati 100

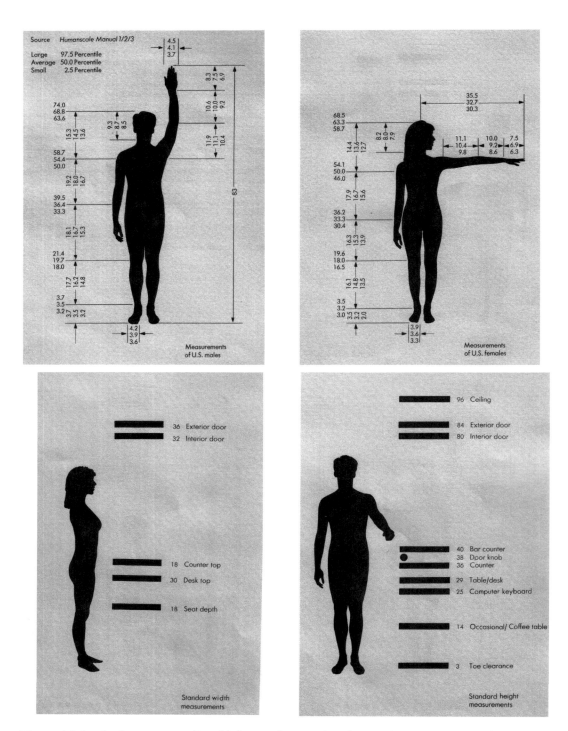

Figure A1-1 *Anthropometry*: (Read left to right, top then bottom) Measurements of US Males & Females. Standard width and height measurements for humans. Courtesy of Pentagram Design.

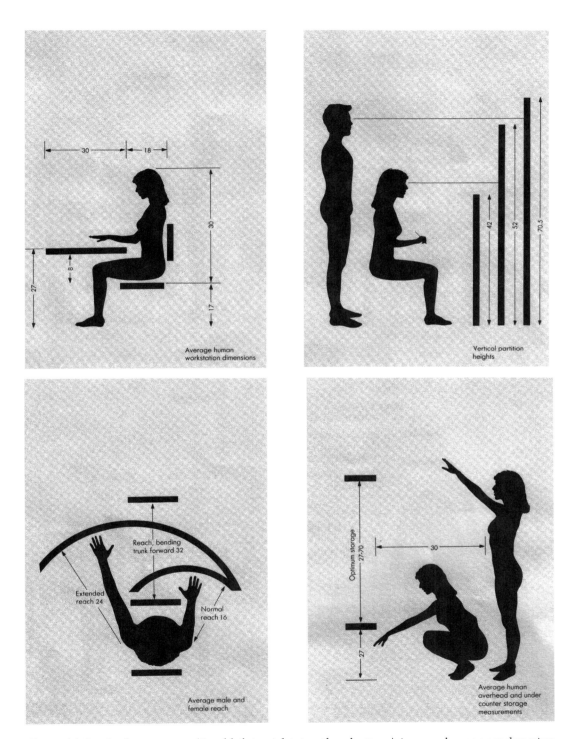

Figure A1-2 *Anthropometry*: (Read left to right, top then bottom) Average human workstation dimensions. Vertical partition heights. Average male & female reach. Average human overhead and under counter storage measurements. Courtesy of Pentagram Design.

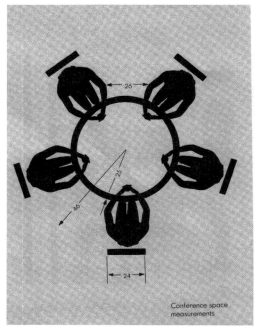

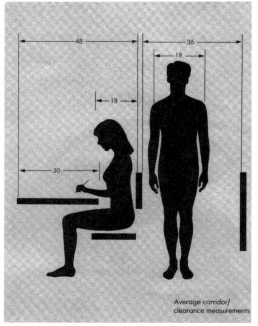

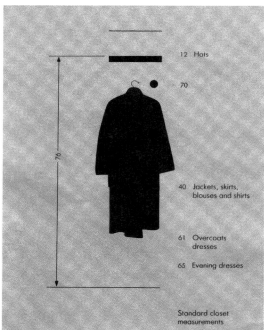

Figure A1-3 *Anthropometry*: (Read left to right, top then bottom) Conference space measurements. Average corridor/clearance measurements. Standard closet measurements. Courtesy of Pentagram Design.

BUCKLAND FILMOGRAPHY

Wilfred Buckland's filmography lists him as: Art Director, Production Designer, Art Department, Second Unit Director or Assistant Director, and Miscellaneous Crew.

This list was compiled from The Internet Movie Database, click: www.imdb.com and AFI Catalog of Silent Films, click: http://www.afi.com/members/catalog/SearchResult.aspx?s=1&TBL=PN &Type=HP&ID=154725&pName=%20%20Wilfred%20Buckland These films are worth watching.

Almost Human	(1927)
Always Audacious	(1920)
Amarilly of Clothes-Line Alley	(1918)
American Consul, The	(1917)
Anton the Terrible	(1916)
Blackbirds	(1915)
Call of the East, The	(1917)
Call of the North, The	(1914)
Captive, The	(1915)
Carmen	(1915)
Cheat, The	(1915)
Chimmie Fadden	(1915)
City of Dim Faces, The	(1918)
City of Masks, The	(1920)
City Sparrow, A	(1920)
Clown, The	(1916)
Conrad in Quest of His Youth	(1920)
Crooked Streets	(1920)
Cruise of the Make-Believes, The	(1918)
Crystal Gazer, The	(1917)
Cumberland Romance, A	(1920)
Dancin' Fool, The	(1920)
Deuce of Spades, The	(1922)
Devil Stone, The	(1917)
Don't Change Your Husband	(1919)
Excuse My Dust	(1920)
Eyes of the Heart	(1920)
Forbidden Woman, The	(1927)
Fourteenth Man, The	(1920)
Furnace, The	(1920)
Girl of the Golden West, The	(1915)
Girl Who Came Back, The	(1918)
Goat, The	(1918)
Hawthorne of the U.S.A.	(1919)

Continues

Continued

Held by the Enemy	(1920)
Her Country First	(1918)
Joan the Woman	(1916)
Johanna Enlists	(1918)
Lady in Love, A	(1920)
Less Than Kin	(1918)
Little American, The	(1917)
Little Princess, The	(1917)
Male and Female	(1919)
Masquerader, The	(1922)
M'liss	(1918)
Mrs. Temple's Telegram	(1920)
Old Wives for New	(1918)
Omar the Tentmaker	(1922)
One More American	(1918)
Plow Girl, The	(1916)
Public Opinion	(1916)
Pudd'nhead Wilson	(1916)
Ragamuffin, The	(1916)
Reaching for the Moon	(1917)
Roaring Road, The	(1919)
Robin Hood	(1923)
Romance of the Redwoods, A	(1917)
Secret Sin, The	(1915)
Selfish Woman, The	(1916)
Something to Do	(1919)
Soul of Kura-San, The	(1916)
Soul of Youth, The	(1920)
Source, The	(1918)
Squaw Man, The	(1918)
Stella Maris	(1918)
Such a Little Pirate	(1918)
Sweet Kitty Bellairs	(1916)
Thou Art the Man	(1920)
Trail of the Lonesome Pine, The	(1916)
Victoria Cross, The	(1916)
We Can't Have Everything	(1918)
Whispering Chorus, The	(1918)
Widow's Might, The	(1918)
Wild and Woolly	(1917)
Woman God Forgot, The	(1917)
Woman Next Door, The	(1919)
You Never Can Tell	(1920)
Young Romance	(1915)
You're Fired	(1919)

DAILY GEAR LIST	
What do you put in your bag? This practical list will keep you effective and wired through every phase of the process. The additional lists below it suggest items you might need in-office and on location.	
HARDWARE	**SOFTWARE**
CARRY BAG	
PDA	**Microsoft Office XP**
Laptop 20GB+ capacity CD-RW burner DVD-RW burner Infrared download capability WI-FI capability	**Adobe—Photoshop CS** **Adobe—Illustrator CS** **Adobe—Acrobat 7**
Digital Camera USB connectivity	**Nemetschek—VectorWorks 11**
Wireless-camera phone	**Discreet—3D Studio Max 7**
DVCAM or MiniCAM Betacam SP quality & a fraction of the price	**Macromedia—Flash MX** **Appropriate back-up discs for EVERYTHING**
Pocket scale rule	**Crew Mobile List** Credit card size
Laser level and Laser Range Meter Quick and accurate	**One-liner** Half-size packet **Shooting Schedule** Half-size packet
Inclinometer Determine height of tall objects	**Pocket Ref** Shirt pocket size: 3.2" × 5.4" × 0.9" Weight 8 ounces
Extra charged batteries for EVERYTHING	**6′ wooden folding ruler**
OFFICE	
External Hard drive System back-up	**Music CDs**
Printer LaserJet B/W for fast volume	**Appropriate back-up discs for EVERYTHING**

Continues

Continued

Printer
Epson Stylus series for excellent
color work
Scanner
Canon series for dependable
1,200 dpi scans
External CD-RW burner
System back-up
Copies for everyone

LOCATION

Rubbermaid Canisters
Bubble wrap and Styro p-nuts

Padlocks
Multiple key sets

Oversize Printer   **Appropriate back-up discs**
Good for in-house graphics on
a large scale

12" Wheelie
Measure up to 999' on terrain

Fly Strips
They hang from the ceiling

Solar Anti-Mosquito Guard
It hangs from a chain around your neck

DESIGN REFERENCE BOOKS

This is a basic list of design reference books. Some of them are first edition copies; newer editions exist for many of them. I offer these as a starter library for first-time art directors and film designers. After more than two decades of art directing, and steady purchase of reference materials for a handful of films, the library has grown to just under five hundred books.
Let this serve as a warning.

Continues

Continued

BOOK NAME	AUTHOR	PUBLISHER	ISBN, PHONE #, Email
Man and His Symbols	Carl G. Jung	Doubleday & Co. Inc. New York: 1964	0-385-05221-9
Seeing With the Mind's Eye: The History, Techniques and Uses of Visualization	Mike Samuels, M.D., & Nancy Samuels	Random House, Inc. New York: 1975	0-394-73113-1
The Power of Myth	Joseph Campbell	Doubleday & Co. Inc. New York: 1988	0-385-24773-7
ARCHITECTURE			
A Field Guide to American Houses	Virginia & Lee McAlester	Alfred A. Knopf New York: 1988	0-394-51032-1
Architectural Graphic Standards, 6th edition	Ramsey & Sleeper	John Wiley & Sons New York: 1970	0-471-70780-5
Sir Banister Fletcher's A History of Architecture, 18th edition	J. C. Palmes	Charles Scribner's Sons New York: 1975	684-14207-4
ART HISTORY			
A Basic History of Art, 2nd edition	H. W. Janson	Harry Abrams, Inc. New York: 1971	0-13-062356-3
Arts & Ideas, 3rd edition	William Fleming	Holt, Rinehart & Winston, Inc. New York	N / A
Gardiner's Art Through the Ages, 5th edition	Horst De La Croix Richard G. Tansey	Harcourt, Brace & World, Inc. New York: 1970	N / A

Continues

Continued

BOOK NAME	AUTHOR	PUBLISHER	ISBN, PHONE #, Email
FILM THEORY			
Film Directing Shot by Shot: Visualizing from Concept to Screen	Steven Katz	[to be filled in. . . .]	0-941188-10-8
Grammar of the Film Language	Daniel Arijon	Silman-James Press Los Angeles: 1976	1-879505-07-X
How to Read a Film: The Art, Technology, Language, History, and Theory of Film and Media, Revised edition	James Monaco	Oxford University Press New York: 1981	0-19-502802-3
INFORMATION & SOURCEBOOKS			
American Cinematographer Manual, 8th edition	Rob Hummel	The ASC Press Hollywood: 2001	0-935578-15-3
Art Directors Guild Member-ship Directory	Christa Munro, Ed.	Art Directors Guild Los Angeles: 2005	818.762.9995 Office
Backstage Handbook: An Illustrated Almanac of Technical Information, 3rd Edition	Paul Carter	Broadway Press Louisville: 2000	0-911747-39-7
Handbook of Ornament	Franz Sales Meyer	Dover Publications, Inc. New York: 1957	0-486-23480-0

Continues

Continued

BOOK NAME	AUTHOR	PUBLISHER	ISBN, PHONE #, Email
Pocket Ref, 3rd Edition	Thomas J. Glover	Sequoia Publishing,	ISBN: 1-885071-33-7 (soft cover) ISBN: 1-885071-45-0; (hard cover) Library of Congress Catalog Card Number: 2002091021
Surfaces: Visual Research for Artists, Architects, and Designers	Judy Juracek	W. W. Norton & Co. New York: 1996	0-393-73007-7
The Elements of Style: A Practical Encyclopedia of Interior Architectural Details	Stephen Calloway, Ed. Elizabeth Cromley, Ed.	Simon & Schuster New York: 1991	0-671-73981-6
The Entertainment Sourcebook	The Association of Theatrical Artists and Craftspeople (ATAC)	Applause Theatre Books New York: 2003	1-55783-597-1
The MacMillan Visual Dictionary	Natalie Chapman, Ed.	MacMillan Publishing Co. New York: 1992	0-02-528160-7
The Styles of Ornament	Alexander Speltz	Dover Publications, Inc. New York: 1959	486-20557-6
Thomas Guide 2005: Los Angeles County [digital edition available]	Thomas Bros.	Rand McNally Co. Irvine: 2005	0-528-95514-4 0-528-85447-X [dig. Edition]

Continues

Continued

BOOK NAME	AUTHOR	PUBLISHER	ISBN, PHONE #, Email
STUDIO MOULDING & STAFF SHOPS			
Fox Staff Catalog	20th Century Fox Studios	Production Services	310.203.2712 Shop
Moulding Catalog	The Walt Disney Studios	Moulding Shop	818.560.5510 andy_meyer@ studio.disney. com
Sony Pictures Studio Staff Shop Catalogue	Sony Pictures Studios	Production Services	310.244.5541 www.spe .sony.com/ studio
The Staff Shop	Paramount Pictures	Staff Shop	213.956.8488
Wood Moulding Catalog	Paramount Pictures	Wood Moulding Dept.	323.956.4242
SUPPLIES, HARDWARE, DECORATIVE ARCHITECTURE			
Architectural Sheet Metal Ornaments	W. F. Norman Corp.	Nevada, MO: W. F. Norman Corp.: 1990's	800.641.4038 Phone
Illustrated Catalogue 124 of Period Ornaments for Woodwork and Furniture	The Decorators Supply Corp.	The Decorators Supply Corp. Chicago: 1990	312.847.6300 Phone
McMaster-Carr Supply Company: Catalog 101	McMaster-Carr	N / A	562.692.5911 Phone [L.A.]
Moes Enterprises Catalog of Authentic Pre-1939 Builders Hardware	Lionel D. Moes	Manchester Sash and Door Company Los Angeles: 1994, reissued	213.759.0344 Phone
The Historical Supply Catalogue	Alan Wellikoff	Rough Hewn Books, Baltimore: 1984	0-9648245-0-7

Continues

ORGANIZATION / RESOURCE	WEB SITE

FILM-POCKET LISTINGS

My invention, FILM-POCKET LISTINGS, developed over ten years of keeping lists both online and off-line. The listing contains a handful of helpful categories to jumpstart searches. Originally, it filled one page and folded neatly into a back pocket before I bought a PDA. But it's still handy. For the most part, it's abbreviated to be quick without extra information: just a description and a Web site address. Additional data, i.e., phone, address exists on each Web site.

As of 12/04 all of these listings still exist. Any suggestions will be gladly included!

ORGANIZATION / RESOURCE	WEB SITE
BOOKS & PUBLISHERS	
CMP BOOKS	http://www.cmpbooks.com
FOCAL PRESS	focalpress.com
HENNESSEY & INGALLS ART + ARCHITECTURE BOOKS	hennesseyingalls.com
LARRY EDMUNDS BOOKSHOP	larryedmunds.com
MICHAEL WIESE PRODUCTIONS	mwp.com
ONLINE DIRECTORIES: L.A., N.Y., HIGH DEF, GAMES	411publishing.com
SAMUEL FRENCH BOOKSTORE	samuelfrench.com
VISUAL REFERENCE PUBLICATIONS, INC.	retailreporting.com
DATABASES	
ACADEMY OF MOTION PICTURE ARTS & SCIENCES	oscars.org

ASSOCIATION OF FILM
  COMMISSIONERS
  INTERNATIONAL
	afci.org

CALIFORNIA ARTS COUNCIL	cac.ca.gov
CALIFORNIA FILM COMMISSION	commerce.ca.gov
CURRENCY CONVERTER	xe.com
DEBBIES BOOK—INDUSTRY RESOURCE	debbiesbook.com

ENTERTAINMENT
  DEVELOPMENT COUNCIL
  OF L.A.
	eidc.com

ENTERTAINMENT SERVICES & TECHNOLOGY ASSOCIATION	esta.org

FILM & TV ACTION
  COMMITTEE— RUNAWAY
  PRODUCTION
	ftac.net

Continues

Continued

ORGANIZATION / RESOURCE	WEB SITE
DATABASES	
FILM HISTORY ON THE INTERNET	http://faculty.mc3.edu/ jeckhard/resource.htm
FILM INDUSTRY NETWORK	filmindustrynetwork.com
FILMMAKING NETWORK	indieclub.com
INDUSTRY PORTAL AND WORLDWIDE DATABASE	moviemakers.com
INDUSTRY SEARCH ENGINE	showbiz.com
INDUSTRY-RELATED WEB DATABASE	industrycentral.net
INTERNET MOVIE DATA BASE	imdb.com
LOS ANGELES FILM FESTIVAL	lafilmfest.com
ONLINE BUSINESS2BUSINESS DIRECTORY	la411.com
THOMAS REGIONAL INDUSTRIAL PRODUCTS & SUPPLIERS	thomasregional.com
UNITED STATES INSTITUTE OF THEATRE TECHNOLOGY	usitt.org
US NAVY DATABASE	aa.usno.navy.mil/data/docs/ RS_OneDay.html
US WEATHER DATABASE	http://www.weathermatrix. net/weather
WEB GUIDE FOR MOVIEMAKERS	webmovie.com
DESIGN	
AMERICAN SOCIETY OF INTERIOR DESIGNERS	asid.org
EVENT PLANNING WEBRING	expoworld.net
INTERNATIONAL INTERIOR DESIGN ASSOCIATION	iida.com
LIBRARY OF CONGRESS	lcweb.loc.gov
THE COSTUME WEG RING	marquise.de/webring/ costumering.html
UNIVERSITY RESIDENT THEATRE ASSOCIATION	urta.com
FILM SCHOOLS	
AMERICAN FILM INSTITUTE	afi.com/education/
NEW YORK FILM ACADEMY	nyfa.com
NYU FILM & TELEVISION	http://filmtv.tisch.nyu.edu/ page/home
SCHOOL OF VISUAL ARTS	schoolofvisualarts.edu

Continues

Continued

ORGANIZATION / RESOURCE	WEB SITE
FILM SCHOOLS	
THE LOS ANGELES FILM SCHOOL	lafilm.com
UCLA SCHOOL OF THEATRE, FILM & TELEVISION	tft.ucla.edu
USC SCHOOL OF CINEMA	www-cntv.usc.edu
GUILDS AND UNIONS	
AMERICAN SOCIETY OF CINEMATOGRAPHERS	theasc.com
ART DIRECTORS GUILD	http://www.artdirectors.org/
DIRECTORS GUILD OF AMERICA	dga.org
INTERNATIONAL ALLIANCE OF THEATRICAL STAGE EMPLOYEES	iatse-intl.org
INTERNATIONAL BROTHERHOOD OF TEAMSTERS	teamster.org
LOCATION MANAGERS GUILD OF AMERICA	locationmanagers.org
PRODUCERS GUILD OF AMERICA	producersguild.org
SET DECORATORS SOCIETY OF AMERICA	http://www.setdecorators .org/
SET DESIGNERS & MODEL MAKERS	local847@earthlink.net
SOCIETY OF MOTION PICTURE & TV ENGINEERS	smpte.org
INDIE ORGS	
AMERICAN FILM INSTITUTE	afionline.org
ASSOCIATION OF INDEPENDENT FEATURE FILM PRODUCERS	aiffp.org
ASSOCIATION OF INDEPENDENT VIDEO & FILMMAKERS	aivf.org
INDEPENDENT FEATURE PROJECT	ifpwest.org
FILM ARTS FOUNDATION— INDIE RESOURCE	filmarts.org
JOBS	
INDUSTRY RESOURCE	filmmaker.com
WORLDWIDE DATABASE	craigslist.org
HOLLYWOOD CREATIVE DIRECTORY	hcdonline.com/jobs/ default.asp

Continues

Continued

ORGANIZATION / RESOURCE	WEB SITE
JOBS	
INDUSTRY-RELATED WEB DATABASE	entertainmentcareers.net
WORLDWIDE INDUSTRY DATABASE	mandy.com
WORLDWIDE JOB & RELOCATION DATABASE	monster.com
LIBRARIES & MUSEUMS	
AMERICAN MUSEUM OF MOVING IMAGES	ammi.org
LOS ANGELES PUBLIC LIBRARY	lapl.org
MUSEUM OF TELEVISION & RADIO	mtr.org
NEW YORK PUBLIC LIBRARY	nypl.org/research/lpa/ lpa.html
THE INTERNET PUBLIC LIBRARY	ipl.org
THE LIBRARY OF MOVING IMAGES	libraryofmovingimages.com
VIRTUAL LIBRARY MUSEUM— WORLDWIDE MUSEUMS	icom.museum/vlmp/ world.html
WORLDWIDE ARTS RESOURCES	http://wwar.com
LOS ANGELES MOVIE STUDIOS	
20th CENTURY FOX STUDIOS	http://www.foxstudios.com/ flash/main.htm
COLUMBIA-TRISTAR [SONY STUDIOS PICTURES]	http://www .sonypicturesstudios.com/
DISNEY STUDIOS	http://corporate.disney.go .com/corporate/ studio_operations.html
MIRAMAX FILM CORPORATION	http://www.miramax.com
PARAMOUNT STUDIOS	http://www.paramount.com/ studiogroup/
UNIVERSAL PICTURES	http://www .filmmakersdestination .com/globalnav/gnf.pl? url=http%3A//www .filmmakersdestination.com/ main.html&referrer= http%3A//studio .universalstudios.com/
WARNER BROS.	http://wbsf.warnerbros .com/home.html

FILMMAKER'S CODE OF ETHICS

1. When filming in a neighborhood or business district, proper notification is to be provided to each merchant or neighbor who is directly affected by the company (this includes parking, base camps, and meal areas). Attached to the filming notification distributed to the neighborhood, the following should be included:
   a. Name of company
   b. Name of production
   c. Kind of production, e.g., feature film, movie of the week, TV pilot, etc.
   d. Type of activity and duration, i.e., times, dates, and number of days, including prep and strike
   e. Company contacts, i.e., first assistant director, unit production manager, location manager
2. Production vehicles arriving on location in or near a residential neighborhood shall not enter the area before the time stipulated in the permit, and they shall park one by one, turning off engines as soon as possible. Cast and crew shall observe designated parking areas.
3. Every member of the crew shall wear a production pass (badge) when issued.
4. Moving or towing of the public's vehicles is prohibited without the express permission of the municipal jurisdiction or the owner of the vehicle.
5. Do not park production vehicles in or block driveways without the express permission of the municipal jurisdiction or driveway owner.
6. Cast and crew meals shall be confined to the area designated in the location agreement or permit. Individuals shall eat within their designated meal area, during scheduled crew meals. All trash must be disposed of properly upon completion of the meal.
7. Removing, trimming, and/or cutting of vegetation or trees is prohibited unless approved by the permit authority or property owner.
8. Remember to use the proper receptacles for disposal of all napkins, plates, and coffee cups that you may use in the course of the working day.
9. All signs erected or removed for filming purposes will be removed or replaced upon completion of the use of that location unless otherwise stipulated by the location agreement or permit. Also remember to remove all signs posted to direct the company to the location.
10. Every member of the cast and crew shall keep noise levels as low as possible.
11. Do not wear clothing that lacks common sense and good taste. Shoes and shirts must be worn at all times, unless otherwise directed.
12. Crew members shall not display signs, posters, or pictures on vehicles that do not reflect common sense or good taste, i.e., pinup posters.

Continues

Continued

13. Do not trespass onto other neighbors' or merchants' property. Remain within the boundaries of the property that have been permitted for filming.
14. The cast and crew shall not bring guests or pets to the location, unless expressly authorized in advance by the company.
15. All catering, crafts service, construction, strike, and personal trash must be removed from location.
16. Observe designated smoking areas and always extinguish cigarettes in butt cans.
17. Cast and crew will refrain from the use of lewd or improper language within earshot of the general public.
18. The company will comply with the provisions of the parking permit.

IATSE 2004 MEMBERSHIP DIRECTORY			
LOCAL	**ADDRESS**	**BUS. REP./TITLE**	**PHONE/FAX**
IATSE	WEST COAST OFFICE 10045 Riverside Drive Toluca Lake, CA 91602	Joseph A. Aredas, International Representative in Charge	P 818-980-3499 F 818-980-3496
IATSE	NEW YORK OFFICE 1430 Broadway, 20th Floor New York, NY 10018 Web site: www.iatse-intl.org	Thomas C. Short, President James Wood, General Secretary & Treasurer	P 212-730-1770 F 212-921-7699 F 212-730-7809
B-192	AMUSEMENT AREA EMPLOYEES 10999 Riverside Dr., #301 North Hollywood, CA 91602	Donna Marie Covert, Business Agent	P 818-509-9192 F 818-509-9873
33	THEATRICAL & TV STAGE EMPLOYEES 1720 W. Magnolia Blvd. Burbank, CA 91506	Peter Marley, TV Business Agent James Wright, Theatre Business Agent	P 818-841-9233 F 818-567-1138

Continues

Continued

LOCAL	ADDRESS	BUS. REP./TITLE	PHONE/FAX
44	AFFIL. PROPERTY CRAFTSPERSONS 12021 Riverside Drive North Hollywood, CA 91605 Web site: www.local44.org	Stewart McGuire, Business Agent	P 818-769-2500 F 818-769-1739
80	MOTION PICTURE STUDIO GRIPS 2520 W. Olive Ave. Burbank, CA 91505 Web site: www.iatselocal80.org	Thom Davis, Business Agent	P 818-526-0700 F 818-526-0719
600	INTERNATIONAL CINEMATOG-RAPHERS GUILD 7715 Sunset Blvd., #300 Hollywood, CA 90046 Web site: www .cameraguild.com	Bruce Doering, National Executive Director Steve Flint, Western Regional Director Tim Wade, Business Agent	P 323-876-0160 F 323-876-6383
683	FILM TECHS OF P.D. IND 9795 Cabrini Dr., #204 Burbank, CA 91504 P.O. Box 7429 Burbank, CA 91510-7429	Dan Quiroz, Business Agent	P 818-252-5628 F 818-252-4962
695	INT'L SOUND/CINETECHNICIANS 5439 Cahuenga Blvd. North Hollywood, CA 91601	Jim Osborne, Business Agent	P 818-985-9204 P 323-877-1052 F 818-760-4681
700	MOTION PICTURE EDITORS GUILD 7715 Sunset Blvd., #220 Hollywood, CA 90046 Web site: www .editorsguild.com	Ron Kutak, Executive Director Kathy Repola, Asst. Executive Director	P 323-876-4770 F 323-876-0861

Continues

Continued

LOCAL	ADDRESS	BUS. REP./TITLE	PHONE/FAX
705	MOTION PICTURE COSTUMERS 4731 Laurel Canyon Blvd., #201 Valley Village, CA 91607	Buffy Snyder, Business Agent	P 818-487-5655 F 818-487-5663
706	MAKE-UP ARTISTS & HAIR STYLISTS 828 N. Hollywood Way Burbank, CA 91505 Web site: www.local706.org	Leonard Engelman, Business Agent Susan Cabral/ Ebert, Asst. Business Agent Butch Belo, Asst. Business Agent	P 818-295-3933 F 818-295-3930
728	STUDIO ELECTRICAL TECHNICIANS 14629 Nordhoff St. Panorama City, CA 91402 Web site: www.iatse728.org	Norm Glasser, Business Agent	P 818-891-0728 F 818-891-5288
729	MOTION PICTURE SET PAINTERS 1811 W. Burbank Blvd. Burbank, CA 91506-1314 Web site: www.ialocal729.com email: ialocal729 @compuserve.com	George Palazzo, Business Agent	P 818-842-7729 F 818-846-3729
767	MOTION PICTURE STUDIO FIRST AID 14530 Denker Ave. Gardena, CA 90247-2323 Web site: www.iatse767.org	Rana Platz-Petersen, RN, Business Agent	P 310-352-4485 P 818-655-5341 F 310-352-4485

Continues

Continued

LOCAL	ADDRESS	BUS. REP./TITLE	PHONE/FAX
768	THEATRICAL WARDROBE 13245 Riverside Dr., 3rd Floor Sherman Oaks, CA 91423	William N. Damron, Jr., Business Agent	P 818-789-8735 F 818-905-6297
790	ILLUSTRATORS & MATTE ARTISTS 13245 Riverside Dr., 3rd Floor Sherman Oaks, CA 91423 email: local790@ earthlink.net	Marjo Bernay, Business Agent	P 818-784-6555 F 818-784-2004
800	ART DIRECTORS GUILD & SCENIC, TITLE AND GRAPHIC ARTISTS 11969 Ventura Blvd., #200 Studio City, CA 91604 Web site: www .artdirectors.org Web site: www.artist816.org	Scott Roth, Executive Director Missy Humphrey, Associate Executive Director	P 818-762-9995 F 818-762-9997
829	UNITED SCENIC ARTISTS 29 W. 38th St. New York, NY 10018	Michael McBride, Business Agent	P 212-581-0300 F 212-977-2011
	5225 Wilshire Blvd. Los Angeles, CA 90036 Web site: www.usa829.org	Charles Berliner, West Coast Rep.	P 323-965-0957 F 323-965-0958
839	THE ANIMATION GUILD 4729 Lankershim Blvd. North Hollywood, CA 91602 Web site: www.mpsc839.org	Steve Hulett, Business Agent	P 818-766-7151 F 818-506-4805

Continues

Continued

LOCAL	ADDRESS	BUS. REP./TITLE	PHONE/FAX
847	SET DESIGNERS & MODEL MAKERS 13245 Ventura Blvd., #301 Sherman Oaks, CA 91423 email: local847@ earthlink.net	Marjo Bernay, Business Agent	P 818-784-6555 F 818-784-2004
871	SCRIPT SUPERVISORS/ CONTINUITY & ALLIED PRODUCTION SPECIALISTS GUILD 11519 Chandler Blvd. North Hollywood, CA 91601 Web site: www.ialocal871.org	Lainie Miller, Business Agent	P 818-509-7871 F 818-506-1555
884	STUDIO TEACHERS P.O. Box 461467 Los Angeles, CA 90046 Web site: www .studioteachers.com	Polly Businger, Business Agent	P 310-652-5330
892	COSTUME DESIGNERS GUILD 4730 Woodman Ave., #430 Sherman Oaks, CA 91423 Web site: www .costumedesignersguild.com email: cdgia@earthlink.net	James J. Casey, Jr., Executive Director	P 818-905-1557 F 818-905-1560

L.A. BACKINGS	

This is a short list but a comprehensive one.
Once you've investigated the Web sites and understand the range of possibilities, this list won't look so small. Pacific Studios catalogues make up for their lack of a Web site. The custom translite service they provide is peerless.

Please note that while the following list is current, there is no guarantee as to how long any individual Web site will remain valid. Also note that providing you with this list does not constitute an endorsement of any of the Web sites nor the services, claims, competitions, or courses they offer.
Michael Rizzo 12/2004

ORGANIZATION	**WEB SITE**
Grosh Scenic Rentals 4114 Sunset Boulevard Hollywood, CA 90029 Toll Free: 1-877-363-7998 Phone: 323-662-1134 Fax: 323-664-7526	http://www.grosh.com/index.asp
JC Backings J.C. Backings Corporation 10202 West Washington Blvd. Culver City, CA 90232 Rental Contacts Lynne M. Coakley Jim Spadoni 310-244-5830 Office 310-244-7949 Fax Custom Work Quotes Painted Backing Quotes Lynne M. Coakley Jim Spadoni 310-244-5830 Photo Backing Quotes Tod Coakley 310-841-0123 Office 310-850-0448 Cell	www.jcbackings.com/home.html
Pacific Studios 8315 Melrose Avenue, Los Angeles 90069 Phone: 323-653-3093	No Web site

L.A. SOUNDSTAGES		
This list is credited to the Entertainment Industry Development Corporation, click:http://www.eidc.com/Location_Information/Soundstages/eidc/owa/dis_ByStage/alphastages.htm		
Please note that while the following list is current, there is no guarantee as to how long any individual Web site will remain valid. Also note that providing you with this list does not constitute an endorsement of any of the Web sites nor the services, claims they offer. Michael Rizzo 12/2004		

STAGE NAME	CITY	WEB SITE
ABC Prospect Studio	Los Angeles	310-557-7777
ACME Stage	North Hollywood	www.acmestage.com
Arroyo Studios	Sylmar	818-837-9837
Avalon Studios	N. Hollywood	818-508-5050
Axel Stages	Burbank	818-556-6182
Action Space	Los Angeles	www.actionspace.com
Barker Hangar	Santa Monica	www.barkerhangar.com
Barwick Studios, LLC	Los Angeles	www.barwickstudios.com
Ben Kitay Studios, LLC	Hollywood	www.benkitay.com
Boyington Film Productions	Los Angeles	323-933-7500
Bruce Austin Productions (BAP)	Burbank	818-842-0820
CBS-MTM Studios (Radford Studios)	Los Angeles	818-760-5000
CBS Television City	Los Angeles	323-463-1600
Carthay Studios	Los Angeles	213-938-2101
Century Studio Corporation	Culver City	www.centurystudio.com
Chandler Toluca Lake Studios	North Hollywood	818-763-3650
Chandler Valley Center Studios	Van Nuys	www.valleystudios.com
Chaplin Stages	Los Angeles	323-856-2682
Cole Avenue Studios	Hollywood	www.colestages.com
Complex Studios	Los Angeles	www.thecomplexstudios.com
Culver Studios	Culver City	310-202-1234
Delfino Stages	Sylmar	www.delfinostudios.com
Disney Studios	Burbank	818-560-5151
Dreamworks SKG	Burbank	www.dreamworks.com
Edgewood Stages	Los Angeles	323-938-4762
Empire Burbank Studios	Burbank	818-840-1400

Continues

Continued

STAGE NAME	CITY	WEB SITE
GMT Studios	Culver City	www.gmtstudios.com
Glendale Studios	Glendale	www.glendalestudios.com
Gosch Productions	N. Hollywood	www.gosch.net
Hangar 9 Studios	Santa Monica	310-392-5084
Hayvenhurst Studios	Van Nuys	818-909-6999
Hollywood Center Studios/Las Palmas Lot	Hollywood	www.hollywoodcenter.com/
Hollywood National Studios	Hollywood	323-467-6272
Hollywood Stage	Hollywood	323-466-4393
Hyperion Stage	Los Angeles	323-665-9983
ICN Productions	West LA	310-826-4777
KCET Studios	Los Angeles	323-953-5258
Keith Harrier Production Service	Hollywood	323-930-2720
LA Center Studios	Los Angeles	www.lacenterstudios.com
Lacy Street Production Center	Los Angeles	323-222-8872
Lindsey Studios/Warren Entertainment Center	Valencia	661-257-9292
Metro Goldwyn Mayer	Santa Monica	310-449-3000
Mack Sennett Stage	Los Angeles	323-660-8466
Media City Teleproduction Center	Burbank	www.mediacitystudios.com
Miramax Film Corporation	New York City	212-941-3800
NBC-Burbank	Burbank	www.nbc.com
NBC Hollywood Sunset Gower	Hollywood	323-617-0153
Nickelodeon	Glendale	www.nick.com
North Field Properties/ Hangar 8	Santa Monica	310-392-9000
Norwood Stage	Culver City	310-204-3323
Occidental Studios	Hollywood	www.occidentalstudios.com
Oceanside Studios	Santa Monica	310-399-7704
P.K.E. Studio	Culver City	310-838-7000
Paladin Stages	West Hollywood	323-851-8222
Panavision Stages	Woodland Hills	818-316-1000
Paramount Pictures	Hollywood	213-956-5000

Continues

Continued

STAGE NAME	CITY	WEB SITE
Pasadena Production Studios 39	Pasadena	818-584-4090
Production Group	Hollywood	www.production-group.com
Quixote Studios	West Hollywood	www.quixote.net
Raleigh Studios	Hollywood	323-466-3111
Raleigh Studios Manhattan Beach	Manhattan Beach	www.raleighstudios.com
Ray-Art Studios	Canoga Park	www.rayartstudios.com
Ren-Mar Studios	Hollywood	323-463-0808
Riverfront Stages	Sylmar	www.riverfrontstages.com
San Mar Studios	Hollywood	323-465-8110
Santa Clarita Studios	Santa Clarita	www.sc-studios.com
Screenland Studios I	Burbank	818-843-2262
Shrine Auditorium	Los Angeles	members.aol.com/shrineaud/
Shutter Studio	Hollywood	323-957-1672
SmashBox Studios	Culver City	www.smashboxstudio.com
Solar Studios	Glendale	818-240-1893
Sony Pictures Studios	Culver City	www.spe.sony.com/studio/
South Bay Studios	Long Beach	310-762-1360
South Lake Stage	Burbank	818-953-8400
Studio 57	North Hollywood	818-985-1908
Sunset Gower Studios	Hollywood	323-467-1001
Sunset Stage	Hollywood	323-461-0282
Ten9Fifty Studios	Culver City	310-202-2330
The Lot	West Hollywood	http://www.thelotstudios.com
Turner Broadcasting System	Atlanta	404-827-1700
Twentieth Century Fox	Beverly Hills	310-369-0900
Universal Studios	Universal City	http://universalstudios.com/studio/hollywood/
VPS Studios	Hollywood	323-469-7244
Valencia Entertainment	Valencia	www.valenciaentertainment.com
Walt Disney Studios	Burbank	www.stu-ops.disney.com
Warner Bros.	Burbank	www.wbsf.com
West Valley Studios	Chatsworth	818-998-2222
World Television Productions	Hollywood	323-469-5638

TABLE OF FRAMING HEIGHTS

Historically there are twice as many framing shots used in filmmaking. I have included the most fundamental ones in this table.

Extreme Close-up	*ECU*
Medium Close-up	*MCU*
Full Close-up	*FCU*
Medium Shot	*MS*
Full Shot	*FS*

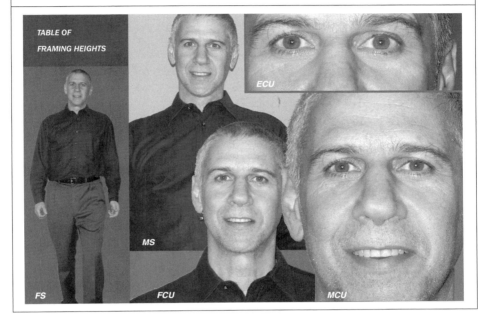

THE CINEMARATI 100: A FEW OF OUR FAVORITE MOVIES

The List compiled by Bryant Frazer, December 2001 gives the reader an idea of what's hot and not in terms of viewable films.
Click: http://www.cinemarati.org/features/canon2.shtml
It's a good basic list.

RANK	MOVIE	DIRECTOR	YEAR
1	Casablanca	Curtiz	1942
2	Citizen Kane	Welles	1941
3	2001: A Space Odyssey	Kubrick	1968
4	Dr. Strangelove, or How I Learned to Stop Worrying and Love the Bomb	Kubrick	1964
5	Rear Window	Hitchcock	1954
6	Apocalypse Now	Coppola	1979
6	This Is Spinal Tap	Reiner	1984
6	Vertigo	Hitchcock	1954
9	The Godfather	Coppola	1972
10	The Princess Bride	Reiner	1987
11	Brazil	Gilliam	1985
11	Singin' in the Rain	Donen/Kelly	1952
13	Monty Python and the Holy Grail	Gilliam/Jones	1975
14	The Searchers	Ford	1956
15	A Clockwork Orange	Kubrick	1971
16	It's a Wonderful Life	Capra	1949
17	Raiders of the Lost Ark	Spielberg	1981
18	GoodFellas	Scorsese	1990
19	Psycho	Hitchcock	1960
19	Pulp Fiction	Tarantino	1994
19	Taxi Driver	Scorsese	1976
22	Raising Arizona	Coen	1987
22	Schindler's List	Spielberg	1993
22	The Shawshank Redemption	Darabont	1994
25	Annie Hall	Allen	1977
26	The Conversation	Coppola	1974
26	Fight Club	Fincher	1999
26	Young Frankenstein	Brooks	1974
29	Se7en	Fincher	1995
29	Seven Samurai	Kurosawa	1954
29	The Wild Bunch	Peckinpah	1969
32	Close Encounters of the Third Kind	Spielberg	1977
33	Bringing Up Baby	Hawks	1938
33	Groundhog Day	Ramis	1993

Continues

Continued

RANK	MOVIE	DIRECTOR	YEAR
35	American Beauty	Mendes	1999
36	The Godfather, Part II	Coppola	1974
36	The Third Man	Reed	1949
38	Airplane!	Abrahams/Zucker/ Zucker	1980
39	Raging Bull	Scorsese	1980
40	The Graduate	Nichols	1967
41	Jaws	Spielberg	1975
42	The Empire Strikes Back	Kershner	1980
43	Star Wars	Lucas	1977
44	Say Anything	Crowe	1989
45	The 400 Blows	Truffaut	1959
45	Alien	Scott	1979
48	The Producers	Brooks	1968
48	Fargo	Coen	1996
49	North by Northwest	Hitchcock	1959
50	A Christmas Story	Clark	1983
51	Memento	Nolan	2000
51	Moulin Rouge!	Luhrmann	2001
53	Do the Right Thing	Lee	1989
53	The Treasure of the Sierre Madre	Huston	1948
55	"What's Opera, Doc?"	Jones	1957
55	Toy Story	Lasseter	1995
57	Blue Velvet	Lynch	1986
57	E.T.	Spielberg	1982
59	City Lights	Chaplin	1931
59	Rashomon	Kurosawa	1950
61	Braveheart	Gibson	1995
61	Sullivan's Travels	Sturges	1941
61	The Wizard of Oz	Fleming	1939
64	The General	Keaton	1927
65	Gone With the Wind	Fleming	1939
66	Back to the Future	Zemeckis	1985
66	Blazing Saddles	Brooks	1974
66	The Maltese Falcon	Huston	1941
66	The Manchurian Candidate	Frankenheimer	1962
66	Willy Wonka and the Chocolate Factory	Stuart	1971
71	Beauty and the Beast	Trousdale/Wise	1991
71	The Big Sleep	Hawks	1946
71	Blade Runner	Scott	1982
71	Bonnie and Clyde	Penn	1967

Continues

Continued

RANK	MOVIE	DIRECTOR	YEAR
71	A Night at the Opera	Wood	1935
71	Saving Private Ryan	Spielberg	1998
71	When Harry Met Sally	Reiner	1989
78	Monty Python's Life of Brian	Jones	1979
78	Requiem for a Dream	Aronofsky	2000
78	Roxanne	Schepisi	1987
81	The Hudsucker Proxy	Coen	1994
81	Lawrence of Arabia	Lean	1962
81	The Sweet Hereafter	Egoyan	1997
81	Three Colors: Red	Kieslowski	1994
85	Crouching Tiger, Hidden Dragon	Lee	2000
85	The Exorcist	Friedkin	1973
85	Magnolia	Anderson	1999
88	Exotica	Egoyan	1994
89	Bulworth	Beatty	1998
89	Dawn of the Dead	Romero	1978
89	Superman	Donner	1978
89	Toy Story 2	Lasseter	1999
93	Babe	Miller	1995
93	Duck Soup	McCarey	1933
93	The Elephant Man	Lynch	1980
93	Miller's Crossing	Coen	1990
93	Shallow Grave	Boyle	1994
98	"The Wrong Trousers"	Park	1993
99	Field of Dreams	Robinson	1989
100	Invasion of the Body Snatchers	Siegel	1956
100	Reservoir Dogs	Tarantino	1992

APPENDIX B

B	**CONTRACTS**	Box-Equipment Rental Inventory Crew Deal Memo I-9 Form

BOX/EQUIPMENT RENTAL INVENTORY

PRODUCTION COMPANY _____

SHOW _____ PROD # _____

EMPLOYEE _____ POSITION _____

ADDRESS _____ SOC.SEC. # _____

_____ PHONE # _____

LOAN OUT COMPANY _____ FED. I.D. # _____

RENTAL RATE $_____ PER ☐ DAY ☐ WEEK

RENTAL COMMENCES ON _____ ☐ SUBMIT WEEKLY INVOICE
☐ RECORD ON WEEKLY TIME CARD

INVENTORIED ITEMS:

_____
_____
_____
_____
_____
_____
_____
_____
_____
_____
_____
_____
_____
_____
_____
_____
_____
_____
_____
_____
_____
_____
_____
_____

Please note: 1.   *Box and equipment rentals are subject to 1099 reporting.*
2.   *The Production Company is not responsible for any claims of loss or damage to box/equipment rental items that are not listed on the above inventory.*

EMPLOYEE SIGNATURE_____ DATE _____

APPROVED BY_____ DATE _____

© ELH

CREW DEAL MEMO

PRODUCTION COMPANY _____   DATE _____

SHOW _____   PROD # _____

EMPLOYEE'S NAME _____   SOC. SEC. # _____

ADDRESS _____   PHONE # _____

_____   MOBILE # _____

START DATE _____   FAX # _____

JOB TITLE _____   PAGER # _____

UNION/GUILD _____   ACCOUNT # _____

RATE (In town) _____   Per ☐ Hour ☐ Day ☐ Week for a ☐ 5- ☐ 6-day week

(Distant location) _____   Per ☐ Hour ☐ Day ☐ Week for a ☐ 5- ☐ 6-day week

ADDITIONAL DAY(S) @ _____

OVERTIME _____   After _____ hours & _____ After _____ hours

☐ BOX/EQUIPMENT RENTAL _____   Per ☐ Day ☐ Week

☐ CAR ALLOWANCE _____   Per ☐ Day ☐ Week

☐ MILEAGE REIMBURSEMENT _____   Per Mile

> Note: Any equipment rented by the Production Company from the employee must be inventoried before rental can be paid.

TRAVEL & HOTEL ACCOMMODATIONS _____

_____

_____

_____

EXPENSES—PER DIEM _____

☐ LOANOUT

CORP. NAME _____   FED. ID # _____

ADDRESS (If different from above) _____

_____

AGENT _____   AGENCY _____

ADDRESS _____   PHONE # _____

_____   FAX # _____

EMPLOYER OF RECORD _____

ADDRESS _____   PHONE # _____

_____   FAX # _____

IF AWARDED SCREEN CREDIT, HOW WOULD YOU LIKE YOUR NAME TO READ?

_____

_____

APPROVED BY _____   TITLE _____

ACCEPTED BY _____   DATE _____

© ELH

273

INSTRUCTIONS
PLEASE READ ALL INSTRUCTIONS CAREFULLY BEFORE COMPLETING THIS FORM.

Anti-Discrimination Notice. It is illegal to discriminate against any individual (other than an alien not authorized to work in the U.S.) in hiring, discharging, or recruiting or referring for a fee because of that individual's national origin or citizenship status. It is illegal to discriminate against work eligible individuals. Employers **CANNOT** specify which document(s) they will accept from an employee. The refusal to hire an individual because of a future expiration date may also constitute illegal discrimination.

Section 1 - Employee. All employees, citizens and noncitizens, hired after November 6, 1986, must complete Section 1 of this form at the time of hire, which is the actual beginning of employment. **The employer is responsible for ensuring that Section 1 is timely and properly completed.**

Preparer/Translator Certification. The Preparer/Translator Certification must be completed if Section 1 is prepared by a person other than the employee. A preparer/translator may be used only when the employee is unable to complete Section 1 on his/her own. However, the employee must still sign Section 1.

Section 2 - Employer. For the purpose of completing this form, the term "employer" includes those recruiters and referrers for a fee who are agricultural associations, agricultural employers or farm labor contractors.

Employers must complete Section 2 by examining evidence of identity and employment eligibility within three (3) business days of the date employment begins. If employees are authorized to work, but are unable to present the required document(s) within three business days, they must present a receipt for the application of the document(s) within three business days and the actual document(s) within ninety (90) days. However, if employers hire individuals for a duration of less than three business days, Section 2 must be completed at the time employment begins. **Employers must record: 1)** document title; **2)** issuing authority; **3)** document number, **4)** expiration date, if any; and **5)** the date employment begins. Employers must sign and date the certification. Employees must present original documents. Employers may, but are not required to, photocopy the document(s) presented. These photocopies may only be used for the verification process and must be retained with the I-9. **However, employers are still responsible for completing the I-9.**

Section 3 - Updating and Reverification. Employers must complete Section 3 when updating and/or reverifying the I-9. Employers must reverify employment eligibility of their employees on or before the expiration date recorded in Section 1. Employers **CANNOT** specify which document(s) they will accept from an employee.

- If an employee's name has changed at the time this form is being updated/ reverified, complete Block A.

- If an employee is rehired within three (3) years of the date this form was originally completed and the employee is still eligible to be employed on the same basis as previously indicated on this form (updating), complete Block B and the signature block.

- If an employee is rehired within three (3) years of the date this form was originally completed and the employee's work authorization has expired **or** if a current employee's work authorization is about to expire (reverification), complete Block B and:
  - examine any document that reflects that the employee is authorized to work in the U.S. (see List A or C),
  - record the document title, document number and expiration date (if any) in Block C, and complete the signature block.

Photocopying and Retaining Form I-9. A blank I-9 may be reproduced, provided both sides are copied. The Instructions must be available to all employees completing this form. Employers must retain completed I-9s for three (3) years after the date of hire or one (1) year after the date employment ends, whichever is later.

For more detailed information, you may refer to the INS Handbook for Employers, (Form M-274). You may obtain the handbook at your local INS office.

Privacy Act Notice. The authority for collecting this information is the Immigration Reform and Control Act of 1986, Pub. L. 99-603 (8 USC 1324a).

This information is for employers to verify the eligibility of individuals for employment to preclude the unlawful hiring, or recruiting or referring for a fee, of aliens who are not authorized to work in the United States.

This information will be used by employers as a record of their basis for determining eligibility of an employee to work in the United States. The form will be kept by the employer and made available for inspection by officials of the U.S. Immigration and Naturalization Service, the Department of Labor and the Office of Special Counsel for Immigration Related Unfair Employment Practices.

Submission of the information required in this form is voluntary. However, an individual may not begin employment unless this form is completed, since employers are subject to civil or criminal penalties if they do not comply with the Immigration Reform and Control Act of 1986.

Reporting Burden. We try to create forms and instructions that are accurate, can be easily understood and which impose the least possible burden on you to provide us with information. Often this is difficult because some immigration laws are very complex. Accordingly, the reporting burden for this collection of information is computed as follows: **1)** learning about this form, 5 minutes; **2)** completing the form, 5 minutes; and **3)** assembling and filing (recordkeeping) the form, 5 minutes, for an average of 15 minutes per response. If you have comments regarding the accuracy of this burden estimate, or suggestions for making this form simpler, you can write to the Immigration and Naturalization Service, HQPDI, 425 I Street, N.W., Room 4307r, Washington, DC 20536. OMB No. 1115-0136.

EMPLOYERS MUST RETAIN COMPLETED FORM I-9
PLEASE DO NOT MAIL COMPLETED FORM I-9 TO INS

Form I-9 (Rev. 11-21-91)N

U.S. Department of Justice
Immigration and Naturalization Service

OMB No. 1115-0136

Employment Eligibility Verification

Please read instructions carefully before completing this form. The instructions must be available during completion of this form. ANTI-DISCRIMINATION NOTICE: It is illegal to discriminate against work eligible individuals. Employers CANNOT specify which document(s) they will accept from an employee. The refusal to hire an individual because of a future expiration date may also constitute illegal discrimination.

Section 1. Employee Information and Verification. *To be completed and signed by employee at the time employment begins.*

Print Name: Last	First	Middle Initial	Maiden Name

Address *(Street Name and Number)*	Apt. #	Date of Birth *(month/day/year)*

City	State	Zip Code	Social Security #

I am aware that federal law provides for imprisonment and/or fines for false statements or use of false documents in connection with the completion of this form.

I attest, under penalty of perjury, that I am (check one of the following):
- ☐ A citizen or national of the United States
- ☐ A Lawful Permanent Resident (Alien # A_____)
- ☐ An alien authorized to work until ___/___/___
  (Alien # or Admission #) _____

Employee's Signature	Date *(month/day/year)*

Preparer and/or Translator Certification. *(To be completed and signed if Section 1 is prepared by a person other than the employee.) I attest, under penalty of perjury, that I have assisted in the completion of this form and that to the best of my knowledge the information is true and correct.*

Preparer's/Translator's Signature	Print Name

Address *(Street Name and Number, City, State, Zip Code)*	Date *(month/day/year)*

Section 2. Employer Review and Verification. To be completed and signed by employer. Examine one document from List A OR examine one document from List B and one from List C, as listed on the reverse of this form, and record the title, number and expiration date, if any, of the document(s)

List A	OR	List B	AND	List C

Document title: _____

Issuing authority: _____

Document #: _____

Expiration Date *(if any):* ___/___/___   ___/___/___   ___/___/___

Document #: _____

Expiration Date *(if any):* ___/___/___

CERTIFICATION - I attest, under penalty of perjury, that I have examined the document(s) presented by the above-named employee, that the above-listed document(s) appear to be genuine and to relate to the employee named, that the employee began employment on *(month/day/year)* ___/___/___ **and that to the best of my knowledge the employee is eligible to work in the United States. (State employment agencies may omit the date the employee began employment.)**

Signature of Employer or Authorized Representative	Print Name	Title

Business or Organization Name	Address *(Street Name and Number, City, State, Zip Code)*	Date *(month/day/year)*

Section 3. Updating and Reverification. To be completed and signed by employer.

A. New Name *(if applicable)*	B. Date of rehire *(month/day/year) (if applicable)*

C. If employee's previous grant of work authorization has expired, provide the information below for the document that establishes current employment eligibility.

Document Title: _____   Document #: _____   Expiration Date (if any): ___/___/___

I attest, under penalty of perjury, that to the best of my knowledge, this employee is eligible to work in the United States, and if the employee presented document(s), the document(s) I have examined appear to be genuine and to relate to the individual.

Signature of Employer or Authorized Representative	Date *(month/day/year)*

Form I-9 (Rev. 11-21-91)N Page 2

LISTS OF ACCEPTABLE DOCUMENTS

LIST A	OR	LIST B	AND	LIST C
Documents that Establish Both Identity and Employment Eligibility		**Documents that Establish Identity**		**Documents that Establish Employment Eligibility**

LIST A

Documents that Establish Both Identity and Employment Eligibility

1. U.S. Passport (unexpired or expired)

2. Certificate of U.S. Citizenship *(INS Form N-560 or N-561)*

3. Certificate of Naturalization *(INS Form N-550 or N-570)*

4. Unexpired foreign passport, with *I-551 stamp or* attached INS Form *I-94* indicating unexpired employment authorization

5. Alien Registration Receipt Card with photograph *(INS Form I-151 or I-551)*

6. Unexpired Temporary Card *(INS Form I-688)*

7. Unexpired Employment Authorization Card *(INS Form I-688A)*

8. Unexpired Reentry Permit *(INS Form I-327)*

9. Unexpired Refugee Travel Document *(INS Form I-571)*

10. Unexpired Employment Authorization Document issued by the INS which contains a photograph *(INS Form I-688B)*

OR

LIST B

Documents that Establish Identity

1. Driver's license or ID card issued by a state or outlying possession of the United States provided it contains a photograph or information such as name, date of birth, sex, height, eye color and address

2. ID card issued by federal, state or local government agencies or entities, provided it contains a photograph or information such as name, date of birth, sex, height, eye color and address

3. School ID card with a photograph

4. Voter's registration card

5. U.S. Military card or draft record

6. Military dependent's ID card

7. U.S. Coast Guard Merchant Mariner Card

8. Native American tribal document

9. Driver's license issued by a Canadian government authority

For persons under age 18 who are unable to present a document listed above:

10. School record or report card

11. Clinic, doctor or hospital record

12. Day-care or nursery school record

AND

LIST C

Documents that Establish Employment Eligibility

1. U.S. social security card issued by the Social Security Administration *(other than a card stating it is not valid for employment)*

2. Certification of Birth Abroad issued by the Department of State *(Form FS-545 or Form DS-1350)*

3. Original or certified copy of a birth certificate issued by a state, county, municipal authority or outlying possession of the United States bearing an official seal

4. Native American tribal document

5. U.S. Citizen ID Card *(INS Form I-197)*

6. ID Card for use of Resident Citizen in the United States *(INS Form I-179)*

7. Unexpired employment authorization document issued by the INS *(other then those listed under List A)*

Illustrations of many of these documents appear in Part 8 of the Handbook for Employers (M-274)

Form I-9 (Rev. 11-21-91)N Page 3

APPENDIX C

C	FORMS	Check Request Form
		Crew Information Sheet
		Invoice Sheet
		Mileage Log
		Petty Cash Sheet
		Purchase Order Form

CHECK REQUEST

DATE _____   AMOUNT $ _____

SHOW _____   PROD # _____

COMPANY _____

ADDRESS _____   PHONE # _____

_____   FAX # _____

CHECK PAYEE _____   PHONE # _____

ADDRESS _____   FAX # _____

_____   ATTN: _____

PAYEE SS # OR FEDERAL ID # _____ CORPORATION: ☐ YES ☐ NO

☐ PURCHASE ☐ RENTAL ☐ DEPOSIT ☐ ADVANCE ☐ SERVICE ☐ 1099 ☐ ASSET

DESCRIPTION	CODING	AMOUNT

INCL. TAX IF APPLICABLE _____

TOTAL $ 0.00
_____

CHECK NEEDED: DAY _____ DATE _____

TIME _____ ☐ A.M. ☐ P.M.   ☐ WITHIN NORMAL PROCESSING TIME

WHEN READY, PLEASE: ☐ MAIL ☐ HOLD FORPICKUP ☐ GIVE TO _____

CHECK REQUESTED BY _____ DEPT _____

APPROVED BY _____ DATE _____

(INVOICESUBSTANTIATIONMUST FOLLOW THISREQUEST)

© ELH

278

CREW INFORMATION SHEET

Please fill in the following information completely and return this form to the Production Office. Thank You.

SHOW _____

NAME _____

POSITION _____ DEPARTMENT _____

HOME ADDRESS _____
_____

MAILING ADDRESS (if different) _____
_____

HOME PHONE # _____ PAGER # _____

HOME FAX # _____ MOBILE PHONE # _____

E-MAIL ADDRESS _____

☐ Check here if you DO NOT want any of the above information on the Crew List

☐ Check here if you just want your pager and mobile numbers on the Crew List

SOCIAL SEC # _____ BIRTHDAY (month/day) _____

LOAN-OUT Co. _____ FED. ID # _____

START DATE _____ UNION _____

EMERGENCY CONTACT _____

RELATIONSHIP _____ HOME PHONE # _____

MOBILE PHONE # _____ WORK PHONE # _____

TRAVELING PREFERENCES (We will try to accommodate your preferences to be best of our ability.)

AIRLINE SEAT (check one)   ☐ Window   ☐ Middle   ☐ Aisle   ☐ Bulkhead   ☐ No Preference

AIRLINE MEAL (check one)   ☐ Vegetarian   ☐ Non-Dairy   ☐ Kosher   ☐ No Preference

AIRLINE _____   ACCOUNT # (Please list your frequent flyer account numbers.)

_____   _____

_____   _____

_____   _____

_____   _____

ACCOMMODATION PREFERENCES

HOTEL ROOM LOCATION: ☐ Ground Level   ☐ In the Back   ☐ Near the Front   ☐ No Preference

BED SIZE: ☐ King   ☐ Queen   ☐ Two Beds

ROOMS: ☐ Smoking   ☐ Non-Smoking

IF AVAILABLE, I WOULD LIKE THE FOLLOWING IN MY ROOM:

☐ Refrigerator   ☐ Microwave   ☐ Extra Rollaway   ☐ Desk   ☐ Modem Line

The above information is solely for Production Office records and will be kept strictly confidential.

© A Stephen A. Marinaccio II form

INVOICE

TO _____   DATE _____

_____

_____

_____

FROM _____

(Address) _____

_____

(Phone #) _____

PAYEE SS# OR FEDERAL ID# _____ 1099 ☐

FOR SERVICES RENDERED ON_____ OR WEEK/ENDING_____

DESCRIPTION OF SERVICE/RENTAL/CAR ALLOWANCE	AMOUNT DUE

TOTAL AMOUNT DUE $ 0.00

EMPLOYEE SIGNATURE _____

APPROVED BY _____

PAID BY CHECK # _____   DATE _____

© ELH

280

MILEAGE LOG

NAME _____   WEEK ENDING _____

SHOW _____   PROD # _____

DATE	LOCATION		PURPOSE	MILEAGE
	FROM	TO		

TOTAL MILES _____ .0

_____ .0   MILES @ _____   ¢ PER MILE = _____ $ _____ .00

APPROVED BY _____   DATE _____

PD. BY CHECK# _____   DATE _____

© ELH

INDIVIDUAL PETTY CASH ACCOUNT

NAME _____   DEPT _____

SHOW _____   PROD # _____

FLOAT $ _____

DATE	CHECK#/CASH RECV'D FROM	AMOUNT RECV'D	ACCOUNTED FOR	BALANCE

PETTY CASH ACCOUNTING

NAME _____ DATE _____ ENVELOPE NUMBER [_____]

PICTURE _____ AMOUNT RECEIVED $ _____

POSITION _____ DEPT _____ ☐ CHECK ☐ CASH CHECK # _____

DATE	RECEIPT NUMBER	PAID TO	PAID FOR	ACCOUNT	AMOUNT

UPM _____ APPROVED _____   TOTAL RECEIPTS _____ $ 0.00

AUDITED _____ ENTERED _____   AMOUNT ADVANCED _____

PETTY CASH ADVANCE/REIMBURSEMENT   CASH/CHECKRET'D _____

RECEIVED IN CASH: $ _____ ON _____   REIMBURSEMENT DUE _____

SIGNATURE

NOTE: Tape receipts to 8 ½ x 11 sheets of paper and number each to correspond with numbers listed above. Receipts are to be originals; each must be dated and clearly indicate what it is for. Circle date, vendor, and total amount on each receipt.

© ELH

PURCHASE ORDER

DATE _____ P.O. # _____

SHOW _____ PROD # _____

COMPANY _____

ADDRESS _____ PHONE # _____

_____ FAX # _____

VENDOR _____ PHONE # _____

ADDRESS _____ FAX # _____

_____ CONTACT _____

VENDOR SS # OR FEDERAL ID # _____ CORPORATION ☐ YES ☐ NO

☐ PURCHASE   ☐ RENTAL   ☐ SERVICE   (Indicate if amount being charged is per show, day, week, or month.)

DESCRIPTION	CODING	AMOUNT

SET #(s) _____   INCL. TAX IF APPLICABLE _____

TOTAL COST _____ $ 0.00

IF TOTAL COST CANNOT BE DETERMINEDAT THIS DATE, ESTIMATE OF COSTS WILL NOT EXCEED$ _____

IF P.O. IS FOR A **RENTAL**, PLEASE INDICATE RENTAL DATES   FROM _____ TO _____

ORDER PLACED BY _____   DEPT. _____

APPROVED BY _____   DATE _____

© ELH

APPENDIX D

D	PRODUCTION LISTS	Breakdown Sheet
		Call Sheet Front
		Call Sheet Back
		Day-Out-of-Days
		Location List
		One-Line Schedule
		Set Breakdown Item Page
		Shooting Schedule

BREAKDOWN SHEET

SHOW_____ BREAKDOWN PAGE #_____

LOCATION _____ PROD #_____

☐ STAGE   ☐ LOCAL LOCATION   ☐ DISTANT LOCATION   DATE _____

SCENE #s		DESCRIPTION ☐ INT. ☐ EXT.		STORY DAY ☐ DAY ☐ NIGHT ☐ DAWN ☐ DUSK	# OF PAGES
					TOTAL PAGES

NO.	CAST	ATMOSPHERE	PROPS /SET DRESSING
		CAMERA	**WARDROBE**

STAND-INS	SPECIAL EFFECTS	VISUAL EFFECTS

STUNTS	TRANSPORTATION / PIC. VEHICLES	SOUND / MUSIC

MAKEUP / HAIR	ELECTRIC / GRIP / CRANES	SPECIAL EQUIPMENT

SPECIAL MAKEUP EFFECTS	ANIMALS / LIVESTOCK / WRANGLERS	OTHER
		☐ TEACHER / WELFARE WORKER

286

CALL SHEET

PRODUCTION COMPANY _____ DATE _____

SHOW _____ DIRECTOR _____

SERIES EPISODE_____ PRODUCER _____

PROD # _____ DAY # _____ OUT OF _____ LOCATION _____

IS TODAY A DESIGNATED DAY OFF? ☐ YES ☐ NO SUNRISE _____ SUNSET _____

CREW CALL_____ ANTICIPATED WEATHER_____

LEAVING CALL_____ ☐ Weather Permitting   ☐ See Attached Map

SHOOTING CALL _____ ☐ Report to Location   ☐ Bus to Location

SET DESCRIPTION	SCENE #	CAST	D/N	PAGES	LOCATION

CAST	PART OF	LEAVE	MAKEUP	SET CALL	REMARKS

ATMOSPHERE & STAND-INS	

NOTE: No forced calls without previous approval of unit production manager or assistant director. All calls subject to change.

ADVANCE SCHEDULE OR CHANGES

Assistant Director _____ Production Manager_____

© ELH

PRODUCTION REQUIREMENT

SHOW:		PROD #:		DATE:	
Production Mgr.		Gaffer		Cameras	
1st Asst. Dir		Best Boy			
2nd Asst. Dir		Lamp Oper.		Dolly	
2nd 2nd Asst. Dir		Lamp Oper.		Crane	
DGA Trainee		Lamp Oper.		Condor	
Script Supervisor		Local 40 Man			
Dialogue Coach				Sound Channel	
Prod. Coordinator		Prod. Designer			
Prod. Sect'y		Art Director		Video	
Prod. Accountant		Asst. Art Dir.			
Asst. Accountant		Set Designer		Radio Mikes	
Location Mgr.		Sketch Artist		Walkie/talkies	
Asst. Location Mgr.					
Teacher/Welfare Worker		Const. Coord.		Dressing Rooms	
Production Assts.		Const. Foreman		Schoolrooms	
		Paint Foreman		Rm. For Parents	
Dir of Photography		Labor Foreman			
Camera Operator		Const. First Aid		Projector	
Camera Operator				Moviola	
SteadyCam Operator		Set Director			
Asst. Cameraman		Lead Person		Air Conditioners	
Asst. Cameraman		Swing Crew		Heaters	
Asst. Cameraman		Swing Crew		Wind Machines	
Still Photographer		Swing Crew			
Cameraman-Process		Drapery			
Projectionist					
		Technical Advisor		**SUPPORT**	
Mixer		Publicist		**PERSONNEL**	**TIME**
Boomman		**MEALS**		Policemen	
Cableman		Caterer		Motorcycles	
Playback		Breakfasts		Fireman	
Video Oper.		Wlkg. Breakfasts rdy @		Guard	
		Gallons Coffee		Night Watchman	
Key Grip		Lunches rdy @ Crew @			
2nd Grip		Box Lunches			
Dolly Grip		Second Meal			
Grip					
Grip					
Grip		**DRIVERS**		**VEHICLES**	
		Trans. Coord.		Prod. Van	
Greensman		Trans. Capt.		Camera	
		Driver		Grip	
S/By Painter		Driver		Electric	
Craftservice		Driver		Effects	
First Aid		Driver		Props	
		Driver		Wardrobe	
Spec. Efx		Driver		Makeup	
Spec. Efx		Driver		Set Dressing	
		Driver		Crew Bus	
Propmaster		Driver		Honeywagon	
Asst. Props		Driver		Motorhomes	
Asst. Props		Driver		Station Wagons	
		Driver		Mini-buses	
Costume Designer		Driver		Standby Cars	
Costume Supervisor		Driver		Crew Cabs	
Costumer		Driver		Insert Cars	
Costumer		Driver		Generators	
		Driver		Water Wagon	
Makeup Artist		Driver		Picture Cars	
Makeup Artist		Driver			
Body Makeup					
Hairstylist		Stunt Coord.			
Hairstylist		Wranglers			
		Animal Handlers		Livestock	
Editor				Animals	
Asst. Editor					
Apprentice Editor					

DEPARTMENT	SPECIAL INSTRUCTIONS

288

DAY-OUT-OF-DAYS

PRODUCTION COMPANY

PRODUCTION TITLE

EPISODE TITLE

PRODUCTION #

SCRIPT DATED

DATE

PRODUCER

DIRECTOR

UNIT PRODUCTION MGR.

FIRST ASST. DIRECTOR

MONTH →
DAY OF WEEK →
SHOOTING DAYS →

NAME	CHARACTER																			TRAVEL	START	FINISH	WORK	IDLE	TOTAL
1																									
2																									
3																									
4																									
5																									
6																									
7																									
8																									
9																									
10																									
11																									
12																									
13																									
14																									
15																									
16																									
17																									
18																									
19																									
20																									
21																									
22																									
23																									
24																									
25																									
26																									
27																									
28																									
29																									
30																									
31																									

© ELH

LOCATION LIST

SHOW _____

PRODUCTION NUMBER _____

SET LOCATION	ACTUAL LOCATION (ADDRESS & PHONE)	DATE & DAYS (PREP/SHOOT/STRIKE)	CONTACTS (OWNER & REPRESENTATIVE)
	( ) -		
	( ) -		
	( ) -		
	( ) -		
	( ) -		
	( ) -		

© ELH

SAMPLE

XYZ PRODUCTIONS

HERBY'S SUMMER VACATION - PROD# 0100

ONE-LINE SCHEDULE

PRODUCER:	SWIFTY DEALS
DIRECTOR:	SID CELLULOID
PRODUCTION MANAGER:	FRED FILMER
1ST ASST. DIRECTOR:	ALICE DEES

FILM SHOOTS - 36 DAYS
TUESDAY, JUNE 1, 20XX
THROUGH
FRIDAY, JULY 17, 20XX

FIRST DAY - TUESDAY, JUNE 1, 20XX

Sc.   1   EXT. PIER AT SUNRISE - Day - 1/8 pg.
                Sunrise over pier at Venice Beach

Scs. 2-13   EXT. VENICE BEACH - Day - 1-6/8 Pgs.
                Steve jogs

Sc.   23   EXT. FRONT OF HOTEL - Day - 1/8 pg.
                Steve jogs up to the front of the hotel

Scs. 46-52   EXT. STRAND IN VENICE - Day - 2-3/8 pgs.
                Steve greets friends on his way out to
                job. He smiles at Laura.

Scs. 87-90   EXT. VENICE STRAND - Day - 6/8 pg.
                Nick and Cory walk together.

Sc.   95   EXT. VENICE STRAND - DAY - 4/8 pg.
                Steve and Laura talk to Herby.

Sc.   101   INT. VENICE RESTAURANT - Day - 1/8 pg.
                Couple nods hello to Seve and Laura.

Sc.   91   EXT. STRAND AREA NEAR PIER - Day - 6/8 pg.
                Marc skates for them.

END OF FIRST DAY   TOTAL PAGES: 6-4/8

291

SET BREAKDOWN ITEM PAGE

SET NAME _____

SHOW _____

LOCATION MANAGER _____

SHOOT DAY _____

MOBILE / PAGER # _____

SCENES _____

EMAIL _____

TOTAL PAGES _____

SERVER/DROP BOX I.D. #_____

| SET NUMBER | INT ☐ | EXT ☐ | DAY ☐ | NIGHT ☐ | LOCATION FOREMAN _____ |
| | | | | | MOBILE / PAGER # _____ |

| LOCATION INFORMATION | ADDRESS | PHONE |
| | CONTACT | |

| STUDIO / STAGE | ADDRESS | PHONE |
| | CONTACT | |

PRODUCTION DESIGN NOTES	RETROFIT ☐
	REPAINT ☐
	SIGNAGE ☐
	GRAPHICS ☐
DATE _____	WHITE MODEL ☐
	DIGITAL MODEL ☐

1ST SCOUT NOTES

DATE _____

2ND SCOUT NOTES

DATE _____

TECH SCOUT NOTES

DATE _____

ART DEPT COORDINATOR	NAME	SET COMPLETION DATE
	PHONE / PAGER #	
	SERVER/DROP BOX I.D. #	
SET DESIGNER	NAME	SHOOT DATE
	PHONE / PAGER #	
	SERVER/DROP BOX I.D. #	

MR2004

XYZ PRODUCTIONS

HERBY'S SUMMER VACATION - PROD# 0100

SHOOTING SCHEDULE

PRODUCER:	SWIFTY DEALS	FILM SHOOTS - 36 DAYS
DIRECTOR:	SID CELLULOID	TUESDAY, JUNE 1, 20XX
PRODUCTION MANAGER:	FRED FILMER	THROUGH
1ST ASST. DIRECTOR:	ALICE DEES	FRIDAY, JULY 17, 20XX

DATE	SET/SCENES	CAST	LOCATION
1ST DAY TUESDAY 6/1/0X	EXT. LAUREL ROAD - Day Day 1 - 1-1/8 pg. Scs. 6, 7, 8 The boys discover a hole in the fence and look through to the other side. NOTES:	1. HERBY 2. JED 3. MARC STAND-INS Herby S.I. Jed S.I. Marc S.I. ATMOS 2 elderly ladies (passers-by)	SWEETWATER ROAD PACIFIC PALISADES PROPS Marc's ball MAKE-UP Cut on Herby's Hand VEHICLES old truck next to fence
	EXT. LAURA'S BACKYARD - Day Day 1 - 1-4/8 pgs. Scs. 9 & 10 The boys see Laura sunbathing by her pool. NOTES:	1. HERBY 2. LAURA 3. JED 4. MARK STAND-INS Herby S.I. Laura S.I. Jed S.I. Marc S.I. SPEC. EFX. Light steam off pool	(SAME AS ABOVE) PROPS Towel Makeup bag Laura's sunglasses WARDROBE Laura's white bikini VEHICLES Laura's Mercedes (in driveway)
	EXT. LAURA'S BACKYARD - Day Day 1 - 2-4/8 pgs. Sc. 11 Steve joins Laura and chases the boys away from the fence NOTES:	1. HERBY 2. LAURA 3. JED 4. MARC 7. STEVE STAND-INS Herby S.I. Laura S.I. Jed S.I. Marc S.I Steve S.I.	(SAME AS ABOVE) WARDROBE Steve in sport shirt & jacket VEHICLES Laura's Mercedes Steve's BMW SPECIAL EQUIPMENT 1 - 60' condor
END OF DAY #1		TOTAL PAGES:	5-1/8 pgs.

□ □ □
□ □ □
□ □ □

APPENDIX E

E FIGURE AND TABLE LIST All images used in this book from Chapter 1 through the Appendix

Figure #	Caption	Color
Fig. 1-1	Film hierarchy (simplified).	
Fig. 1-2	Wilfred Buckland, the first Hollywood art director.	
Fig. 1-3	Production still from *The Cheat*. B) An example of a "Lasky Lighting" effect for the same scene, designed by Wilfred Buckland.	
Fig. 1-4	A) Perspective aerial close-up shot of Robin Hood castle. B) High aerial shot of Robin Hood castle. C) Production shot of the Robin Hood castle: The glass painted matte above the existing set suggests additional architecture within or beyond. D) Interior: Great Hall with the Robin Hood castle. E) Interior: A battle scene is fought just inside the main courtyard entrance of the castle set. F) Holding court just outside the Robin Hood castle walls.	
Fig. 1-5	The Motion Picture Art Director: Responsibilities, functions, and accomplishments. Courtesy of ADG—Local 800 IATSE.	
Fig. 2-1	Art department hierarchy: A functional chart. Courtesy of ADG—Local 800 IATSE.	
Fig. 2-2	Wheel of art department influence.	
Fig. 2-3	The revised art department. Courtesy of Alex McDowell © 2002.	Color plate section
Fig. 3-1	Typical locations folder: Left: Bradford Building, L.A., Top panorama: Ford Theatre, D.C., Middle panorama: Farmhouse, Luxembourg, Bottom panorama: Moab, UT.	Color plate section
Fig. 3-2	Scout notes for N. Carolina locations on *My Fellow Americans*.	
Fig. 3-3	Preliminary set breakdown for *Red Dragon*.	
Fig. 3-4	A) Solar anti-mosquito guard, B) Magnetic angle locator, C) Fly catcher strip, D) Professional Measure Master II™, E) Suunto inclination device, F) Digital distance indicator, G) Scale Master Classic™ digital plan measure, H) Rulers: flat architectural scale ruler, three-sided architectural scale ruler, and a wooden scissor-extension ruler (diagonal). A 12"-diameter measuring wheelie with an extendable tube makes measuring over terrain easy up to 999' without the use of a 500' cloth tape measure (not pictured).	

permission of Oxford University Press, Inc. from HOW TO READ A FILM: THE ART, TECHNOLOGY, LANGUAGE, HISTORY, AND THEORY OF FILM AND MEDIA, 3rd Edition by James Monaco, copyright © 1977, 1981, 2000 by James Monaco.

Fig. 4-18   Sketch of plan and schematic by John Graysmark for *Lifeforce* Cathedral scene, front projection technique.

Fig. 4-19   A) Elevation sketch by John Graysmark showing the onstage, front-projected House of Commons Lobby set (2005). B) Plan sketch by John Graysmark showing the onstage, front-projected House of Commons Lobby set (2005). YOUNG WINSTON © 1972, renewed 2000 Columbia Pictures Industries, Inc. All Rights Reserved—Courtesy of Columbia Pictures.

Fig. 5-1   A comparison of the credit list of six films from *Modern Times* (1936) to *Lord of the Rings: Return of the King* (2004). Courtesy of the New York Times: Baseline/Filmtracker and New Line Cinema.

Fig. 6-1A   Hand-drafted city jail plan—upper and lower levels —by Maya Shimoguchi. MURDER IN THE FIRST © 1994 Warner Bros., a division of Time Warner Entertainment Company, L.P. and Le Studio Canal + (U.S.). All Rights Reserved.

Fig. 6-1B   Hand-drafted city jail elevations—upper and lower levels—by Maya Shimoguchi. MURDER IN THE FIRST © 1994 Warner Bros., a division of Time Warner Entertainment Company, L.P. and Le Studio Canal + (U.S.). All Rights Reserved.

Fig. 6-2   Hand-drafted city jail ceiling: reflected ceiling plan, section through ceiling skylight, and **FSD** of skylight center by Maya Shimoguchi. MURDER IN THE FIRST © 1994 Warner Bros., a division of Time Warner Entertainment Company, L.P. and Le Studio Canal + (U.S.). All Rights Reserved.

Fig. 6-3   Foam sculpted courtroom angels pictured, with art department crew. MURDER IN THE FIRST © 1994 Warner Bros., a division of Time Warner Entertainment Company, L.P. and Le Studio Canal + (U.S.). All Rights Reserved.

Fig. 6-4   Hand-drafted courtroom and judge's chamber sets drawn by Michael Rizzo. Inset: Spotting plan, indicating placement on Stage 12, Culver Studios.

APPENDIX F

F	GLOSSARY	All terms that are "bolded" in the text

180 degree rule
A screen direction rule that camera operators must follow—an imaginary line on one side of the axis of action is made, e.g., between two principal actors in a scene. The camera must not cross over that line; otherwise there is a distressing visual discontinuity and disorientation. Camera placement must adhere to the 180-degree rule.

24 frames per second
Refers to the standard frame rate or film speed, e.g., the number of frames or images that are projected or displayed per second. In the silent era before a standard was set, many films were projected at 16 or 18 frames per second, but that rate proved to be too slow when attempting to record optical film sound tracks, e.g., 24 fps or 24 p.

2nd Unit director
The 1st Unit is the main shooting crew of a movie. Second unit crews are appointed by the director to shoot additional footage. Traditionally, the stunt coordinator heads the second unit on action films. Shooting simultaneously on the regular shooting schedule saves time and money.

Anaglypta™
(Trade name) A type of wallpaper made from the pulp of cotton fiber now used to refer to any type of paper with embossed patterns created by hollow mouldings that can be painted, stained, and aged. It is more flexible and lighter than its similar counterpart Lincresta and was cheaper when it was first produced during the nineteenth century. It is very durable and is most commonly used below the dado rail in halls and stairways. It was invented in 1886 by Thomas Palmer, was adored by the Victorians and Edwardians, and is still in production today.

Anamorphic
Relates to different optical imaging effects; a method of intentionally distorting and creating a wide-screen image with standard film, using a conversion process or a special lens on the camera and projector to produce different magnifications in the vertical and horizontal dimensions of the picture. An anamorphic image usually appears "squished" horizontally, while retaining its full vertical resolution. (See also, **aspect ratio**.)

Animatic
A sophisticated type of preview-storyboard, often shot and edited on video with a soundtrack, or the more comprehensive, updated, graphic version of storyboarding showing typical plan and elevation, as well as camera moves, camera angles with additional shooting equipment, i.e., cranes, etc.

Aspect ratio
The numerical relationship of the height and width of the image frame used in film and television. There are several standard aspect ratios used internationally: The Academy Aperture is 1.33 : 1; European standard wide screen is 1.66 : 1; American standard wide screen is 1.85 : 1; the 70 mm frame is 2.2 : 1; and the anamorphic ratio is 2.35 : 1.

The most common aspect ratio found through the 1950s was called *Academy Aperture*, at a ratio of 1.33 : 1—the same as 4 : 3 on a TV screen. Normal 35 mm films are shot at a ratio of 1.85 : 1. New wide-screen formats and aspect ratios were introduced in the 1950s, from 1.65 : 1 and higher. Cinemascope™ was a wide-screen movie format used in the U.S. from 1953 to 1967, and other anamorphic systems such as Panavision™ have a 2.35 : 1 AR, while 70 mm formats have an AR of 2.2 : 1. Cinerama™ had a 2.77 : 1 aspect ratio, letterboxed videos for wide-screen TVs are frequently in 16 : 9 or 1.77 : 1 AR.

Avant-garde
A French term literally meaning "ahead of the crowd," referring to films made outside the commercial, profit-oriented filmmaking enclave. These films are referred to as art films and are usually experimental films.

AD
A short end version of art director.

Back projection
A photographic technique whereby live action is filmed in front of a transparent screen onto which background action is projected. Back projection was often used to provide the special effect of motion in vehicles during dialogue scenes, but has become outmoded and replaced by blue-screen processing and traveling mattes. Back projection is also known as rear projection, process photography, or process shot as opposed to matte shot.

Example: Any film with a moving vehicle and back-projected street scenes viewed through the back or side windows, such as in *To Catch a Thief* (1955).

Basecamp
A compound word coined by the film industry describing a parking lot or neighborhood in town (Hollywood), or a suite of offices, a converted warehouse space, or large grouping of trailers on location out of town, representing the film studio off premises. Think: the military, a hiking expedition, or the Wild West.

Below-the-Line
Both above and below-the-line are accounting categories describing the divisions of salary level and perks existing in the film business. Above-the-line includes: producers, directors, actors, cinematographers, and some production designers. Below-the-line includes: everyone else.

Billing
Name and title placed within the credits listed on a movie screen, movie poster, or any other advertising of a motion picture.

Blocked
also, *blocking*
Refers to how a director positions actors on a set in order to properly deliver lines as they play a scene.

Bluelines
Another term for blueprints, architectural in origin.

Bluescreen
A process in which actors perform in front of an evenly lit, monochromatic, usually blue or green, background. The background is then replaced in post-production by chromakeying, or allowing other footage or computer-generated images to form the background imagery, around the actor in the foreground footage. Since 1992, most films use a greenscreen. (See also, **greenscreen**)

Bobbinette
A loosely woven theatrical fabric, much like a fine fishnet, used for its invisible quality for onstage scenery. (See also, **sharktooth scrim**)

Borders and legs
Originally a theatrical term for lengths of black velour material, generally called "blacks," tailored to hang in specific arrangements "to frame" the look of onstage scenery. "Masking stage curtains" is a good way to describe blacks. A border is a horizontal black typically 8–10' high, and in widths varying from 30–50'. A leg is a vertical black typically 8–12' wide, and in lengths varying from 12–30'. A border and a pair of legs are used in groups. They are attached to suspended pipes or battens by ties, or small pieces of rope. On film stages, blacks have the same function in terms of scenery—to frame what the camera sees or doesn't see.

Box rental
In addition to salary, a deal memo negotiated with the unit production manager, includes items like PC, digital camera, or scanner rented by the production company from the person signing a contract to work on a film. This rental fee is paid in a check separate to the paycheck and listed separately on an IRS form as additional income.

Breakaway
Refers primarily to glass objects either as plate glass in windows or handheld glasses, cups, plates, etc., used for stunt/mechanical effects gags in a scene. It also refers to destroyable scenery, e.g., explosions.

CADD/CAD
A quick difference between CADD, computer assisted drawing and drafting, and CAD, computer assisted drawing, must be made here. CADD specifically refers to drafting either architecture or scenery, whereas CAD is a generic term encompassing all computer-assisted drawing software.

Call time
The specific time each individual is expected to begin work on a film set. This information is indicated on a call sheet, a page composed by the assistant directorial staff while organizing the daily shooting schedule. Traditionally, call times are day scheduled; nighttime shooting schedules require reporting times at night. (See also, **wrap time**)

Camera Angle Projection
A system of perspective drawing for cinematography whereby the dimensions on a plan and elevation can be processed according to the camera angles of a given lens and aspect ratio, i.e., degree of convergence. Using these elements of this system, one can draw an accurate elevation sketch of any set. Harold Michelson—storyboard artist, concept illustrator, and art director—invented this perspective drawing system.

Card model
A white model. (See also, **white model**)

CGI
Computer Generated Imagery.

Chroma
also, *hue*
An attribute of a color derived from splitting a beam of light with a prism producing red, orange, yellow, green, blue, indigo, violet. The light primaries are red, blue, and green; the pigment primaries are red, blue, and yellow. (See also, **hue**)

Chromakey
also *chromakeying*
An electronic/computerized technique that allows for specific color elements (chroma) to be replaced with different picture elements. In simple terms, this is done by separating out the three, primary light colors (chroma) of red, blue, and green onto separate channels and using them to manipulate different aspects of the captured image during the development process.

Colortrans
A large-scale color photograph printed on a flexible, translucent material. It is the name of a category of photographic backdrop lit from both back and front surfaces, as opposed to painted backdrop, lit just on its front side. (See also, **translite**)

Composite
The process and product of combining of two images onto a single piece of 35 mm film. One component of the composite image is typically foreground action and the other component is background imagery shot elsewhere. The process involves the use of matting or replacing imagery.

Contract Services
The Roster, a listing of available art directors in good standing in the Art Directors Guild, Local 800, is maintained by the Contract Services Administrative Trust Fund (CSATF) and is separate and apart from the Guild. To get onto the Roster, one must apply to Contract Services and have worked on a total of no less than 30 days for one or more signatory companies within the one-year period immediately preceding application

for Roster placement. Contract Services also arranges health care, education and other benefits for Union members.

Cover set
Scenery pre-built, easily dressed, and ready for shooting on a soundstage or other interior space, given inclement weather conditions and a possible disruption of the shooting schedule.

C-stand
A piece of grip equipment combining the use of an adjustable C-clamp on the neck of a sturdy, metal, and a three-legged stand.

Cyclorama
A continuous length of fabric at least 20 feet high or a built scenery wall the same size, used as a fixed backdrop to suggest sky or similar volumes of space on a stage.

Dado
Another term for chair rail, a decorative moulding placed on a wall at about waist height to stop chair backs from marking the wall. It also provides a convenient level to stop wallpapering.

Dailies
A previous day's work shot by principal and second unit shooting crews shown at the end of the next day's shooting. Dailies or rushes are always viewed after the fact.

Descenders
A British term used by paratroopers in free-fall simulator training. Adopted by the American film industry, free-fall simulators revolutionized high-fall stunts.

Drop
Shorthand for backdrop. (See also, **paint frame**)

Dupe
Shortened version of duplicate as it refers to the copy of a photographic image.

Duvetyne
A felt-like, black fabric in extra-wide widths used as backing pieces for theater, TV, and film sets.

Ellipsis
The shortening of the plot duration of a film achieved by deliberately omitting intervals or sections of the narrative story or action. An ellipsis is marked by an editing transition, e.g., a fade, dissolve, wipe, jump cut, or change of scene to omit a period or gap of time from the film's narrative.

Experimental film
Refers to a low-budget or Indie film not oriented toward profit-making, challenging conventional filmmaking by using camera techniques,

imagery, sound, editing, and/or acting in unusual or creative ways. (See also, **avant-garde**)

Examples: *Un Chien Andalou* (1929), *The Seventh Seal* (1957), *Amerika* (1972–1983), *Pink Flamingos* (1972), *Eraserhead* (1976), *Zenotropa* (1991).

Exposition
The initial plot layout of a film revealed within the first ten minutes as a psychological or emotional "hook" to dramatically enroll the attention of the audience.

Feeding tent
A large, rented tent set up on location with tables and chairs as a meal place for the crew.

Flat
also, *flattage*
A scenery wall.

Frames per second
also, *fps*
Present-day films are usually run through a camera or projector at a frame rate, that is, running speed or camera speed of 24 fps. Older films, made at 18 fps, appear jerky and sped-up when played back at 24 fps—this technique is referred to as *undercranking*. Overcranking refers to changing the frame rate, i.e., shooting at 48 or 96 fps, thereby producing slow-motion action when viewed at 24 fps.

Example: The William Tell Overture sequence in *A Clockwork Orange* (1971) is an example of undercranking. Action films often use overcranking for film explosions so that the action is prolonged.

FSD
Shortened version of full size detail. A drawing in actual size indicating up-close detail for exact building purposes.

Fuller's earth
An older name for a taupe colored, powdery substance used primarily to age set dressing or reduce glare on reflective surfaces that the camera sees when shooting. The new term used is "Movie Dirt."

Gaffer
A film electrician. English electricians are called "sparks."

Gimbal
also, *gimbaled*
Traditionally, this cinematic term refers to the mechanism responsible for the spinning of a room or similar interior scenery piece. In contrast, the common use of the term refers to the mechanism that keeps an object, like a compass, horizontal regardless of outside movement—it is related to the working principles of a gyroscope.

Green light
The formal OK given by a film studio to the producer or UPM of film production office to begin pre-production activity.

Greenscreen
A newer technique similar to bluescreen, using a chromakey green background in place of an evenly lit blue background. Research has shown that substantially better results could be gained by filming on green instead of blue, as the sensitivity of modern film stock was more sensitive to separating key green light from other foreground colors. (See also **chromakeying**)

Hero
A term referring to any set, set piece, item of set dressing, prop, or vehicle relating to a main character—male or female. It is used as an adjective and can refer to a hero or villain, i.e., the hero getaway car, or the hero honeymoon suite.

High concept
As in "high concept film." The idea of a sound bite used in pitching or advertising the concept of a film, simply stated and easily understood by everyone, i.e., a pathetic nerd is secretly an invincible superhero.

Highly directional
This phrase refers to the reflective quality of a front projection screen. 3M-screen material reflects most stage light back to the camera with little ambient light loss; the surface-silvered mirror has a 50/50 reflective/see-through capacity and a perfect ability to both reflect and transmit light.

Hot set
A set or location being actively shot on or used by the shooting crew of a film.

Hue
also, *chroma*
An attribute of a color derived from splitting a beam of light with a prism producing red, orange, yellow, green, blue, indigo, violet. The light primaries are red, blue, and green; the pigment primaries are red, blue, and yellow. (See also, **chroma**)

Icon, Iconic
(Gr. *eikono- < eikon*, image) A simile or symbol. An icon is *an image* that is what it *is*. Human emotions captured on the screen are icons that can be read in any language—they are universal. When we watch Roberto Benigni (*Life Is Beautiful*) win the 1998 Academy Award for best actor, we understood joy. In the "language of film," which includes semiology, or the study of systems of signs, there is a signifier and the signified. An icon is a sign in which the signifier (image) represents the signified (meaning) through its likeness or close similarity to it.

In-camera
This term refers to any processing or optical work done primarily with mattes within the body of the camera, in order to composite companion pieces of film shot for the same scene.

Index
One of three "signs" or metaphorical imagery used in film language. As an image, a sign presumes a sign(ifier) and that which is sign(ified) within the visual syntax of a film. A sign or visual image can be: 1) an Icon or an image that *is* what it is: a screaming face is horror; or 2) an Index, an image that suggests an inherent relationship: a wad of bills given to a prostitute; or 3) a Symbol, an image representing a meaning through convention: a flag symbolizes patriotism. Semantics, you say? Yes, film being a visual language is full of denotative and connotative images.

Indie
also, ***independents or independent films***
Small, low-budget companies, mini-majors, or entities for financing, producing, and distributing films, i.e., Miramax, New Line Cinema, Polygram, working outside of the system or a major Hollywood studio. California-based Miramax, although the leader in the independent film movement in the early nineties, has become so powerful and successful that it has lost most of its independent studio status. Indie refers to a movie, director, distributor, or producer not associated with a major Hollywood film studio, often with groundbreaking subject matter designed for sophisticated audiences, and not necessarily produced with commercial success as the goal (like mainstream films).

Example: Indie films include Jim Jarmusch's *Stranger Than Paradise* (1984) and Kevin Smith's *Clerks* (1994). The cable TV *Independent Film Channel* showcases Indie films.

Insert shot
Usually a close-up shot of a prop or an actor shot at a later time, out of sequence to the scene it was originally part of. This requires organizing set dressing and wall sections of the related scenery to be set up for shooting on the revised shooting day.

In-studio
The shooting of a motion picture in a proper film studio as opposed to on location.

Intermittent movement
It is the heart, or essential component, of any motion picture camera comprised of an assembly located just behind the camera lens and aperture, or light opening within the lens mount. The intermittent movement has a double function: it physically pulls the film down by the sprocket holes on either side of the filmstrip, and it alternately exposes the film by "intermittently" blocking the light with a rotating shutter frame by frame.

Key frame
A single shot image of a digital sketch or model, used in previsualization as a visual template.

Lincresta
A type of wall covering made of wood pulp strengthened with linseed oil, gum, and resins. It is usually spread over canvas and given an embossed pattern with engraved metal rollers. It can be painted or stained, and it is both waterproof and durable making it perfect for hallway walls and ceilings. It was invented in 1877 by

Frederick Walton and, like Anaglypta, was commonplace in Victorian and Edwardian homes. Not much later, it was also embossed out of pressed tin for the same uses. It is still made today.

Locked-off
A stationary camera supported by a tripod or camera pedestal base.

Magazine
A spool of film.

Majors
Refers to the major Hollywood motion picture producer/distributor studios at the present time, i.e., 20th Century Fox, Disney Studios, DreamWorks SKG, MGM/UA, Paramount Pictures, Sony-Columbia/Tri-Star, Warner Bros., and Universal, in contrast to the smaller, mini-major production-distribution companies, i.e., Miramax, New Line Cinema, and Polygram that compete directly with the bigger studios.

Martini shot
The last shot of the last scene of the day—jut before wrap time.

Matte shot
The optical process of combining (or compositing) separately-photographed shots—usually actors in the foreground and the setting in the background—onto one print through a double exposure that does not meld two images on top of each other, but masks off, or makes opaque, part of the frame area for one exposure and the opposite area for another exposure. It is a photographic technique whereby a painting or artwork from a matte artist—usually painted on glass—is combined with live action footage to provide a convincing setting for the action; also sometimes known as *split-screen*.

McGuffin or MacGuffin
Alfred Hitchcock's term for the device or plot element, e.g., an item, object, goal, event, or piece of knowledge, that catches the viewer's attention or drives the logic or action of the plot and appears extremely important to the film characters, but often turns out to be insignificant, or is to be ignored after it has served its purpose.

Example: "Mistaken identity" at the beginning of *North by Northwest* (1959) and the "government secrets," the uranium ore in *Notorious* (1946), or "the stolen money" in *Psycho* (1960); also the "black bird" in *The Maltese Falcon* (1941) served as a McGuffin.

Metaphor
A filmic device in which a scene, character, object, or action may be associated, identified, or interpreted as an implied representation of something else. (See also, **symbol** and **trope**)

Miniature
also, ***miniature shot*** or ***model***
Small-scale models photographed to give the illusion that they are full-scale objects.

Example: The spacecraft in *2001: A Space Odyssey* (1968).

Mise en scène

A French phrase literally meaning, "putting in the scene" in physical or spatial terms within the frame. In film theory, it refers to staging action that covers or records an entire scene within the frame of the film, and the arrangement, composition, and content of the visual elements before the camera, usually in a long-shot, including settings, decor, props, actors, costumes, lighting, performances, and character movements and positioning. It includes both technical and non-technical elements that make up a scene's look and feel.

Its opposite, montage or "putting together," refers to the time element of filmmaking. These twin elements of cinematic space and time fuel the engine of the process. Mise en scène is what an art director does.

MoCap

Motion capture describes the process of tracking the movement of an actor with tiny sensors fitted in regular patterns over the surface of a form-fitting suit and head cap. This information is fed to the hard drive of a computer and digitally manipulated for storytelling.

Montage

Literally, "putting together;" refers to a filming technique, editing style, or form of movie collage consisting of a series of successive short shots or images that are rapidly juxtaposed into a coherent sequence to suggest meaning, i.e., dissolves, fades, superimpositions, and wipes are often used to link the images in a montage sequence. An accelerated montage is composed of shots of increasingly shorter lengths.

Example: The breakfast scene in *Citizen Kane* (1941), the ambush scene in *Bonnie and Clyde* (1967), the 45 second shower scene in *Psycho* (1960) with 78 camera setups and 50 splices for the shooting of the scene.

Motion pictures
also, ***movies***, ***pic(s)***, ***pix***,
or ***moving pictures***

A series of photographic images arranged in a vertical or horizontal strip moving at a constant speed and projected with light (or electronically) onto a screen for information or entertainment purposes.

Example: Edweard Muybridge's "animal animation" or "persistence of vision" experiments in the late nineteenth century is one of the earlier examples of motion picture experimentation.

MOW

Shortened version of *Movie of the Week*.

Murphy's Laws and corollaries

Rules of life and work. Murphy's Law ("If anything can go wrong, it will") was born at Edwards Air Force Base in 1949. Go to http://dmawww.epfl.ch/roso.mosaic/dm/murphy.html

One-liner
also, ***one-line schedule***

A shortened version of the shooting schedule composed by the UPM and 1st assistant director. (See also, **shooting schedule**)

Onionskin

A term used to describe pieces of yellow tracing paper torn from rolls of various lengths, used to quickly sketch ideas in the designing/drafting process. It is commonly known as *tracing paper*.

Optical printing

In photographic terms, there are two ways of printing an image: contact printing by placing a negative transparency against a piece of photographic paper, and optical printing or taking a picture of a picture. This is done by placing a transparency in front of a light box, composing and focusing the positive image on the viewfinder, balancing light intensity with regard to lens aperture and shutter speed, and making a negative from the exposed film. Contact printing two strips of film, emulsion to emulsion, in an optical or process camera accomplishes optical printing in moviemaking.

Optical printing is another aspect of adding to or subtracting from original film stock footage, concerning itself primarily with master positives and dupe negatives.

PA

Shortened version of production assistant; gopher; intern.

Paint frame

A large wooden framework mounted to a vertical, mechanical lifting device, pulling it up out of a trough in a warehouse floor. Scenic artists stand on the floor beside it and paint large backdrops from top to bottom as the lifting device assists in positioning the drop.

PD

Shortened version of production designer.

Pick-ups

Individual shots or mini scenes added to the larger movie at a later time (See also, **second unit**).

Picture plane

The imaginary plane of sight through which an audience views a scene. In the theater, the proscenium arch is a physical picture plane or frame through which it views the drama of the play it is watching; in film, whatever scenery the camera is shooting can act as a similar, viewing frame of the drama. It is composed either intentionally or subliminally, but is there nonetheless.

Picture vehicle

This term is synonymous with hero vehicle and refers to the car, motorcycle, bus, truck, etc. of the main character in a movie.

Post-production

The time in film production when the editing of all previously shot footage, sound editing, foley, and optical/visual effects compositing takes place.

POV

also, ***omniscient point-of-view***

Shortened version of point of view. In the process of storytelling, every scene, shot, or character has a viewpoint. A film in which the narrator knows and sees everything occurring in a story, including character thoughts, action, places, conversations, and events; in contrast to subjective point-of-view.

Practicing visual presence
My phrase, explaining the active state of creativity when visualization and the creation of an artifact are fully engaged.

Pre-production
The planning stage in a film's production *before* principal photography commences, involving script treatment and editing, scheduling, previsualization, set design and construction, casting, budgeting and financial planning, and scouting/selection of locations; in contrast to post-production. (See also, **production** and **post-production**)

Process camera
Optical printing is accomplished in a process or optical camera. (See also, **optical printing**)

Production
"The production" refers to the film project itself. "Production" refers to the production office staff and its activity.

Production design
Refers to a film's overall design, continuity, visual look, and composition, i.e., color palette, graphics, previsualization, set design and construction, costumes, set dressing, props, locations, etc., that are the responsibility of the production designer. The art department refers to the people in various roles, e.g., digital concept artists, set designers and draft persons, set decorator and staff, concept illustrators, graphic designers, and storyboard artists, who work under the production designer's supervision. The art director is responsible for the film's physical settings, budget, and the combined efforts of all art department crew.

Raked
A surface like a set floor angled up and away from the camera.

Rekkie
also, *recce*
A New Zealand term for scout or drive.

Re-shoot
Additional photography on specific scenes previously shot. This typically happens after the end of principal photography.

Retrofit
Making specific physical changes to a location site to insure that the design concept is seamless and believable.

Right-to-work
As in "a right to work state." In the U.S., some states comply with IATSE in terms of maintaining union organized shows and some do not. Right-to-work states are the latter, and have more relaxed policies regarding who is hired and how filmmaking can operate. Right-to-work states are the opposite of signatoried states. (See also, **signatory**)

Rotoscoping

Rotoscoping was a technique of tracing each frame of live action and then hand painting in the silhouette, invented by Max Fleischer, the pioneer cartoonist who created Betty Boop and Popeye. The time-sensitive technique was regularly used in filmmaking in the twentieth century until digital editing software was developed based on its principles, to do the work more efficiently.

Scout

The activity of looking for an appropriate location for a film shoot. Scouts or rekkies are organized and conducted by the locations department.

Scouting

Looking for shootable locations.

Second unit

A smaller shooting crew assigned to shoot matching pieces of a scene, to later be edited into the larger scene(s) of a film.

Sequel

A cinematic work that presents the continuation of characters, settings, or events of a story in a preceding movie; in contrast to a prequel. A sequel is also known as a follow-up, serial, series, spin-off, or remake.

Example: *The Maltese Falcon* (1941) followed by *The Black Bird* (1975); *National Velvet* (1944) followed by *International Velvet* (1978). Sequels generally tend to be inferior products—with some exceptions—such as *The Godfather, Part II* (1974), *Toy Story 2* (1999), *The Empire Strikes Back* (1980).

Set

The environment—an exterior or interior locale—where the action takes place in a film. When used in contrast to location, it refers to an artificially constructed time/place, supervised by the film's art director. It can be a physical space or a virtual environment created digitally. "Strike" refers to the act of taking apart a set once filming has ended.

Example: The War Room set, production-designed for *Dr. Strangelove, Or: How I Learned to Stop Worrying and Love the Bomb* (1964), or *The Polar Express* (2004).

Sharktooth scrim

A tightly woven theatrical fabric, much like a fine burlap, used for its transparency qualities for onstage scenery work. (See also, **bobbinette**)

Shooting schedule

This is the master list for the shooting process, painstakingly compiled by the unit production manager, and 1st assistant director, but ultimately the responsibility of the latter. It distills the script breakdown into workable, daily units of the total number scenes to be shot, item by item needs of the shooting crew requested per department for that particular day, and general notes or reminders for everyone connected to the shooting crew.

Signatory

A film company, film studio, or any other filmmaking entity that has signed a basic agreement with the Union to provide adequate working conditions, benefits, and appropriate salaries to members of IATSE, The International Alliance of Theatrical and Stage Employees. Companies making films in "right to work" states in America are most likely not signatory companies. (See also, **right-to-work state**)

Skin

A fiberglass or vacuum formed sheet of fake architectural texture like brick, stone, rock, shingle, slate, Spanish roofing tile, lincresta, logs, sandbags, soundproof panels, fluted columns, and cornice moulding.

Special effects
also, *F/X*, *SFX*, *SPFX*, or *EFX*

A broad term used by the film industry but specifically referring to mechanical or physical effects such as wind, rain, fog, fire, pyrotechnics as squibs and miniature explosions, i.e., a gunshot, animatronics, or use of electronic puppets in both interior and exterior sets.

Spotting plan

A ground plan for a set indicating placement on a soundstage or warehouse space in relationship with loading doors and distance from existing walls and other sets sharing the space.

Staff shop

That department of a film studio complex housing an inventory of carved plaster moulds used as 3D templates for fiberglass copies. From these moulds vacuum formed copies are also made, although "staff moulding" traditionally refers to horizontal bands of ornately carved, classically derived moulding in varying widths and motifs.

Step printer

A step printer is an apparatus that develops film whether it is 35 mm film from a reflex camera or a 35 mm movie camera. Photographic printing page or fine grain film stock is exposed to light and holds the reverse image of negative placed between it and the light source.

Stop-motion animation

A special-effects animation technique where objects, such as solid 3-D puppets, figures, or models are shot one frame at a time and moved or repositioned slightly between each frame, giving the illusion of lifelike motion. Stop-motion was one of the earliest special-effects techniques for science-fiction films, now replaced by CGI and animatronics; also known as stop-frame motion.

Example: The stop-motion animation in the first great monster movie, *King Kong* (1933).

Storyboard

A sequential series of illustrations, stills, rough sketches, or captions, sometimes resembling a comic or cartoon strip of events, as seen through the camera lens, that outline the various shots or provide a visual synopsis for a proposed film story or for a complex scene. The storyboards are displayed in sequence for the purpose of mapping out and crafting the various shot divisions and camera movements in an animated or live-action film. A blank storyboard is a piece of paper with rectangles drawn on it to represent the camera frame for each successive shot; a sophisticated type of preview-storyboard, often shot and edited on video, with a soundtrack. (See also, **animatic**)

Strips

A quick term for the production boards used in determining the shooting schedule for a movie. Literally, they are narrow, stiff pieces of colored cardboard slipped into predesigned frames, indicating various aspects of scenes to be shot.

Subjective point-of-view

A film in which the narrator has a limited point-of-view regarding the characters, events, action, places, thoughts, conversations, etc. (See also, **POV** and **omniscient point-of-view**)

Example: Scout, daughter of Atticus Finch in *To Kill a Mockingbird* (1962).

Superimpose

also, *superimposition*

Placing one image on top of another to create a greater psychological effect.

Example: In Hitchcock's *Vertigo* (1958) during Scottie's nightmare sequence his face is superimposed over a drawing.

Symbol

An object in a film that stands for an idea, representing a second level of meaning, e.g., an open window or flying bird = freedom, a dew-laden rose = beauty, etc. The more a symbol is repeated, the greater its significance in a film. (See also, **icon**, **metaphor**, and **trope**)

Syntagmatic

Referring to syntax or the organization of the elements that make up a sentence or film image and how each element relates to the other parts of that sentence or image. In "film language," which is different from written language, the elements of space and time are a vital part of the equation. (See also, **mise en scène** and **montage**)

Telefilm

Refers to a feature-length motion picture made for television; also known as telepic or telepix.

Trades

Refers to the professional magazines and publications that report the daily or weekly entertainment news of the entertainment industry.

Example: *Variety*, the *Hollywood Reporter*, *Boxoffice Magazine*, and *Below the Line News*.

Translite

A large-scale photograph printed on a flexible, translucent material. It is the general term of a category of photographic backdrop lit from both back and front surfaces, as opposed to painted backdrop, lit just on its front side. Translites are black/white or color. (See also, **colortrans**)

Transpo

The transportation department comprised of members of the teamsters union; the wheels of filmmaking.

Trope

In literary terms, "a rose is a rose is a rose," is what it is: a rose. It is the opposite of a trope. In film semiology, a rose is love is death, is a trope—a more complex image. So, a trope is a universally identified image imbued with several layers of contextual meaning creating a new visual metaphor. (See also, **metaphor** or **symbol**)

UPM

Shorthand version of Unit Production Manager. A production office crewmember supervising the finances of a film project.

VFX

Shorthand version of visual effects as opposed to SFX, special effects.

Visual concept

It is shorthand for a longer explanation; it abbreviates words into symbols or indexes; it is an image that defines the central idea of a movie.

Visual effects
also, *VFX*

Visual and audio fantasy illusions that cannot be accomplished normally, i.e., travel into outer or inner space. Many photographic or optical and filmic techniques are used to produce digital effects, bluescreen or greenscreen chromakeying, (MOCAP) motion capture, in-camera effects, and the use of miniatures/models, mattes, or stop-motion animation. Considered a subcategory of special effects; it refers to anything added to the final picture that was not in the original shot. The visual effects supervisor coordinates visual effects.

Walk through

Touring a set in-progress or a new set to be shot with the director, cinematographer, and any required department heads for comments or last looks.

White model

A physical model constructed in $1/8$" or $1/4$" scale and made from white fomecore or Bristol board. It is derived from drafting at the same scale to enable the viewer an in-hand, 3D concept of scenery. (See also, **card model**)

Widescreen

Refers to projection systems in which the aspect ratio is wider than the 1.33 : 1 ratio that dominated sound film before the 1950s; in the 1950s, many widescreen processes were introduced to combat the growing popularity of television, such as an anamorphic system known as Cinemascope™, a non-anamorphic production technique in which the film is run horizontally through the camera instead of vertically known as VistaVision™, and Todd-AO and Super Panavision that both used wider-gauge film; also known as *letterboxing*.
    Example: *Oklahoma!* (1955) and *Around the World in Eighty Days* (1956).

Wild, or **wild wall**

A partial or full wall in an interior set designed to be removed to allow shooting crew and camera access for easier shooting ability.

Wrap
The formal end of shooting a film.

Wrap time
The actual time the company stops shooting on any given day on the shooting schedule, or at the end of principal photography. With call time, and breaks during the day, wrap time is noted by the assistant directing staff and script supervisor, recorded, and reported to the studio. (See also, **call time**)

Z-film
Refers to a very low-budget, independently made, non-union, less than B-film grade movie, usually featuring first-time director and actors. Quickly made for the teenaged youth market, Z-films are amateurish-looking but with campy appeal. They incorporate exploitative subject matter and include surfing films, motorcycle flicks, cheap horror films, etc. Z-films often become prime candidates for cult film status.

Example: American International Pictures specialized in Z-films, such as *Gas-S-S-S!* (1970), *The Incredible Two-Headed Transplant* (1971), and *Invasion of the Bee Girls* (1973).

Zoptic special effects
A revolutionary 3D process invented by cameraman Zorian Perisic, incorporating a camera system and a projector with synchronized zoom lenses.

Example: The unique flying sequences in the *Superman* movies. A projected background scene remains constant while the camera zooms in on the foreground subject.

APPENDIX G

G	**INDEX**

NOTE: Color plates are found between pages 142 and 143.